Sport and Physical Education in China

Sport and Physical Education in China contains a unique mix of material written by both native Chinese and Western scholars. Contributors have been carefully selected for their knowledge and worldwide reputation within the field, to provide the reader with a clear and broad understanding of sport and PE from the historical and contemporary perspectives which are specific to China. Topics covered include: ancient and modern history; structure, administration and finance; physical education in schools and colleges; sport for all; elite sport; sports science & medicine; and gender issues.

Each chapter has a summary and a set of inspiring discussion topics.

Students taking comparative sport and PE, history of sport and PE, and politics of sport courses will find this book an essential addition to their library.

James Riordan is Professor and Head of the Department of Linguistic and International Studies at the University of Surrey.

Robin Jones is a Lecturer in the Department of PE, Sports Science and Recreation Management, Loughborough University.

Sport and Physical Education in China

Edited by
James Riordan and Robin Jones

ISCPES
International Society for Comparative Physical Education and Sport

London and New York

First published 1999
by E & FN Spon,
11 New Fetter Lane, London EC4P 4EE

Simultaneously published in the USA and Canada
by Routledge
29 West 35th Street, New York, NY 10001

E & FN Spon is an imprint of the Taylor & Francis Group

© 1999 James Riordan and Robin Jones, selection and editorial matter; Individual chapters, the contributors

The right of James Riordan and Robin Jones to be identified as the Authors of their contributions has been asserted by them in accordance with the Copyright, Designs and Patents Act 1988

Typeset in Sabon by
J&L Composition Ltd, Filey, North Yorkshire
Printed and bound in Great Britain by
MPG Books Ltd, Bodmin

British Library Cataloguing in Publication Data
A catalogue record for this book is available
from the British Library

Library of Congress Cataloging in Publication Data
Sport and physical education in China / [edited by] James Riordan and
    Robin Jones.
      p.   cm.– (ISCPES book series)
    Includes bibliographical references and index.
    ISBN 0–419–24750–5 (hardbound). –ISBN 0–419–22030–5 (pbk.)
    1. Sports–China–History   2. Physical education and training–
    China–History.   I. Riordan, James, 1936-   .   II. Jones, Robin
    (Robin E.)   III. Series.
    GV651.S655   1999
    613.7'0951—dc21   98–51481
                                     CIP

ISBN 0–419–24750–5 (hbk)
ISBN 0–419–22030–5 (pbk)

Contents

	List of figures	vii
	List of tables	viii
	Notes on contributors	x
	Series' editor's preface	xii
	Dedication	xv
	Foreword	xvii
	Note on pronunciation	xix
	Map of China	xx
1	**Sport in China** ROBIN JONES	1
2	**Recreation and sport in Ancient China: Primitive society to** **AD 960** MIKE SPEAK	20
3	**The emergence of modern sport: 960–1840** MIKE SPEAK	45
4	**China in the modern world: 1840–1949** MIKE SPEAK	70
5	**Sport and physical education in school and university** ROBIN JONES	90
6	**Elite sport** DENNIS WHITBY	120
7	**Professional training** DENNIS WHITBY, ZHU PEILAN AND ZHANG BAOLUO	142

 8 Chinese women and sport   159
    JAMES RIORDAN AND DONG JINXIA

 9 The emergence of professional sport – the case of soccer   185
    ROBIN JONES

10 China and the Olympic movement   202
    HAI REN

11 Sports science   214
    DENNIS WHITBY

12 Sports medicine   231
    FRANK H. FU

13 Mass fitness   243
    SHIRLEY REEKIE

    Appendix: Administration of sport   255
    SHIRLEY REEKIE

    Index   273

Figures

Map of China   xx

1.1 General structure of the Chinese sports system up to
2 March 1998   16

1.2 Administrative sections of the State Physical Culture and
Sports Commission in January 1998   17

1.3 Structure of the Chinese sports system after 2 March 1998   18

5.1 The Chinese education system   92

9.1 Graph comparing the number of Asian countries with all
countries taking part in the preliminary and qualifying
rounds of each World Cup, 1930–94   187

10.1 Comparison of research papers and introductory articles   209

12.1 Silk painting of 'Daoyin' found at the grave of Emperor Ma
(475–221 BC)   233

12.2 Wu Quan Xi – postural exercises imitating animals   234

12.3 Ban Duan Jin – postural exercises   235

12.4 Tai Chi Quan   236

Tables

1.1	Chronology of change, 1978–98	5
1.2	Results of drugs tests in China, 1997	7
5.1	Kinds of key and non-key schools in China	91
5.2	Transfer rates from middle schools to universities, vocational schools and work	93
5.3	National age group standards – female, 9 years	95
5.4	Points awarded for standards achieved in official competition	96
5.5	Middle school PE standards for 'graduation'	96
5.6	National Age Group Norms, male, 18 years	97
5.7	Standards for transfer from junior to senior middle school	98
5.8	Overall content of a key middle school timetable	101
5.9	Courses followed by PE students at East China Normal University	106
5.10	Elective courses for PE students at East China Normal University	107
5.11	Fitness test record for students at special sports schools	111
8.1	Chinese women's and men's contribution to China's results in the summer Olympics, 1984–92	162
8.2	China's performance at the winter Olympics, 1984–92	162
8.3	Numbers of male and female competitors in Olympic teams, 1988: countries with established sports traditions	163
8.4	Chinese women's comparative contribution, 1988 and 1992 summer Olympics	163
8.5	Respective numbers of male and female professional coaches, 1990	177
9.1	World Cup preliminary and qualifying rounds 1930 to 1994 – Asian countries taking part	188
9.2	FIFA-Coca Cola world soccer rankings	189
9.3	Structure of the Chinese professional soccer league, 1996	189
9.4	Soccer clubs and national teams playing in or against China in recent years	192

9.5   Country of origin of overseas players in Japanese J-League,
      August 1996   198
10.1 Summary of China's participation in the 23rd, 24th, 25th
      and 26th Olympic Games   207
10.2 Content change of Olympic studies in China in different
      periods   209
13.1 Test items for young people in the National Fitness
      Standards   248
13.2 Test items for adults in the National Fitness
      Standards   249

Contributors

Frank Hoo-kin Fu is Professor and Dean of the Faculty of Social Sciences, Director of the Dr Stephen Hui Research Centre for Physical Recreation and Wellness, Hong Kong Baptist University. He is the author of *The Development of Sport Culture in the Hong Kong Chinese* (HKBU Press, 1993) and is a recognized international authority on sports medicine in and outside China.

Dong Jinxia is an ex-Chinese gymnast who now coaches the Chinese women's national gymnastics team, as well as lecturing at the Beijing Sports University. She has been conducting research into 'Society, Women and Sport in Modern China', and is registered for her doctorate at the University of Glasgow in Scotland.

Robin Jones is lecturer in sports studies at Loughborough University and is the United Kingdom's leading expert on Chinese sport. He has travelled extensively in China, taught PE and sport for a number of years in Singapore, and has written on many aspects of sport and PE in China. In his introductory chapter, he sets the tone for our book in maintaining that,

> to understand the contextual position of sport in China – its 'Chineseness' – demands a much fuller awareness of Chinese culture, conditions and values, and that is a complex task.

Shirley Reekie was trained in sports studies in England, but teaches international PE and sport at San Jose State University in the USA. She is a competitive rower and sailor, and has made sport in China a special research topic, having spent several months living in China (Fujian Province). She is President of the International Society for Comparative Physical Education and Sport.

Hai Ren is a professor at the Beijing University of Physical Education where he is also Director of the Centre for Olympic Studies and is widely known, both within and outside China, for his work in this field. He is an executive member of the International Society for Comparative Physical Education and Sport.

James Riordan is Academic Head of the School of Language and International Studies, and Director of the International Sports Studies Centre at the University of Surrey. He has written several books on sport and PE in communist countries, including *Sport in Soviet Society* (CUP, 1978), *Sport under Communism* (Hurst, 1981) and *Sport, Politics and Communism* (MUP, 1991).

Mike Speak originally trained as a linguist (French and Swedish), but has spent his career in physical education. He was Deputy Director of Sport at the University of Lancaster before becoming Head of the PE and Sports Science Unit at the University of Hong Kong, where he has taught for some twenty years. He has made a special study of Chinese sports history.

Dennis Whitby, Director of the Hong Kong Sports Institute, coached at the highest level in China for a number of years, and travelled extensively in the country to observe sports facilities, talent and attitudes. His three chapters provide a valuable insight into Chinese sport, based on visits to China over the last fifteen years and his own coaching experience in Beijing.

Series' editor's preface

Prior to 1970, texts concerned with comparative and international issues and dimensions were relatively rare. A few American commentators devoted some attention to developments in sport in the then Soviet Union and also produced, through assembled descriptive accounts, information on health, physical education and recreation in a number of countries around the world. After 1970, there was an increasing interest in international aspects of physical education, testimony to which was the plethora of descriptive articles contributed to professional journals by American physical educators. In the main, these articles represented information derived from observational educational or 'touristic' visits to be shared with colleagues. Generally, they were not seen to qualify as comparative research reports and reflected the broader situation of comparative studies in physical education and sport trailing behind reported research in the 'parent' area, 'comparative education'. However, some significant developments in scholarly activity were marked by two seminal texts in the field: Bennett, Howell and Simri (1975) and Riordan (1978).

A major initiative in the international development of the comparative physical education and sport domain was the formation of the International Society for Comparative Physical Education and Sport (ISCPES) in 1978, since when it has been at the forefront of the promotion of comparative physical education and sport studies. This society is a research and educational organization with the expressed purpose of supporting, encouraging and providing assistance to those seeking to initiate and strengthen research and teaching programmes in comparative physical education and sport throughout the world. ISCPES holds biennial international conferences, publishes conference proceedings, an international journal and monographs, sponsors (in the form of patronage) research projects and, with this text on physical education and sport in China, has now launched a book series.

The idea of an ISCPES book series originated in an initial concern about the dearth of published analytical literature in the comparative and transnational/cross-cultural domains of physical education and sport. Since the early 1970s, with few exceptions such as seminal work by Riordan, there has been a continuing predisposition, in textbooks with a 'first order' comparative or international approach, towards description rather than analytic interpretation. There has been a concentration on the 'what' and a neglect of the essential ingredients of 'truly' regarded comparative study – the 'why' and 'how'. The volumes in this book series are aligned with the expressed purposes of comparative and cross-cultural study and serve to progress comparative and international studies beyond description.

The primary purpose is for the titles in the series individually and collectively to result in extending knowledge of national systems and 'problem' themes and topics. As such they will represent a significant contribution to the progression of comparative, cross-cultural and international studies in physical education and sport. Physical education and sporting activity have a ubiquitous global presence. At the same time, they are subject to culturally specific 'local' (national and/or community) interpretations, policies and practices. Inevitably, therefore, similarities and differences are encountered at these 'local' levels. The collection of volumes to feature in the book series illustrates the nature and extent of the variations.

The intention with all titles in this series is to present explanations and/or interpretations so as to provide an analytic dimension rather than mere descriptive narration for the nature and scope of national delivery systems in selected countries as well as to address issues which are pervasively important in global and local cross-cultural contexts. The overriding aim of the series is not only to provide texts which will cover constituent elements of cross-cultural and international aspects of physical education and sport, but also to facilitate deeper awareness and understanding in a variety of geographical political area and thematic issues settings.

Each volume focuses on a national or regional political entity (China, Germany, Australasia, the Gulf States, etc.) or a thematic issue (women and sport, adapted physical activity, the development of elite sport, comparative methodology, etc.). Each text can be used on an individual basis to extend knowledge and understanding. More importantly, the volumes can be taken together as an integrated basis for informed comparisons of national systems and thematic issues, thereby serving the overall purpose of contributing to critical awareness and analysis amongst confirmed and potential comparativists and young scholars at both undergraduate and postgraduate levels.

The template for the content of the 'area' study volumes is set by this first title in the series. Each volume in the series will have a contextualizing introduction, followed by chapters focusing on historical developments, organizational structures, policies and programmes in physical education in educational settings, sport delivery systems, including issues of institutional development of excellence in sport and sport for all policies and practices. Such a template facilitates awareness of similarities, variations and differences between the countries.

REFERENCES

Bennett, B., Howell, M., and Simri, U. (1975) *Comparative Physical Education*, Champaign, Illinois: Human Kinetics.

Riordan, J. (1978) *Sport in Soviet Society*, Cambridge: Cambridge University Press.

Ken Hardman
Series Editor

Dedication

ISCPES acknowledges the generous donation of Sheikh Ahmad-al-Fahad al Sabah, President, Olympic Council of Asia, member of the International Olympic Committee (IOC), President of the National Olympic Committee of Kuwait and Vice-President of the Association of National Olympic Committees (ANOC). Sheikh Ahmad's donation to the ISCPES Trust Fund for publications and to establish a book series is dedicated to the name and memory of his father, Sheikh Fahad al-Ahmad al-Sabah, who was tragically killed at the outset of the Gulf War.

Sheikh Fahad was the younger brother of the Emir of Kuwait, H.H. Sheikh Jaber al-Ahmad al-Sabah. After a distinguished military career, Sheikh Fahad, at the age of 29, became President of the Kuwait Olympic Committee, an office held until the time of his death on 2 August 1990. He was a prominent sports personality in Asia. His most distinctive achievement was the founding of the Olympic Council of Asia (OCA). As President of the OCA, Sheikh Fahad was instrumental in enhancing the international status of the Asian Games as a sporting spectacle. Other presidential and vice-presidential offices held were both national (Kuwait Football and Basketball Associations) and international (Arab Sports Union, Arab Basketball Federation, Asian and International Handball Associations, Association of National Olympic Committees). Sheikh Fahad was also a member of the Olympic Movement Commission of the IOC as well as a member of the IOC Executive Board from 1985 to 1989. His extensive commitment to sport was also reflected in his founding of several Kuwait national bodies: karate, taekwando and yachting and rowing federations. He was an active huntsman and breeder of fine Arabian horses. His broader interests embraced support of many sports-related charities, music, poetry and writing, an affinity with which resulted in his founding of the Asian Sports Writers Association. Recognition of his various contributions to the international arena included military honours, honorary citizenship of Japan and an Honorary Doctorate in Law from Seoul University, South Korea, OCA and ANOC Merit Awards.

Like his eldest son, Sheikh Ahmad, at the present time, the late Sheikh Fahad was a strong advocate of fair play in sport and believed in the special role of sport in contributing to global peace, harmonious co-existence and prosperity. In associating with these ideals, ISCPES is indebted to Sheikh Ahmad for his financial support, one tangible result of which is this book series.

Ken Hardman
Editor-in-Chief, ISCPES book series

Foreword

James Riordan

This book was prepared with the best of intentions: to bring together scholars from East and West to write a clear and objective account of Chinese sport and physical education. That such a book is needed by students of comparative sport, and by those professionally and casually interested in sport, is evident from the dearth of material available in English,[1] and by the status of China in the world today.

Not only is China the most populous state on earth, with over a billion people, but it is in rapid transition to a nation of considerable world import politically, commercially, militarily – and in terms of sport. Its athletes, who only made their debut at the Olympic Games in 1984, are increasingly attracting world attention, not always for the right reasons.

Yet it is western ignorance about China and its sport that so often fosters suspicion and induces false conclusions. The Chinese themselves, only now emerging from political isolation, have contributed to the general mystique surrounding their society. To some extent, this has been a feature of all erstwhile communist states whose scholars were for long outside the mainstream of world scholarship. They spoke, if they spoke at all, in shibboleths and arcane formulae, presenting the ideal for the actual, the transitory political line for the last word in science.

In today's China, all that is changing. Yet the imprint of the past is still perceptible in much of the sports scholarship. It is a problem which soon became apparent as we sought contributors in China. In the end, we had to turn principally to western scholars with a knowledge of Chinese language and culture and who were themselves involved in sport. All the authors have a long association with Chinese sport, have lived in China and have spent their professional lives both teaching and coaching sport.

Not all the chapters are written in the usual descriptive analytical way. The three chapters by Dennis Whitby are written partly in narrative/diary form, comparing and contrasting impressions gained at different periods when visiting the same institutions in China. He therefore provides a personal insight into significant changes made over the decade he describes.

NOTE

1 Two major books exist in English on sport in China. Howard G. Knuttgen, Ma Qiwei and Wu Zhongyuan (eds), *Sport in China* (Human Kinetics, Champaign, Illinois 1990) is a well-intentioned collection of conference papers covering important aspects of sport in China old and new. All fourteen chapters were written by Chinese authors and many bear the imprint of recent political dogma. Susan Brownell, *Training the Body for China* (University of Chicago Press, 1995) is an excellent personal account of 'sport in the moral order' of China, written from an anthropological standpoint.

Note on pronunciation

The Chinese language comprises many dialects that frequently make it impossible for people in one part of the country to speak to those in another, although the written characters may be understood by everyone. To address this problem, the Chinese government have adopted one spoken form, referred to as 'putonghua', which is used in schools, television, and for all other public or official occasions. In addition, to facilitate the transcription of the written form of the Chinese language into Romanized script (used in the early stages of learning in primary schools and also by non-Chinese), the People's Republic of China introduced a standardized 'spelling' system known as Pinyin. Although this is now almost universal, other systems do exist such as the older Wade-Giles system. Inevitably, there can be considerable confusion to a foreigner in recognizing the same word spelt in totally different ways (Peking and Beijing being one example), not to mention the problems created over the spoken language by the many dialects.

This book largely uses the pinyin system, although some of the references in the historical chapters are better left in their dialect form, and other sections contain dialect variations. It would not be appropriate to try to standardize every one of these variations.

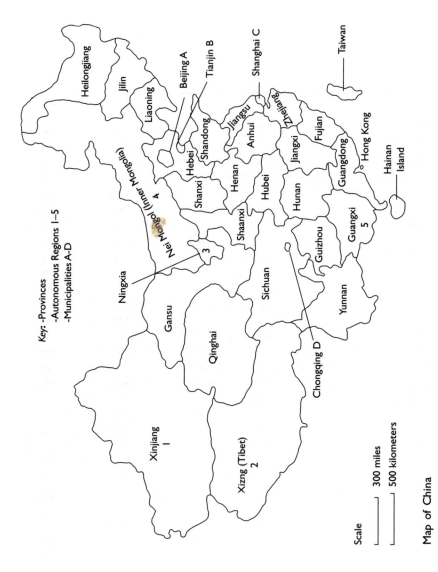

Key: -Provinces
-Autonomous Regions 1-5
-Municipalities A-D

Heilongjiang

Jilin

Liaoning

Beijing A

Tianjin B

Shanghai C

Taiwan

Jiangsu

Shandong

Anhui

Zhejiang

Hebei

Fujian

Hong Kong

Nei Mongol (Inner Mongolia)

Shanxi

Henan

Hubei

Jiangxi

Guangdong

Hainan
Island

4

Shaanxi

Hunan

Guangxi

5

Ningxia

3

Guizhou

Gansu

Sichuan

Yunnan

Chongqing D

Qinghai

Xinjiang

1

Xizng (Tibet)

2

Scale

300 miles

500 kilometers

Map of China

Chapter 1

Sport in China

Robin Jones

With increasing regularity, the People's Republic of China is appearing in western news bulletins, television documentaries, newspapers, feature articles, films – and of course sporting record books – coinciding, it so happens, with the end of the twentieth century. Historians will look back and surely mark the last hundred years as hugely significant in the chain of events that have led to the present position of China as an emerging world superpower. The nation's status as a superpower is heavily dependent on the fact that it is the most populous country in the world and that potentially it holds the key to the growth of the world economy. But there are other reasons for seeing China as pre-eminent. First, it has the fastest growing economy in the world, sustaining an average annual growth of around 10 per cent over the last decade.[1] Second, it is well placed in the Pacific Rim to stand alongside other economies in the region – South Korea, Singapore, Malaysia, Japan, Australia, and even the United States (California, notably). Third, it has a long tradition as a trading nation from the times of the Silk Road[2] to the nineteenth century links with western countries. And fourth, China has a very distinct sense of identity; even though in much of its history the country has been dominated by others, it has nevertheless remained relatively untainted by outside influences.

The first half of the twentieth century saw the demise of Imperial China, the defeat of Nationalist China and the rise of Communist China. During the same period the country had to withstand the ravages of the Second World War and occupation by the Japanese (1938–45),[3] involvement in the Korean War (1950–3) and its own Civil War (1946–9).[4] It also had to accept the trade concessions forced upon the country by western powers in the earlier years.[5] The second half of the century, although markedly different from the first, was nevertheless enormously diverse. During the first twenty-five years following the founding of the People's Republic in 1949, government policies variously led to failure, disaster, famine, revolution and stagnation. It is clear that China in the twentieth century has been in a constant state of flux. As the millennium comes to an end, world communism has collapsed inwards, leaving China as one of the few countries basing their policies on socialist principles – and there is much to suggest that even that is in name only.

The long tradition of China has given it a rich and distinct cultural heritage, combining as it does the secular and the non-secular philosophies of Confucianism, Taoism and Buddhism over a period of more than 2,500 years.[6] During this period, China not only developed and refined forms of exercise that were in complete contrast to those in the West, but also developed folk games similar to the European precursors of soccer and hockey.[7] However, the arrival of explorers, traders and missionaries from afar also exposed China to western ways in the last 600 years and marked one of the curiosities of Chinese history in that, whilst there was an inward flow of people and ideas from outside, the country did not develop its unique talents in the way that the western nations did. China did not become a fermenting vessel of industrial, commercial and academic ideas, but rather was the recipient of those from outside.

We might ask how, if China was in such turmoil during the twentieth century, did sport manage to find a niche. Despite the civil unrest between the Guomindang[8] and the Communists, the struggle against the Japanese invasion and the relative poverty of the peasant population, Chinese traditional sports together with 'new' sports brought in by 'foreigners'[9] continued to survive and (later) flourish. This is as much a comment on the resilience of sport as it is on Chinese society, but it serves to emphasize two important aspects of sport in twentieth-century China. First, that whatever the Communist revolution led to – such as the emancipation of women (for example from bound feet and concubinage), the freeing of peasants from the land, official rejection of Confucianism, eradication of the bourgeoisie and the mercantile class – it did not (and could not) eradicate the influence of tradition in every area of life. Although Mao Zedong had railed against the 'Four Olds' – old culture, old ideology, old customs, old habits – in the early years of the People's Republic, the tradition of *tai ji quan* and other martial arts, for example, remained intact. They are, after all, a silent and individual affair that do not need any overt display or team work in order for them to be practised; even though they have strong symbolic links with the past, their development as a form of health therapy insulated them from criticism as a threat to the new society.

Second, in adopting western sports such as track and field, China was entering the international arena of sport. This matched in some way the move towards the four modernizations of the post-Maoist era: agriculture, science and technology, industry and national defence. The rapid development of international sport in the final decades of this century has relied heavily on the input of science and technology. But it has also created a modern and fashionable image in the designer clothes market that is influential in setting trends for young people. Thus, as China has opened her doors to the West, sport has been able to present itself as being uniquely Chinese (in traditional sport) and forward looking and modern (in Olympic sport). This combination of tradition and the modern is a constantly recurring theme in China and can be seen in many ways: in cliches such as 'crossroads', 'interface', and 'turning point'; in architecture, where the swept lines of the old roofs contrast with the cubic shapes of modern high rise buildings; in the transport system, where the old tricycle rickshaws ply their trade alongside the new Japanese and German taxi cars; in the countryside, where the water buffalo breathes the fumes of the mechanized tractor, and the hand threshers at rice harvest go home to their colour televisions.

In what ways does the Chinese system of sport differ from that of other (former) Communist countries, such as the Soviet Union and the German Democratic Republic? For all the unrest and even open animosity that existed between the USSR and China in the 1960s, the essential features of the two sports systems were virtually identical, inasmuch as they were both 'centralized' and part of a sporting hierarchy that operated from government down to county and district level. The circumstances under which they operated, however, were different. It is fair to say that by the mid-1980s, when the Gorbachov reforms in the USSR were presaging the political collapse of the Soviet system, China was beginning to realize the need for change to its own system – change that had been assiduously espoused by Deng Xiao Ping (the late, former leader of China). The collapse of the former USSR was a warning against early political reform. If Communism was unable to survive in Eastern Europe, it was because, de facto, it simply was not providing the improvements to living standards that might have been expected to attract popular support. Deng was a reformer by nature, and his determination drove the government to take a reformist line – the open door policy of 1979/ early 1980s, the four modernizations programme (of agriculture, industry, science and technology, and defence), and the establishment of Special Economic Zones (for example Shenzhen in southern China) are testimony to this. China under Deng first accepted, and has since built on, some measure of co-operation with the West, but although Communism has subsided elsewhere, it still underpins the official policies of the country. It was under the leadership of Deng, following the death of Mao in 1976, that China adopted an 'open door' policy, gradually allowing more western influence (largely in the form of trade) into the country, encouraging the adoption of market principles, permitting entrepreneurial activity, all carrying the clear message that reform was possible and even desirable.

Under those conditions, and with the example of the former Soviet Union, the events leading to the clash between the government and those clamouring for reform in Tian An Men Square (and elsewhere in China) in the summer of 1989 were perhaps predictable. The political clampdown that followed Tian An Men did not, however, halt the economic realism that was dominating government policy, and sport has flourished in this new climate. This has been apparent in the following:

- Decentralization has allowed provinces some autonomy in establishing programmes for sport according to their own perceived needs
- Rationalization has led to a streamlining of the numbers of people employed in sports administration
- Accountability has meant that, for the first time, new ways of financing sport are being explored as the government gradually reduces its support
- The sports system is having to learn to cope with media attention to the growing success of Chinese athletes and the attendant scandals that have surfaced over drug abuse, coaching dissent, walk outs and disputes.

Are the reforms part of the civilizing process noted by Howell[10] or is the 'soy paste vat'[11] of Chinese culture so bound by tradition that reform is nothing more than a reshuffling of the same cards? Curiosity about the West (a poor term because it encompasses many different patterns and ideas) has inevitably been fuelled by the media and knowledge that the family of Communist states is now virtually non-existent. The Olympic Games and world championships in various sports (especially soccer, tennis and basketball) were created in the West and have become the dominant role model for the sporting aspirations of emerging nations. So powerful is this model and so standardized are international sports that there seems little room for indigenous sports. China, then, has little option but to reform her sports according to IOC, FIFA or IAAF rules – a major factor in the reform process.

On 2 March 1998, sweeping changes to the structure of Chinese government were announced at the Ninth National People's Congress in Beijing. Eleven out of forty ministries and other offices of the State Council were to be closed, including the State Physical Culture and Sports Commission. It was also announced that provincial Sports Commissions would close, and the number of employees in government offices would be reduced by 50 per cent by the end of 1998. Was this a complete surprise, or were there earlier signs that, in retrospect, were a portent of things to come? A reduction in the size of the Sports Commission had already occurred at the beginning of the 1990s and, in 1993, views expressed by Chinese academics and sports officials regarding the failure of Beijing to win the nomination for the 2000 Olympic Games suggested that the failed bid would add to the pressure for reform of the sports system, although at the time closure of the Sports Commission was not mentioned.

Whilst the pattern of reform was evident at the beginning of 1998, it was certainly not the start of the process, nor was it complete. Basic reform began in the 1980s – the USA, UK and Germany were examples of countries that were looked at and, by 1992/3, structural reform was under way. The pattern of reform was evident: sport was being separated from government, and was adopting, broadly, a western approach. However, the separation was not total. The government would continue to give some funding to the training system and to the competitive programme in Olympic sports. Under the training system reforms, different levels of funding emerged: parents would have to contribute towards their children's involvement in sport at the introductory level (payment for coaching sessions); the government would help at medium level (providing coaches and special sports schools); and finally at the top level, the government would fund training only for those sports unable to attract major sponsors, leaving sponsors to fund the rest (soccer, basketball and volleyball are in the vanguard of sponsorship). For competitive sport, the government will now only fund the Olympic sports programme, thus making national priorities quite transparent. The strong links with government, noted by Zhang Li[12] are weakening, as an independent tier of organization, separate from government, emerges. Table 1.1 gives a simple chronology of some of the changes identified.

Economic and political reforms are having a major impact on sport. In 1995 the five-day week was adopted throughout the country; income levels have risen, with greater disposable margins; the economic boom is bringing an air of confidence; industrial growth is strong; inward investment is high; consumer goods are expanding; and an embryonic leisure industry is emerging. As leisure time increases with the long weekend, and as prosperity grows, more attention is being given by sports leaders to the provision of Sport for All (or rather, Recreation for All, in the broader sense). Four key target groups have been identified:

1   the elderly – that is, those around retiring age (males, 60; females, 55);
2   young people;
3   the rural population;
4   blue collar workers.

Table 1.1 Chronology of change, 1978–98

1978/79	Deng Xiao Ping comes to power. Start of the reform era; open door policies and modernization programme take root.
1980s	The collapse of Communism and the decade of change in Eastern Europe.
1990s	Re-alignment of policies with the free market under the banner 'Socialism with Chinese characteristics'.
1995	New government regulations for sport; new professional soccer leagues formed; soccer management centre planned.
1996	Soccer management centres established; basketball and volleyball management offices follow suit.
1997	Sports Commission restructured; management offices for all major sports planned. Provincial Regulations appear in some provinces.
1998	Major government restructuring announced by State Council; State Sports Commission to close; closure of provincial sports commissions also announced. All China Sports Federation to become the government's sports office, listed directly under the State Council, with loss of ministerial status.

To analyse what China expects from sport, reference is made to government regulations that have been formulated during the 1990s. New regulations covering sport were published in 1995,[13] containing eight chapters, with fifty-six clauses, the key features of which reflected:

- the move towards market forces and commercialism;
- the separation between government agency and sport agency;
- concern for mass sport, leisure and free time;
- sport management issues – as opposed to simply sport provision;
- the active promotion of sponsorship;
- retention of state concern for nationalism, socialism, morality and discipline;
- recognition of international concerns over substance abuse in sport;
- the rights of athletes to careers after sport and the state's duty to provide opportunity for job training;
- importance given to school physical education – compulsory, daily PE, evaluation alongside academic performance, national standards, school sports clubs and health and fitness checks.

The 1995 regulations set the framework for the development of sport in China, certainly into the next century, but it was unclear, at the time, whether there would be further reductions in government control over sport and whether market forces were expected to completely prevail. The regulations were relatively clear about policy, but less clear about implementation and, as the following examples show, retained the hallmarks of sports policies in Communist countries, as well as marking the change towards a free market.

> Regulation 3
> Sport is valued for its contribution to the economic, social and military development of China . . .
> Regulation 24
> China promotes the development of competitive sport and encourages athletes to improve the level of their sports skills, in order to raise the standard of sports competition, and gain honour for the country.
> Regulation 17
> Schools must include Physical Education to develop the moral, intellectual, and physical qualities of the students.

The departure from the traditional pattern of state provision lies in Regulation 42, 'Sports organizations are encouraged to raise money through sponsorship by business companies and individuals.' Here was a clear sign that reform was part of an ongoing, planned process, rather than an end product in itself. This process is still unfinished and, by 1997, a number of provinces were formulating local versions of these regulations, that spelled out in greater detail the responsibilities of local authorities in sports planning and provision.[14]

The regulations represent the sporting aspirations of China and focus constructively on past traditions, present realities and future possibilities. International recognition, almost automatically, follows Olympic success and, by reaching fourth place in the medal tables at Atlanta in 1996, China undoubtedly attracted much acclaim for its success in events such as diving and gymnastics. But China has also attracted negative publicity as its sportsmen and women were found guilty of drug abuse on a number of occasions. Of course, it is true to say that no country has solved the problem of substance abuse in sport, and China, by Article 50 of the 1995 Regulations, recognizes the problem, 'athletes found guilty will be punished according to the rules; people in charge will also be held responsible'. In a summary chapter of the same regulations, Wu Shao Zu, the head of the Sports Commission, emphasizes that there should be a strict ban on drugs, with rigorous testing, management and enforcement of the laws.[15] Figures published recently in China show the scale of abuse. Table 1.2 lists six sports in which Chinese sportsmen and women have been found guilty.

The negative publicity associated with drugs abuse in sport is certainly most unwelcome to the sports leaders in China; nevertheless, there has been a sceptical response from the sporting world when Chinese athletes have been found guilty. Amidst the tangle of hypocrisy over the drugs issue, China is undoubtedly having to face comparison, however unfairly, with former

Table 1.2 Results of drugs tests in China, 1997*

Total number of tests	3,540		
Number of out-of-competition tests	1,893		
	Male	*Female*	*Total*
Number of athletes testing positive	6	18	24
Sport	*Number*		
Athletics	13		
Weightlifting	7		
Wrestling	1		
Boxing	1		
Cycling	1		
Sailing/canoeing	1		

Source: *China Daily*, 7 April 1998. (The table does not include recent cases involving swimmers.)

Note
* Ten of the positive urine samples, not confirmed until 13 March 1998, were at the 8th National Games (Shanghai, October 1997).

Communist countries, especially the GDR. The complaint often levelled against GDR and USSR athletes was that having the full state machinery behind the sport effort gave an unfair advantage to their athletes, when compared to those who received no state support. This complaint was further compounded as the extent of the use of banned substances by the Germans gradually came to light after the collapse of the GDR. The 1995 Chinese regulations thus display a measure of real concern on the part of the government. However, as the government relaxes its control of sport, and commercialism rushes in, any reduction of the problem seems likely to become more difficult.

Whilst China is the world's longest surviving civilization, there are, today, regional and other differences (apart from geography and climate) that have an impact on sport. China can broadly be divided into three bands, running north to south: the heavily populated eastern seaboard, the immediate hinterland in the centre of the country and the more remote, less densely populated region to the west. These three bands also divide the country into rich, average and poor areas. Using the Chinese National Games as an example, they have only been held in four centres (Beijing, Guangzhou, Shanghai and Sichuan) partly because not all the provinces could afford to host them.[16] All the locations, with the exception of Sichuan, are in the seaboard belt. Sichuan, in the middle belt, hosted part of the 7th National Games in 1993, which were divided between Beijing and Sichuan roughly in the ratio 2:1. The southern province of Guangzhou, bordering Hong Kong and containing the Special Economic Zone of Shen Zhen, is considered by the Chinese to be wealthy, whilst Xin Jiang Province on the north-west border is considered poor. Spending on sport is thus not evenly distributed throughout the country, making some provinces strong in sport and others weak. In addition, China has several minority nationalities that have their own strengths in local sports.

An example of the growing leisure industry can be found in Wen Jiang County, Sichuan Province, where the local authorities decided a few years ago to encourage horse racing. Money from local companies, together with further investment and advice from Hong Kong, resulted in a 1,200 metre oval rececourse being opened in 1995 complete with on-course tote betting. Over 100 horses are stabled at the course – some owned by hotel companies – and a team of jockeys live there; they ride horses once a week on Saturday afternoons with a card of six races. Several hundred spectators watch the races either on closed circuit television in lounges under the stands, live at the rails or from the indoor restaurant above the finish. The racecourse company may take around 40,000 yuan during the meeting, with winnings on the tote set at 70 per cent. Although lacking in 'silks and high fashion', the development of this racecourse represents a marked change from the situation just a few years ago when such activities were frowned on by the government. It is interesting to note that Hong Kong (which officially became an integral part of the People's Republic of China on 1 July 1997) has an extremely lucrative horse racing and betting industry which over the years helped to fund many public projects in the city. The Wen Jiang project is some distance from the scale of Hong Kong horse racing, but the potential for sport to fund other activities is obvious.

Is there any evidence yet that the arrival of professional sport – principally soccer – is affecting other sports? The aspirations of young schoolboys, the demise of less glamorous sports, the reduction of available funding for minority sports, the development of new facilities and stadiums are all signs that a new sports culture – like the soccer culture – is growing. The power of television in this process is also important; it is significant that during the football season, from about March to November, one professional match from the top division is broadcast live on the national network at each stage of the league competition. In the top division (twelve clubs up to 1998, then increasing to fourteen), the average attendance is about 19,000, with the soccer fans of Sichuan being noted for their strong support, including a nucleus that follow the provincial team to away matches in other provinces. Professional soccer and its league system have continued to flourish in China, with the game firmly established as the most popular spectator sport in the country. Overseas players and coaches contribute significantly to the top league clubs, and the national team continues to strive for international success. Soccer was the first sport to go down the professional route, to achieve a large measure of independence from state control, gain substantial sponsorship and generate a sport culture in China that, hitherto, was more associated with western sport. The soccer transfer market is already making transfer deals totalling hundreds of thousands of US dollars[17] and disputes over contracts have occurred, leading to the sacking of players. The 'hiring and firing' system of accountability in the West will doubtless apply to other sports, especially high profile sports, as the stakes increase.

By 1996, other sports had moved in the same direction as soccer, as first basketball and then volleyball adopted a similar structure; the management of sport in China was under review and the overall government plan was to shift responsibility for the running of sport away from the state towards clubs. Soccer had been the guinea pig for the experiment, and management centres for soccer were established that focused on the grassroots development of the sport. The professional game lacked the sort of infrastructure that would nurture new players: junior leagues, competitions, training and coaching programmes, soccer sports schools and links with clubs. The management centre's task was to provide these. Government input to the management centres took several forms, but importantly, finance and personnel were available. The soccer management centre received 3 million yuan (about US$350,000) from the State Sports Commission in 1997 and, as part of the restructuring and reduction of the Commission itself, some Commission staff switched employment to the soccer (and other) management centres. Significantly, however, in contrast to the government money, around 30 million yuan (about US$3,500,000) in commercial sponsorship flowed into the soccer management centre.[18]

Professional soccer only started in 1993, so it is still rather early to say whether a major shift is occurring, but there is some effect discernible in schools as students set up their own informal soccer teams, outside school hours. However, there is no strong evidence yet that schools are themselves changing their physical education curriculum to embrace soccer.

The period of reform in China, stemming from the early 1980s, is now firmly set. Indeed, looking at the degree of change, it is difficult to imagine how the reform process can be halted without enormous upheaval. In the cities, urban life is increasingly dominated by commerce. Every level of society is being driven more and more by economic pressures. Schools, colleges, universities and even the army are now allowed by the government to have 'commercial interests'[19] and the economic tradition, built up during the early years of the People's Republic, whereby parents and grandparents would 'save' as a matter of course, is being replaced by a 'spend' culture among young people. The renowned sinologist Joseph Needham (who died in 1995) suggested that one of the reasons why China, in the nineteenth and twentieth centuries, did not match the economic growth of the West was because, traditionally, the mercantile class in China was never highly respected.[20] This was also the case in the early days of the People's Republic, but success of the economic reforms is now creating an air of respectability for economic enterprise. The emergence of professional sport may help to promote a popular view of 'wealth creation', especially as the arrival of the superstar (cash bonuses for those athletes who win gold medals, for example) demonstrates that being successful is officially recognized both financially and morally. Often in the past the view was expressed that seeking a career in sport was associated with a lack of intelligence. There was the feeling that young people in the provincial sports schools were not academically minded. Mah Jun Ren's 'Army' (the group of women athletes who set world records in middle and long distance track events in the early 1990s under coach Mah) was described as being 'from peasant families . . . used to eating bitterness'.[21] If this suggests that the status of sport has been traditionally lower than in other established careers, the attention now being given to professional sport may encourage people to see sport in a different light. Young people, fans of the new professional teams, are also well acquainted with the sporting superstars of the West, such as Michael Jordan, Carl Lewis, Jurgen Klinsman and Linford Christie[22] and the attendant glamour attached to their lifestyles. The public can see sport on national and local television, although the government has not yet made available, nationally, statellite channels such as Star TV from Hong Kong. There are also sports newspapers, some exclusively for soccer,[23] on general sale to the public.

At the beginning of the 1990s, China began to prepare her bid to hold the

2000 Olympic Games. This would have been the ultimate success for sports leaders and a powerful affirmation to the public that the government sports policy was 'correct'. In the months before the IOC decision to award the Games to Sydney, Chinese women athletes (and later swimmers) astonished the sports world with record breaking performances in the 1,500, 5,000 and 10,000 metre track events. The timing could not have been better – nor the disappointment at the failed bid more intense. Soon after the IOC decision to hold the Games in Sydney (the final voting was 45–43), the 'super athletes' of Mah Jun Ren were in open dispute with their coach, and drugs scandals brought Chinese swimming public shame. Suddenly, in the space of just a few months, the full-blooded optimism of Chinese sports leaders was viewed by the West with increasing scepticism. Also facing sports leaders was the painfully obvious fact that in the Olympic arena at least, China, as the world's largest country, was falling far short of its potential – notwithstanding its prowess in certain events. Comments by sports leaders at the time in 1993, suggested that a failed 2000 bid would lead to an increased pace of reform of sport,[24] and subsequent events have shown this to be taking place. The sense of common purpose, referred to earlier, is now less easy to distinguish with the arrival of the sponsor, the foreign coach, the foreign player, the TV/media interest, the commercial contract. There is a danger that reduced spending by government will create uncertainty for those parts of the sports system remaining under the government wing, including sports science.

Also indicative of the future direction of Chinese sport is the decline in non-Olympic sports and, conversely, the increasing importance of the Olympic programme. The Chinese National Games (those under the People's Republic of China, post-1949, not to be confused with National Sports Games that took place in China pre-1949) started in 1959 and, held every four years (with some breaks between 1966 and 1976), have become a very important part of the national and international sporting effort of the country, also reflecting the reformist trend. Brownell[25] suggests that the Chinese National Games, held in Guangzhou, southern China, in 1987, already displayed strong moves towards a western pattern. The 7th National Games (1993, held partly in Chengdu, Sichuan province and partly in Beijing) comprised competitions in forty-three events, thirteen of which were not in the Olympic programme. Sports leaders were saying[26] that future Games would be further trimmed back, in line with the Olympic programme. By the time of the 1997 National Games (held in Shanghai), this had happened. With the exception of wushu, the programme of events in Shanghai was Olympic, which in itself was not remarkable, but the abandoned sports were those that were typically included in the family of sports followed by Communist nations – such as radio controlled model boat racing, radio orienteering, board games and fin swimming (a sport virtually unheard of in the West, but a feature of competitive sport in China until the mid-1990s). They were expendable in the new order of things. Without alternative sources of funding, such as a national lottery, it is possible that China's fledgling success in international sport will cause a division of sports into those that may be described as high profile and those that operate at a more parochial level. Various groupings of sport may be discerned:

1   Olympic sports
2   International sports – high profile, e.g. soccer, tennis
3   Indigenous/traditional sports – e.g. wushu
4   International/'Communist' sports – low profile, e.g. fin swimming
5   Non-physical sports, e.g. board games

The first two categories will continue to receive help from the government as part of the image building process. The third category will attract attention as being 'uniquely' Chinese or Oriental. The fourth category will not be supported by the government or may even cease altogether, and the fifth category will be separated from the Olympic effort and assigned to their own federations for support and development. This division would represent a realignment of Chinese sport that would bring it more into line with western models.

A major part of understanding Chinese sport, especially for the westerner, is an appreciation of the wide range of lifestyles that confront the visitor. It would be a mistake to assume that, because China is making substantial economic and sporting progress, all aspects of life are progressing equally. Several factors should be noted.

1   *The rural–urban differences*. China is administratively governed on five levels: the state, the province, the county, the city and the townships/villages. Within and between these levels, the provision for sport can vary substantially. The largest province, Sichuan, has a population of 100 million people divided into almost 200 counties, together with city populations of several million in Chengdu and Chongqing.[27] Provision for sport is thus a huge task when set against other government priorities. Whereas most European countries have developed community facilities for sport and have extensive networks of sports clubs, China has only rudimentary provision at present. Nor is such provision evenly distributed. The large cities are relatively rich in facilities compared to the smaller towns and villages, but because three-quarters of China's population live in the 'countryside', the problem of lack of facilities is more acute. It is easy to understand why China has developed Sport for the Elite in advance of Sport for All. The introduction of the five-day week (after a transition period of alternate five- and six-day weeks) has, for the city dweller especially, substantially altered the pattern of life and brought forward the time when the public expectation of Sport for All is likely to rise significantly.

2   *Transport and communication.* For provincial sports teams, for soccer clubs and the wealthier fan, for the urgent meeting or the special occasion, travel around China is usually by air. A flight from Guangzhou in the south to the capital Beijing takes about four hours. Land-based transport between cities or provinces is a slow and time consuming affair, in crowded conditions, although between some of the major cities – Beijing, Shanghai, Tianjin, Nanjing – there are new road and rail networks that give a fairly rapid link. Beyond that, there is a shortage of good transport communications, making much of inter-city or inter-town travel a tedious task. The larger rivers provide important links, too, but these arteries are slow and time consuming. A river trip from Chongqing in central China on the Chang Jiang (Yangstze River) to Shanghai on the east coast takes four-and-a-half days (about two days by train). Road links between small towns and villages may only be along uneven, unfinished tracks on which vehicles lurch and bounce alarmingly. Within the cities, people use bus, taxi or bicycle, all of which are convenient, although they produce congestion, especially at peak hours, and there is a constant battle between cyclist and motorist which slows everything down! All of this does not prevent Chinese people from travelling short or long distances, but it does impose certain constraints on human movement that have a direct impact on sport. Even with the five-day week, there is still insufficient time to get to nearby places on a regular basis, such as would be needed by inter-town or inter-village sports leagues. The improvement of this aspect of Chinese life would seem to be crucial for the long-term development of sport at club level.

3   *The pressure of economic change.* 'No money, no honey' is a phrase used to describe the economic situation facing Chinese citizens today. It is a situation driven by two factors. First, government economic reform is forcing a restructuring of industry – including the industry of sport (for example soccer). For some, this has been a golden opportunity to start up in business (Li Ning, ex-gymnastics champion, has established his brand name sportswear) and gain a degree of financial independence. For others, it has undermined their previous financial security that stemmed from the government's 'iron rice bowl' policy. They have little opportunity or ability to 'xia hai' – the Chinese term for 'jumping into the sea' or 'getting your feet wet', that is, setting up in business. Such people are exposed to fluctuations in the market economy, where bonuses may go up with profits but down with losses. Second, although the economic reforms have led to rapid growth, China experienced high inflation during the 1990s (which the government, in 1998, is planning to reduce to 3 per cent). Those families with two reasonable incomes can absorb inflation, though presumably not forever, whilst others have to seek a third income from somewhere and yet others have to lower their standard of living, which may already be marginal. With the economy growing and salary differentials

increasing, there are those whose lifestyles are becoming more affluent and for whom leisure is becoming significant. All the same, 100 yuan for a ticket to watch the Chinese national soccer team (August 1995, Sichuan) is still beyond the means of many people. Economic pressures in an inflationary economy have thus reduced leisure opportunities for some.

4 *The status of sport and exercise.* It is true that China has responded to the government's four reforms, in agriculture, industry, science and technology and defence, but only in the 1990s has the government begun to pay serious attention to fitness and lifestyle, through the Fitness for All project (1995). *China Daily*[28] reported that a survey in Guangdong Province had shown women intellectuals to be taking too little exercise and that more education was needed in this field. The impression is that, with notable exceptions, sport has yet to become a regular and active part of Chinese lifestyle. Exceptions would include school physical education, special sports schools and traditional activities, such as *tai ji quan* and *qigong*, but as Reekie shows, in Chapter 13 of this volume, city life offers far more opportunity for participation in sport than the countryside – yet it is the latter where the large majority of the population live. The value of sport and exercise, although changing, has yet to become recognized by everyone.

5 *Traditional Oriental sports. Tai ji quan, qi gong* and *wushu* are very distinctive forms of exercise that the Chinese have practised for centuries. Asia in general has developed several forms of exercise that have no real counterpart in the West, although many are also practised there now. The Asian forms have become stylized and ritualized – even reified, for example sumo wrestlers throwing salt, the display of *kata* in judo, and *tai ji quan* – in quite different ways from western competitive sports. Surrounding the martial arts of China, there is still an aura of mystery, a sense of something different. Sports science does not dominate the training and practice of these ancient forms of exercise. International federations have not sanitised the activity by chopping away tradition and replacing it with 'competition rules'. For those westerners who take them up, China is still the dominant, defining body for practice, training, philosophy and the source of inspiration. Keen to become 'masters of the craft', they turn to China for the deepest level of understanding and the highest level of teaching, and whereas Olympic sport is regularly associated with drugs, such scandals do not pervade *wushu*. But even the long traditions of *wushu* are not exempt from evidence of change, and starting in 1998 a 'Dan' system[29] is being introduced in order to standardize the various levels of achievement amongst practitioners 'both at home and throughout the world', and this 'after a thousand years being without such a system'.[30] Besides the merit in the development, there is the risk that the essential Chinese qualities of *wushu* will gradually be lost as the process of standardization follows its course.[31]

CONCLUDING REMARKS

Until the beginning of 1998, the planned restructuring of the State Sports Commission had continued, with the extension of the management centre system to twenty sports, and the reduction of the commission to 380 staff and just twelve departments, for the overall administration of the country's sport. Autonomy for sport was increasing by every move, but just three months later came the announcement, in March 1998, of the closure of the Sports Commission. Part of a whole package of government restructuring designed to lead the drive for a more efficient system, the changes were sweeping in their extent and profound in their potential for the future of China. Figures 1.1, 1.2 and 1.3 outline the structure of the sports system at this time.

In closing the Sports Commission, was the government simply washing its hands of sport, saying that it no longer was interested in the national cause? Was it saying that it no longer could afford to develop it? Or was it yet another move towards a market economy? A gap has been created between government and sport that, for the first time since 1949, amounts to the partial de-politicization of sport. Where do the reforms leave the existing structure of sport? There are, clearly, some sports that are unlikely to become professional in the manner of soccer – gymnastics and swimming for example. The countrywide network of sports schools, ranging from spare time to full time, remains firmly in place, as does the support network of research institutes, and the objective of international success in world and Olympic competition has not changed, which will ensure the continuing involvement of government in overall planning. However, as a more flexible system develops and lifestyles change, as commercialism and professionalism come into sport alongside a growth in participation, the general focus of the system may become more blurred. Formerly, whatever its weaknesses, the sports system was a united and co-operative venture with a sense of common purpose, and this meant concentrating on Olympic success.

The twenty-first century approaches, and sport in the global sense has become a dominant social force through the Olympic and international arenas. But as the achievements and records of champions stretch ever further into the distance, it is important to remember that, for the majority of people, the chance to take part in sport depends on simple factors, such as having enough time and energy, being close to a suitable facility, being able to afford the equipment, getting basic instruction and so on. In the case of China, the strategy for achieving world records or Olympic gold standard is both fairly well understood and in place: early selection and training, full-time expert coaching, the input and support of sports science research, the development of and involvement in top-class competition. Whilst countries may differ in the balance of some of these components, in the way in which they are organized, and in their ability to deliver them, the components for success are fully recognized today. However, to understand the contextual

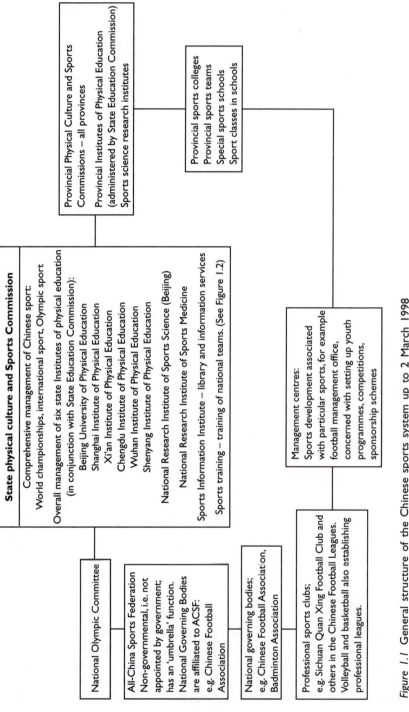

Figure 1.1 General structure of the Chinese sports system up to 2 March 1998

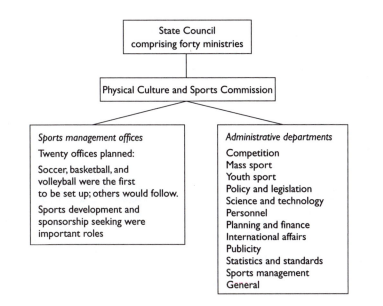

Figure 1.2 Administrative sections of the State Physical Culture and Sports Commission in January 1998

position of sport in China – its 'Chineseness' – demands a much fuller awareness of Chinese culture, traditions and values, and that is a complex task. As China moves towards reforming its sports system, and as the country develops economic strength, the question of 'sport for the many' as opposed to 'sport for the few' is likely to come to the fore, and it is this aspect that will ultimately shape China's sports system.

NOTES

1 A full account of the Chinese economy in the 1990s can be found in S. Long, *China to 2000: Reform's Last Chance* (Economic Intelligence Unit, Special Report M209, 1992).
2 The Silk Road was an ancient caravan route linking China with the West, used from Roman times and taking its name from the silk which was a major Chinese export.
3 The Japanese occupied and controlled the tip of the Liaodong Peninsula prior to 1938; they occupied north-eastern China ('Manchuria') in 1931, and Beijing was under both Chinese and Japanese control in 1936.
4 Although the Chinese Civil War, which led to the founding of the People's Republic on 1 October 1949, is correctly referred to as running from 1946 to 1949, it should be remembered that the conflict between the defeated Guomindang and the Communists stretched back to the 1920s and included the famous Long March of 1934 when the Goumindang hounded the Communists for almost a year, pursuing them for thousands of kilometres before they ran out of steam against the growing threat of Japanese invasion.

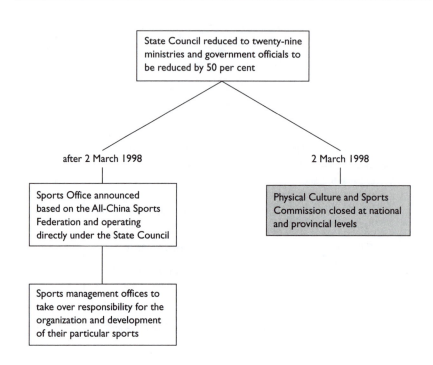

Figure 1.3 Structure of the Chinese sports system after 2 March 1998

5 Nineteenth-century China was a major trading post for western powers, such as Britain, France, Germany and Portugal, disputes over which led to various treaties and, for example, the British takeover of Hong Kong.
6 Confucius, 551–479 BC; Buddhism spread to Northern China from India AD 75–100; Taoism – sixth century BC (following Confucius).
7 Gu Shi Quan, 'Introduction to ancient and modern Chinese physical culture', in Knuttgen, H.G. *et al.* (eds) *Sport in China* (Human Kinetics, 1990).
8 The Guomindang (also spelt Kuomintang) were the Nationalists led by Chiang Kai Shek who were eventually defeated by the Communists and in 1949 fled to (what is now) Taiwan to set up the Republic of China.
9 See J. Kolatch. *Sports, Politics and Ideology in China* (Jonathan David, 1972) for a more detailed account of the arrival of western sports into China.
10 J. Howell, 'Civil society', in Benewick, R. and Wingrove, P. (eds), *China in the 1990s* (Macmillan, 1995).
11 'Soy Paste Vat' is a term used by Bo Yang in his analysis of Chinese culture to describe its complexity. Bo Yang, *The Ugly Chinaman* (Allen and Unwin, 1991).
12 Zhang Li, 'An analysis of the corporate attributes of individual sports associations in China', paper presented at the Asian Conference on Comparative Physical Education and Sport, Shanghai, December 1994.
13 President's Order, Number 55, President Jiang Zemin, 29 August 1995.
14 President's Order, *op. cit.*

15 President's Order, *op. cit.*

16 S.E. Brownell 'The changing relationship between sport and the state in the People's Republic of China', in Landry, F.Z. and Yerles, M. (eds), *Sport: the Third Millennium* (Les Presses de l'Universite Laval, 1991). Brownell comments on the high cost of the National Games, and the inability of many cities to afford to host them. This view was confirmed at the 7th National Games, 1993 (Chengdu and Beijing), in the author's own conversations with sports leaders.

17 *China News Digest*, 27–8 March 1998, p. 4.

18 Figure quoted in author's discussions with the Sports Commission, January 1998.

19 See Godfrey Kwok-yung Yeung, 'The People's Liberation Army and the market economy', in Benewick, R. and Wingrove, P. (eds) *China in the 1990s* (Macmillan, 1995).

20 J. Needham, *Science and Civilisation in China* (Cambridge University Press, 1956, Volume 1, and 1960, Volume 2).

21 Mah Jun Ren, quoted in *The Daily Telegraph*, 18 October 1993, p. 44. There is clear evidence that the educational opportunities for people from the countryside are far below those of city dwellers, as the following figures show:

	All China	Sichuan – cities	Sichuan – countryside	Sichuan – all
University graduates per 10,00 population	15	157	21	31

Source: The Population Census Office of the State Council of China in the *Population Atlas of China* (OUP, 1987)

Although there has been a slight increase in the numbers of students in higher education over recent years to around 0.2 per cent of the population, the above table remains the broad picture (see also S. Long) *China to 2000: Reform's Last Chance* (Economic Intelligence Unit, Special Report M209, 1992).

22 R. Jones, 'Sport in the community in China', paper presented at the ISCPES Conference, Prague, 1994.

23 *Zhong Guo Zu Qiu Bao*, published weekly; *Zu Qiu Shi Jie,* published twice monthly, are examples.

24 Author's conversations with sports leaders at the 7th National Games, Beijing, 1993.

25 S. Brownell, *Training the Body for China* (University of Chicago Press, 1995), pp. 99–119.

26 Author's conversations with sports leaders at the 7th National Games, Beijing, 1993.

27 In 1997, the Chinese government announced plans to change the administrative status of Chongqing to that of 'municipality', with a population expected to grow to 30 million. The new status thus separates Chongqing from its former administrative position as part of Sichuan province. There are three other municipalities in China: Beijing, Tianjin and Shanghai.

28 *China Daily,* 6 September 1995, p. 4. Make Time for Exercise, a survey by the Women's Federation of Guangdong Province, showing that professional women are not sufficiently health conscious.

29 As in Judo, the 'Dan' system will indicate level of achievement.

30 *The Messenger*, 1998, Vol. 9, No. 4, p. 3. (*The Messenger* is the overseas news-letter of Radio Beijing.)

31 Since becoming an Olympic sport in 1964, judo, although rooted in Japan, has lost much of its pre-Olympic Japanese style.

Chapter 2

Recreation and sport in Ancient China

Primitive society to AD 960

Mike Speak

INTRODUCTION

For convenience, this historical introduction is divided into three periods. Ancient China is considered by historians to be that period of Chinese history stretching from the neolithic period to the middle of the nineteenth century or the end of the Qing dynasty in 1840. This chapter describes physical activity and forms of sport up to AD 960. Chapter 3 investigates the second millennium as far as 1840. Chapter 4 follows China into the modern era up to 1949.

Britain came to be regarded, rightly or wrongly, as the cradle of modern sports, in the same way that Greece was identified with the ancient and later modern Olympic Games. Yet the universality of play and recreation does not allow a single country, or even continent, to lay claim to the parenthood of sport. Gernet (1982: 3) has made the point that Chinese civilization has been the guiding spirit for a large section of humanity, and that 'the West which has borrowed from China right down to our day without realising it, is far from recognising its sizeable debt to her'.

Recent progress in international sport by China has sharpened the interest of western observers, but there is a long and respected history of physical culture, recreation and sport in Ancient China which has remained largely unrevealed outside China and even within its borders, but which, in the complex pattern of the history of world sport and recreation, deserves serious attention. The period of history under consideration spawned a wide range of activities, many of which withstand serious scrutiny as the forerunners of modern sport and carried marks of sophistication well in advance of similar activities in the West.

THE DEVELOPMENT OF RECREATIONAL AND SPORTING ACTIVITY IN ANCIENT CHINA

Political and economic influences

One of the problems facing the sport historian in this context is the vastness of the time period involved in the spread of Chinese history, the range of climatic differences and influences, from the cold wastes of Siberia to the tropical heat of the South China Sea, the diversity of peoples inhabiting the vast land mass known as China and the variety of individual cultures and languages involved.

Four cultures have been identified by demographic and anthropological historians, namely: sedentary populations with a highly developed agriculture, nomadic cattle-raisers of the grasslands and deserts, mountain peoples of the huge Himalayan Tibetan complex, and mixed cultures of the tropical zones. The recreational lives of these populations generally reflected the basic background culture. The nomadic peoples enjoyed a lifestyle which was almost permanent training for war, incorporating horse training, hunting and horseback exercises. Mountain peoples endured a hardy lifestyle and were equally warlike in their habits, whereas the sedentary and coastal plain cultures tended to be less aggressive in their approaches to life and recreation.

Chinese civilization, like other great civilizations throughout history, has been a perpetual, dynamic creation, occasionally absorbing external influences from distant civilizations. Time periods are so vast that whole periods of history are often referred to as a homogeneous whole, for example the Ming Dynasty (1368–1644), yet there are variations within each time period and certainly within each region which ensure that a simple treatment is impossible. Political, economic and social systems are living organisms which continually adapt to change and the religious, warrior monarchy of archaic times (1600–900 BC) has nothing in common with the centralized empire administered by paid civil servants established in the third century AD. The political system of the Sung period (AD 960–1279) and the authoritarianism of the Ming dynasty are worlds apart.

The Chinese economy tended towards decentralization. The major river valleys which absorbed the bulk of the population offered ideal conditions for crop cultivation, and China rapidly developed into a major agrarian society, relying on large-scale production of food to support political, economic and social developments. There tended to be a division of labour between males, who tilled the soil, and females, who wove cloth, highlighting the division between physical effort and sedentary role accepted for millennia. The mode of production isolated small groups of people in self-sufficiency, and social intercourse, particularly in large groups, became the exception. This may partly explain the obvious pleasure of social gatherings during festivals. Major mass gatherings were the exception rather than the norm.

Self-sufficiency also curtailed the need for urban-centred economies and substantial commercial trading, and during certain periods of Chinese history, central governments sought to actively confine commercial trade. The reasons were simple: commerce and manufacturing production would compete with agriculture for a labour force and the primary occupation should be protected.

Small farmers also provided the backbone of military forces and corvée labour, and their conversion to an industrial or commercial workforce would compete with this. Change and competition would challenge the traditional authority of the feudal rulers and this was to be prevented. The Han government (206 BC–AD 220) lowered the social status of merchants, forbade them to become officials, increased trading taxes, changed the monetary system to prevent accumulated wealth and monopolized key commodities such as iron and salt.

In summary, even in a highly centralized political system, decentralized economies persisted and were encouraged. No opportunity was offered for national cohesion, festivals retained a fairly local character, and traditional Chinese recreations demonstrated great diversity.

Military, medical, philosophical and social factors

A further factor influencing the nature of physical activity and recreation was the need for military preparation. In most societies, there has been a clear link between military training and physical fitness and there are substantiated interactions in Ancient China. Horsemanship and archery were basic military skills, and both developed social forms. Charioteering and archery were both included in the curriculum of educational establishments for young aristocrats, together with propriety, music, writing and arithmetic. Running, throwing and jumping also evolved from military exercises, and *wushu*, or Chinese martial arts, is an early and inseparable component of Chinese culture. Exercises were performed naturally or with implements and, as cavalry and chariots became supplemented by infantry, a variety of forms of *wushu* were employed for training artisans and foot soldiers. Forms also developed for personal fitness training and for entertainment purposes.

A further major influence on the nature of recreational activity in Ancient China was the development and direction of medical theory. A key element was *Qi* (air) which had an abstract and broader meaning than simply air or oxygen, and whose precise nature is still debatable. The theory of *Qi* emanated from Taoism, which proposed that, in the universe, all was interconnected and interacted, and *Qi* became all-important as the material forming the human body, having responsibility for the physical functions of human beings and connecting the human body to its external environment. Human life depended on the constant interchange between the internal body and the external environment, and breathing came to hold a predominant position in Chinese exercise.

The concept of *Yin* and *Yang* which appeared in the late Western Zhou period (eleventh century BC–771 BC), but was refined and developed in *I Zhuan* (Book of Changes) in the Warring States period (475–221 BC) was also an influential factor. The theory was that all things in the universe possess the nature of *Yin* (a negative, female, cosmic force) and *Yang* (a positive, male force), embodied in natural phenomena such as heaven, earth, wind, water and fire, but also in human society as master and subject, father and son, husband and wife, even and odd numbers, softness and hardness in personality, and virtue and evil in behaviour. The basis of the theory is that all is well when *Yin* and *Yang* are balanced and mutually harmonious.

The medical theory was that good health will result from the balancing of these two agents, yet balance and harmony are not easily achieved. *Jingluo*, or the network of *Qi*, is the channel through which *Qi* flows, connecting all parts of the human body. Where the flow is smooth and uninterrupted, bodily functions will be good, but if stagnation, or blockage, occurs, pain and disease would be likely to follow. Acupuncture is based on the theory of re-opening blocked pathways. Chinese traditional exercises, such as *Dao Yin*, seek to cultivate the *Qi* by the intake of breath and undertaking certain physical exercises to ensure smooth circulation of *Qi* in the network. Methods of breathing are emphasized, but emotional states involving anger, joy, sorrow, likes and dislikes will affect the balance of *Yin* and *Yang*, so that a calm, relaxed state is an essential concomitant of breathing and exercise. A mental approach was inseparably linked to physical exercise, and Chinese physicians recommended gentle, non-vigorous exercise, since vigorous exercise would make it impossible to achieve the harmony of breathing, movement and mood.

Activities associated with the maintenance of health and fitness in China emphasized a harmony of movement, consciousness and breathing to stimulate vital energy. Muscular development was not the primary purpose, and again, reflecting the rural nature of society, many of the movements imitated the motions of animals. Muscular development and beauty was never highly valued by Taoism and Confucianism. External appearance was less important than moral virtue, and virtue and mental health in turn were likely to play a fundamental part in achieving good health and longevity, respected goals. The *Shang Shu* (Book of History), which records affairs in the Xia, Shang and Western Zhou dynasties (2100–771 BC) claims 'of the five happinesses: the first is long life; the second is riches; the third is soundness of body and serenity of mind; the fourth is love of virtue; the fifth an end crowning the life'. There were several schools of exercise, but whatever the variations, all were concerned with longevity and achieving mental and physical harmony, and were more concerned with internal organic function than musculature, strength and vigour.

The simple agricultural life of the sedentary populations allowed experiences of natural life to be absorbed into recreational activity. Imitation of animals occurred in early forms of dance, and also became part of *Dao Yin* and *Wushu* through forms of traditional exercise. Early medicine also reflected the proximity of humans and nature, and in *Shan Hai Jing*, written before 221 BC, sixty-two species of animals and forty-two species of plants are recorded and recommended for medicinal purposes. Exercises were described according to the behaviour of animals, affording a vivid picture to the exponent of how movements should be performed. Taoism also recommended a return to nature, and regarded all creatures as equal, since all had *Qi* and *Yin* and *Yang*, and there should be no discrimination between all living forms. Man was required to live in harmony with nature, according to natural laws and in tune with a natural rhythm. Neo-Taoism, however, moved from a passive acceptance of the need to follow nature's way to a more dynamic reflection of the vigour and freedom of animals. After the Western Han period (206–24 BC), physical exercises took on a greater imitation of wild animals, evidence of which is available in the *Dao Yin* silk painting in the Han tomb of Ma Wang Duai.

Ren (1988) draws attention to certain philosophical factors which helped to shape the nature of sport and physical recreation in Ancient China, and contrasts them with very different ideals and purposes within Greek civilization. Since the nature of sport in a society is likely to reflect the value system of that society, consideration has to be given to the moral, philosophical and social attitudes towards physical activity in Chinese society. Competition in Chinese society was invariably discouraged, and emphasis was placed on harmony. The most influential philosophical schools, Confucianism, from 500 BC, and Taoism, from 100 BC, totally opposed competition. The former had benevolence at its core and strove to maintain a harmonious patriarchal social structure. Conflict, rivalry and competition were likely to damage this harmony. Political life consisted of a complicated hierarchical structure of administration, in which people were ranked according to their socio-economic status. The Empire was divided into thirty-six *Jin* (commanderies), each comprising several *Xian* (sub-prefectures), all with a variety of officials whose duties involved agriculture, taxation, ceremonials, the law, tribute, militia and education. Inequality was universal, between and within classes, and was reinforced to preserve the feudal hierarchy by clothing, residences and ceremonies. There were also three 'cardinal guides' which first appeared in the works of Xun Zi (313–238 BC) and Han Fei Zi (280–233 BC) to regulate social behaviour. These stated that ruler guides subject, father guides son and husband guides wife. These social and moral precepts and hierarchical structures gave little room for competition, and both society and its recreational forms tended to emphasize the cultivation of virtue, self-improvement and recreational pleasure.

The sedentary cultures, rooted in agriculture and politically and commercially estranged from competitive practices, tended towards non-competitive forms of recreation. The process of physical activity was emphasized rather than the outcome. Some activities were associated with health and general physical fitness, others remained co-operative in nature. Activities such as archery often identified and reinforced a hierarchical social order, and many activities concentrated on the cultivation of virtue as a priority. In archery and *touhu* for example, participants were required to demonstrate moral virtue in addition to skill, so that winner and loser equally could gain respect. Indeed Zhou (1991: 71) suggests that, because of the special emphasis placed on moral education and ethics in traditional Chinese society, ancient Chinese sports were overburdened with moral principles.

The emphasis on thoughtful recreation is also revealed in a nine-level hierarchy of competence in board games, with *Wei Qi* (Go), a game played with black and white pieces on a board of a hundred squares, representing the highest form of Chinese wisdom, being fully developed by the Warring States period. *Xiang Qi* was played with sixteen pieces on each side, and both games were attempts to represent forms of complex military strategy.

As in most agricultural societies, festivals had a seasonal nature, often integrated with crop production and seasonal rhythms. There were often religious and contained superstitious undertones, particularly arising from folk legends. Whatever the reason for festivals, however, they became a vital ingredient in the social life of rural communities, and developed, according to Gramet (1932: 180), into 'festivals of union in which people became aware of the bonds which unite them and, at the same time, of their oneness with their natural environment'. Many of the festivals incorporated forms of physical expression. Dragon and Lion dances were both symbolic and physically demanding, and were performed at certain festivals. Dragon boat racing was the major activity on the fifth day of the fifth lunar month and mountain climbing has been associated with the Double Ninth Festival since the Eastern Han period (AD 25–220).

Dance forms are common in most early societies, and in Ancient China served purposes in religious rites, recreation, education, health and fitness. By the Western Han period (206 BC–AD 24) a variety of secular dances for recreational purposes had emerged and involved all social classes. There was a mimicking in early dance forms of animal behaviour, but gradually dance as entertainment emerged, and dancers employed long sleeves, weapons and musical instruments to accompany the dance to entertain audiences. The Han court set up a special institution, *Yue Fu* (Department of Music), and employed the finest artistes from the whole country as professional entertainers.

Summary

This introduction has attempted to offer information on the nature of sport and recreational activity in Ancient China. There are obviously major differences in the nature of sport and recreation during different periods of Chinese history, and in their availability in certain forms to different sections of the population, aspects which need to be further explored. There appears to be evidence, however, that the nature of sport and recreation was often a product of philosophical directions, which stressed co-operation and harmony at the expense of competition. Equally, religious and medical proponents who stressed the therapeutic nature of exercise, breathing and mental state as opposed to the development of strength, musculature and vigour had an important effect on the direction of Chinese physical recreation.

The variety of ethnic groups, geographic locations and traditional occupations also influenced the range and natures of sports practised. In the nomadic and mountainous peoples, more vigorous forms of physical activity were adopted, often linked with horsemanship and preparation for warfare. Conversely, in the agricultural and coastal populations, gentler forms of recreation were practised, and co-operation was the watchword. Festivals provided an opportunity for mass celebration and the practice of communal forms of physical activity and entertainment.

The process of physical activity was often stressed at the expense of outcome, and some activities reinforced the social hierarchy and concentrated on the cultivation of virtue and good behaviour. The relationship between recreation and mental stimulation should also be stressed and was evident in a variety of board games and exercises which evolved. Dance and acrobatic entertainment were prominent in a variety of forms throughout Chinese history, in early times as a form of social expression, but later for the entertainment of imperial courts and the aristocracy. These forms of physical recreation and sport will be illustrated in subsequent descriptions, together with commentary on the significance of activities undertaken.

PHYSICAL ACTIVITIES IN PRIMITIVE CHINESE SOCIETY (3,000–476 BC)

The Neolithic stage of culture in China (8,000–2,000 BC) marked the end of the mesolithic, hunting and gathering phase of history, and saw the start of settled societies, the building of villages, farming, horticulture and the use of pottery. By the eleventh century BC, the surge in social organization was accompanied by sophisticated knowledge and techniques, bronzes, architectural design, the chariot and forms of writing. Excavations of the Shang civilization (sixteenth to eleventh centuries BC) have revealed royal palaces, walled cities, chariots and bronzes reflecting an organized society with a developed aristocracy. The Shang were replaced in power by the Zhou (eleventh century to 771 BC) and evidence of the nature of this society is provided by a chronicle added to the *Annals of Lu*, called *Traditions of Tso*. Society was based on a hierarchy of domains and families who owed their authority to the number of chariots owned, their religious privileges including the right to dance, links with the royal household and possession of treasures. During this period emerged the ideal of the noble warrior and the ethic of honour.

Throughout history, the development of man's physical skills and capacities has served a number of purposes – military, social, educational and health. There were strong links with military preparation during this period, and charioteering, the most sophisticated form of warfare, formed part of the education curriculum for young aristocrats. They were required to drive skilfully, and the primitive design of the chariot and difficulties presented by the terrain required great skill. According to *Shi Jing*, the Book of Songs, chariot races were held amongst the nobility and gambling was involved.

During the Zhou period, the emperor ordered his leaders and commanders to give instruction in military operations, and exercise soldiers in archery, charioteering and wrestling in the first month of the winter. Other natural activities used for military purposes were running, jumping and throwing, which increased in value with the decline of charioteering and the emergence of the infantry soldier. In the state of Wu (sixth century BC), soldiers were trained for seven years, and were required to run the equivalent of 300 *Li* in full armour, carrying weapons, without resting. This form of endurance training appears to have contributed to the Wu's successful attack on the Chu capital in 506 BC. In the state of Lu, a general selected 300 soldiers by placing a jumping hurdle in front of his residence, selection being achieved by those who cleared it three times.

There is also evidence during this period of the emergence of tug-of-war as a military and social activity. This developed during the late spring and autumn Period (770–476 BC) when, according to *Jingchu suishi ji*, a general of the state of Chu taught his sailors the activity in preparation for combat. There is a further suggestion that during the Warring States period, Gong Shubau, a well-known engineer, designed a long rope made from the skin of bamboo to help Chu warships in a naval battle. Gradually, the activity developed into a recreational game, played initially in the south of China. Two teams competed, accompanied by the beating of drums, and during the Han period it became a custom to play the game in January.

Wrestling was yet another activity primarily used for military training. Legend claims that when Huangdi tried to conquer Chiyou, the latter knew how to wrestle, and wrestlers during the Zhou dynasty copied this style. Certain styles incorporated head butting, and legendary battles between the tribes of the yellow Emperor and the Chiyou were later synthesized into entertainment, comprising music, dance, acrobatics, sports and magic.

During the mesolithic period, simple forms of bow and arrow existed for hunting, and gradually refinements were made for military purposes. There is evidence of archery 4,000 years ago in China, but by the period of the Western Zhou, it had developed into an essential military skill and encompassed ritual as well as martial forms. Archery was considered essential for the strength and defence of the nation, but was also used for the selection of feudal dignitaries and officers during the Zhou period. Ritual archery was highly significant and was regulated by complex rules based on social rank. There were several different forms of archery. Great archery formed part of ceremonies to worship divinities and ancestors, and success was based not only on accuracy but physical demeanour and harmony with music. Guest archery was performed when kings paid respect to the emperor and recreation archery took place when the emperor feasted his senior officers. District-drinking archery took place during festivals, whenever the head of a district led people in archery practice, or every three years on the graduation of aristocratic students. Boys of 15 years of age were required to learn charioteering and archery.

Archery also served social and moral purposes. There was an element of competition involved, although this was not regarded as important, and winners were awarded a banner, but targets, bows, arrows and conditions varied according to social status. Ritual archery was accompanied by music and dance and served to confirm the social status and virtue of the archer. Confucius claimed, 'There is no contention between gentlemen. The nearest to it is perhaps archery. In archery they bow and make way for one another as they go up, and on coming down they drink together. Even the way they contend is gentlemanly' (Radice 1979: 68). Also recognized in ritual shooting was the archer's propriety, good character, filial love and love of learning. In *Sheyi* (The Definition of Archery) it is claimed that 'archery can make people virtuous . . . all the wise kings like it'.

Gradually, during the Zhou dynasty, as archery became more ritualized and associated with ceremonies, constraints of space led to the creation of a similar activity, held indoors or outdoors, called *touhu*. The game, which consisted of throwing arrows into a pitcher, soon became popular and detailed rules were drawn up. Confucius noted the changed nature of archery when he claimed, 'In archery, the point lies not in piercing the hide (equivalent to the bull's eye) for the reason that strength varies from man to man. This was the way of antiquity' (Radice 1979: 70).

Outside privileged social circles, and forming part of everyday or festival life, there existed a number of recreational activities. There is evidence of swimming in a pictograph character inscribed on bones and tortoiseshells in the Shang dynasty and, in *Shi Jing* (Book of Songs), there is a hint that women were swimming in this period. Boating is referred to as a recreational activity, and according to Tan (1987: 2) there is evidence in the Book of Songs that women enjoyed fishing, boating, singing and dancing, and certain activities were engaged in beside the river in March, and linked directly or indirectly to the concept of marriage and reproduction.

The period also saw the emergence of board games, which reflected the frequency and complexity of warfare in Ancient China. Two popular forms were developed, complex board strategies were involved, and these eventually developed into forms of chess.

It is doubtful if football emerged during this period, but a popular outdoor game was 'board hitting', consisting of a board being placed in the ground and serving, at a distance of 30–40 paces, as a target for players with sticks. It was traditionally a game for older country people, but was also played by boys during the December festival.

Finally, and almost universally, dance was part of the fabric of social life. A painted bowl dating back to 1,000 BC depicts dancing figures, and a cliff carving in Yunnan Province, which is 3,000 years old, provides evidence of dance, running and pyramid acrobatics. In *Shang Shu* (Book of History), it is claimed that people in primitive society danced in imitation of animal movements, accompanied by the beating of a stone drum. Dance was divided into several forms. The gentle dance praised virtue and kindness, whereas the violent dance praised bravery and military achievement. The great dance, popular during the Huangdi and Zhou dynasties, consisted of seven types of dance, only available to those over 20 years of age. Younger people learned the little dance, which consisted of six forms. During the Zhou dynasty, all gentlemen and learned people danced, and dance served many purposes. Yoshi, a scholar, suggested that the purpose of dance was to train the body and regulate the spirit, to achieve peace of mind, quicken the senses and support social harmony. It served as a means of recreation, as an accompaniment to religious and ceremonial rites, and as a contributor to good health.

There is clear evidence during this early period of Chinese history of a wealth of physical activity, linked often with military or courtly life, but serving ceremonial, educational and recreational functions also. Many of these early forms of activity were to grow more sophisticated and functional as time passed.

PHYSICAL ACTIVITY IN CHINESE FEUDAL SOCIETY (476 BC–AD 220)

A changing society

The age of the Warring States (476–221 BC) was one of transformation in society, economy and culture. There was rapid movement towards a centralized state, a clear division between civil and military functions, and the emergence of a civil service. Uniform rules and laws replaced the rights, privileges and customs of former regimes, and state institutions, reward, punishment and collective responsibility characterized the new state.

There was further evolutionary change from 206 BC to AD 220 during the Han dynasties. The first Chinese Empire was founded by armed unification, and consolidated by the education of princes of other kingdoms at the Chinese court. The administrative system in use in China was extended to the Empire, which was divided into thirty-six, later forty-eight commanderies. Society grew increasingly hierarchical and the whole population was classified into twenty-four degrees of dignity. Measures of length and capacity were standardized, new standard characters devised, common coinage agreed, a network of imperial roads and canals constructed under harsh corvée, and a Great Wall erected on the northern frontier. Scientific and mechanical developments contributed to the increasing wealth of Han society. Steel replaced bronze, progress was made in agricultural techniques and production, the water mill and the wheelbarrow made their appearance, and some families grew rich in the ownership of iron and steelworks.

The period also witnessed the emergence of princely courts. After the initial harshness of the Han and its opposition to learned enemies of the state, culminating in the burning of books in 216 BC and the execution of 400 opponents of the state, the princely courts became centres of intellectual, literary, scientific and artistic activity. Information on the social life of the earlier periods was available in a number of classical documents produced by scribes and annalists. These include the *Shu* (writings) from the Shang court, the *Shih* (poems or odes) sung at ritual ceremonies, sacrifices and banquets, the Annals, which recorded events announced in the temple, and the Analects produced by the disciples of Confucius. The courts retained retinues of jugglers, acrobats and musicians, and the *fu* describe in great detail and in rhythmic and grand style the palaces, parks, hunts and entertainments of the courts.

The emergence of Taoism also gave rise to a change in life habits. Its emphasis on longevity through various techniques of breathing, diet and exercise known as the *yang-sheng* (nourishing the ritual principle), aimed at refining the body to render it invulnerable and able to delay the ageing process.

Physical activity in the military field

As society changed, so did its military organization. In previous eras, the possession of chariots was restricted to a small privileged group, who took part in battles and tournaments in open country to test the courage of conflicting noble houses. In the expansion of the Empire, however, bravery and ritual gave way to the serious business of conquering territory. The decline of chariots and promotion of the infantry saw a growth in importance of the sword, the crossbow and the cavalry. Social change also resulted in the disappearance of the *Shih*, a noble fighting knight, and his remodelling as an educated, politically aware citizen.

Ritual archery declined and the activity took on greater military importance. The state of Wei issued an act which encouraged archery training. Legal cases were decided by archery skills, with the consequence that people practised regularly and the state military machine benefited. There were also major technical developments. Several texts appeared on archery and an official in charge of archery training was appointed. Skill was high at this time and it was claimed that to miss a small target once in a 100 shots would have prevented an archer from being classed as expert.

As charioteering declined, equestrianism increased in importance, and by 307 BC, King Wu Ling of the State of Zhao developed the first cavalry from the northern, barbaric tribes. By 119 BC, the Han put 100,000 cavalry and 140,000 private horses into the field in one campaign, and in 111 BC, the emperor's victory parade incorporated 180,000 cavalry. Training of the cavalry led to recreational offshoots, and polo, which is supposed to have begun during the Eastern Han dynasty, proved popular as did acrobatics and archery on horseback. During the Western Han dynasty (206 BC–AD 24) hunting became a recreational activity for emperors and the nobility, and Liu Che (140–88 BC), the Han emperor, opened a forest hunting park west of Xian which measured hundreds of kilometres in circumference.

A number of sports appeared consisting of physical challenge. Fighting with bare hands and feet emerged, and a form developed which allowed kicking and striking but no holding. The development must have been extensive, as there are references to six texts on hand fighting, which in turn referred to 199 works of thirteen different schools on training hands and feet. *Quan* (boxing) and *Wushu* (martial arts) were more representative of individual forms of challenge, and their separation from collective military training later allowed *Wushu* to incorporate elements from *daoyin* and acrobatics and become a multi-functional activity for health, fitness, self-defence and entertainment.

After the Qin dynasty (221–206 BC), wrestling, which had enjoyed some popularity, lost much of its value and became an entertainment, but tug-of-war and weightlifting grew in popularity. The latter has a long history in China, and during the spring and autumn period (770–476 BC) and the Warring States period (475–221 BC), *kangding* (tripod lifting) and *tuoguan* (lifting a city gate bolt) were popular as demonstrations of strength. During the Western Han dynasty (206 BC–AD 24), when a thriving economy and stable political situation encouraged recreational activity, the court appointed an official to be in charge of *kangding*, and contestants who were victorious in a major competition would be granted an honorary title. Some kings promoted strong men to positions as high officials, an early example of social mobility through sport, and professional weightlifters thrived and demonstrated a wide variety of feats of strength. Other forms of weightlifting during this period were turning and lifting heavy stones and lifting a large wheel.

Fencing and swordplay became increasingly popular and emperors and officers alike carried swords. There were different schools of fencing in different regions, and in the *Han Shu* there were thirty-eight chapters on sword skills. Several physical activities which originated in military form later assumed recreational or entertainment functions. This applied particularly to the *Jiao Di* games which during the Han period became a synthesis of music, dancing, acrobatics, sports and magic. These games were held on various occasions, particularly on holidays and special celebrations, and served to demonstrate to visitor and trade delegations the cultural superiority of the Han. The games included feats of strength, acrobatics, horse-riding, pole climbing, balancing, juggling and dance and feats of hardship, like sword swallowing, together with shuttlecock kicking, kite-flying and dragon dances.

Other forms of social recreational physical activity which added sophistication to earlier raw forms were dance, *touhu* and board games. The Han court greatly encouraged dance, and established a special institute, *Yue Fu*, with eighty-three employees to entertain the court. Social forms of dance emerged which involved all classes of people. In the separation of military and civic authorities, *touhu* began to take on increasing importance for celebrations and special occasions. A symbolic form of archery, it was mainly played by the upper classes and adopted a complex system of rules and behaviour. Lessons in virtuous behaviour, character development and social skills were incorporated, and notions of respect for rank and elders, filial piety, deference, reverence and purity encouraged. Another form of the game was played by professional players and performed as an entertainment.

A rather more curious form of exercise and recreation emerged during this period. The swing was originally used by northern tribes for agility. The standard swing was introduced into central China between 770–476 BC, and the rotating swing had appeared by 475–221 BC. During the Han period, the swing grew more sophisticated and was introduced into the emperor's palace to be used by imperial concubines and their maids. The meaning of swing resembles long life in Chinese pronunciation, and it became symbolic to swing to please the emperor and encourage his long life.

It may be, however, that for western readers the most remarkable development of the whole period was football. There are suggestions in the literature that football may have been played in some form as early as 5,000 BC, but as *cuju* it first appears in historical literature in Sima Qian's *Shi Ji* (Historical Records) in the Han period. There is some doubt as to the precise origins of the game, some historians claiming that the yellow emperor devised the game for the purpose of military training, others that it emerged during the Warring States period, when warfare grew increasingly important to settle political conflict. The game was certainly in existence during this period as both *Shi Ji* and *Zhan Guo Ce* (History of the Warring States) record that the citizens of Linzi, a wealthy city, all enjoyed playing musical instruments, cock-fighting, dog hounds, chess and *cuju*.

Reference has already been made to the increasing demand for cavalry and infantry during this period. Conflict with the northern, nomadic Xiongnu required the Han to improve both cavalry and infantry and, in addition to training in both horseriding and archery, the military used *cuju* as a means of fitness training and identification of talented athletes. The historian Pan Gu (AD 32–92) recorded that when Huo Qubing, a general in the Han army, led his soldiers to the northern borders, he allowed his soldiers to construct a field to play *cuju*. The forms of *cuju* developed in the army had strong competitive characteristics in which teams attacked and defended their goals.

There were various forms of *cuju*, some involving goals such as are used today, others involving holes in the ground as the targets. The game was controlled by referees who were expected to be completely impartial. The game is described in the *Ju Cheng Ming* of the poet Li You (AD 50–130) of the later Han dynasty:

A round ball and a square wall,
Just like the Yin and Yang.
Moon-shaped goals are opposite each other,
Each side has six in equal number.

Select the captains and appoint the referee(s),
Based on the unchangeable regulations.
Don't regard relatives and friends,
Keep away from partiality.
Maintain fairness and peace
Don't complain of other's faults,
Such is the matter of *cuju*.
If all this is necessary for *cuju*.
How much more for the business of life.

Li Yen, in an article called *Cushiming*, also describes the nature of the pitch, surrounded by walls on all four sides. There were six goalkeepers on each team, but the total number of players is unknown. The team who scored most goals was the winner. The game was not only used for military training but also for entertainment purposes. The emperor Gaozu built a huge football pitch (*cujong*) in his palace, and in the preface of Luji's *Cugehang* he mentions that football pitches were not only built at the imperial court, but that the nobles and wealthy citizens also had private pitches.

Festival recreations

A number of physical activities related to seasonal festivals also appear to have originated or evolved during this period. With origins often integrated with legend, and with growing multicultural influences in the Chinese empire, these festivals became an important feature of social life. The Lantern Festival dates from this period and brought the lunar new year holidays to an end. Among the activities associated with the festival, some were of a physical recreation nature, including the dragon dance, in which ten people take on the form of a dragon and cause it to move in different directions. Physically demanding, the activity is still popular in Chinese culture, and a variety of dragon dances can be seen on formal and festival occasions. A dance of similar nature is the lion dance, which required a high level of physical fitness among participants, and which reputedly originated from combining two dances from the western regions of the Han empire. The dragon boat festival, which takes place on the fifth day of the fifth lunar month is supposed to have originated in the Warring States era, when Qu Yuan (340–278 BC), a minister of the State of Chu, urged reforms on a despotic prince. His counsel refused, he wrote a famous poem, *Li Sao*, which expressed his anxieties, and then committed suicide by drowning in the Milo river. Local fishermen tried unsuccessfully to save him or recover the body, and the day has been commemorated by the staging of dragon boat ceremonies and rituals since that period.

The festival of the double ninth, held on the ninth day of the ninth lunar month, originated during the Eastern Han period (AD 25–220), when Huan Jing and his family were advised by his teacher to escape disaster by going into the mountains and drinking chrysanthemum wine. On his return, he found that all his dogs and poultry had been killed. The festival was thereafter celebrated by climbing mountains on that date. The activity of kite flying, which became extremely popular during the Tang dynasty (AD 618–907), can be traced to the Warring States period when, according to Han Fei Ji, Mo Zi constructed a wooden kite which took him three years to complete, to fly for one day.

Health and exercise

There were also important developments in exercise and health during this period. Reliable literary evidence, according to Ren Hai (1991), began to appear about the nature of *Dao yin*.

> To pant, to puff, to hail, to sip, to spit out the old breath and draw in the new, practising bear-hangings and bird-stretchings, longevity his only concern – such is the life favoured by the scholar who practises Dao Yin, the man who nourishes his body, who hopes to live to be as old as Pen-Zu.
> (Ren 1991: 70)

It was believed that *Dao Yin* and massage came from central areas in China, but exactly what the exercises comprised was uncertain. In 1973, however, archaeologists discovered a painting on silk in a tomb in Changsha, Hunan Province. The painting, measuring 50 cm × 100 cm, was dated to the early Han dynasty, according to the burial date of the tomb occupant (168 BC). From the forty-four figures in the painting, several categories could be identified; movements for the treatment of disease, movements imitating the movement of animals, and movements with instruments. It is also worth noting that half of the figures are female, and the variety of dress suggests that figures are from a range of social groups. Exercises were not only characterized by an emphasis on breathing and imitation of animals, but by the harmony of mental and physical effort.

Summary

There is little doubt that the Han period was particularly influential in the proliferation and sophistication of recreational, physical and sporting activities in Ancient China. The changing requirements of both civil and military life led to the evolution of forms of physical activity to serve increased demands. In the military field, these were provided by new and improved forms of activity and training; horseriding, archery, tug-of-war, strength training, martial arts and *cuju*, which aimed to increase the fitness of both cavalry and infantry. In the civil field, recreational forms grew more sophisticated, with *touhu* establishing itself, archery serving social as well as military needs, and dance and a wide variety of entertainments becoming firmly established as part of court and social life. Board games were resurrected and many of the forms of physical recreation also adopted behavioural requirements which were the forerunners of rules, regulations and fair play.

This period, however, was to make its most significant contribution to the future of world sport and physical recreation by the establishment and formalizing of many activities which in modified forms are now part and parcel either of everyday life or competitive sport. Activities which now form part of the Olympic Games or world championship programmes were clearly evolving during this period – fencing, gymnastics, martial arts, archery (which underwent major technical advances), polo, arising from the increased demands for competence in cavalry, weightlifting, boxing, wrestling and football. Other activities which have become part of Asian or world culture, such as tug-of-war, dragon boat racing and board games, were also introduced during this rich period.

THE CHINESE MIDDLE AGES (AD 220–589)

Introduction

The period from the end of the Han dynasty to the period of the aristocratic empires of the Sui and Tang was marked by the decline of the state, dismemberment of Empire and collapse of urban economies. The Chin withdrew to the Yangtse valley, centralization disappeared with the emergence of an hierarchical aristocracy, which held the real power both at court and in the provinces, and state military strength was replaced by half-official, half-private armies of mercenaries recruited by local officials and aristocratic families.

By the fourth century, there were profound differences between warlike, populist, almost illiterate North China and aristocratic, refined, Yangtse China, with its court life, coteries and hermitages. The arrival of Buddhism, from AD 200, brought with it a deep and general transformation in sensibility, and a taste for sumptuousness and ornamentation. The Taoist interest in nature, and its search for procedures capable of prolonging life and sublimating the body, continued alongside the new layman's religion of Buddhism, with its own yoga practices of breathing, contemplation and visualization.

The period was marked also by frequent wars and social unrest, which were to have an effect on the continued development of sport and recreation. No less stifling was the affirmation, according to Gernet (1982: 202), of a sort of literary and artistic dilettantism, a pursuit of aesthetic pleasure for its own sake, which was in complete contradiction to the classical tradition. This emphasis adversely affected the pursuit of the physical in Chinese life.

Physical activity in military life

Archery remained an essential component of military training, and during the period of the Northern Zhou (AD 557–581), archery ceremonies were held during troop reviews. One of the most remarkable persons of the period was the Chongwa, the empress dowager of Emperor Su Zong of the Northern Wei (AD 386–534). The daughter of an army officer, she practised archery as well as the classics, was summoned to the palace to teach Buddhism, became a concubine and, as mother to Su Zong, was proclaimed Empress Dowager in AD 515. She took an interest in the affairs of state but continued to practise archery, and during a hunting expedition, she set up an archery contest and required all officials, whether civil or military, to participate. Some officials apparently were unable to even draw the bow and, after rewarding or punishing officials according to their results, she demonstrated her own skill as an exceptional archer.

There was general antagonism to the martial arts from the literati and officialdom, belittlement affected their development, and there is evidence of literati who enjoyed military exercises being derided for their interest.

Religious and social influences

One of the benefits of the arrival of Buddhism into China for the sports historian is its tradition of depicting scenes from everyday life. Some of the finest examples are in the Mogao Grottoes in Gansu Province, which contain paintings, sculptures and works of decorative and architectural art from AD 386 to 1368. Amongst the various scenes depicted can be identified horseriding, archery, wrestling, *wushu*, swimming, boating, *weiqi* and *qigong*. According to Xie Yunxin (1989: 45), many of the murals depict events in the life of Satyamuni, the prince of Nepal, who founded Buddhism and was fond of sports as a child and young man.

Exercise and Health

The spread of Buddhism and ideas of fatalism, according to Ba (1987a: 47), appear to have had a negative influence on people's faith in the value of health-oriented physical exercise. Many of the writings on health during this period advocated physical immobility and showed a disdain for strenuous activity. There was a shift in emphasis from *daoyin* to medication, and the new belief in medicine led people to put faith in medicaments rather than exercise to bring longevity.

Despite opposition however, *daoyin* still had several advocates. Tao Hou-jung (AD 452–536) reviewed the work of his predecessors, and advocated six different ways of practising *daoyin*. In a book entitled *Records On Ways to Keep Fit and Prolong Life*, he introduced a wide range of health maintenance theories and practices handed down through the centuries, including exercises devised by the celebrated physician Hua Tuo (AD 208). A further significant development in the field of exercise occurred with the arrival in China in AD 527 of an Indian monk called Budhidharma. After a stay of nine years at the Shaolin Temple in Wei, he grew to realize how physically weak and spiritually dejected his fellow monks were. He recommended morning exercise daily, and taught them a drill consisting of the eighteen exercises of Arhat, which was eventually incorporated into the book *Boxing of the School of Shaolin*.

The influence of the literati can be noted in the strengthening of intellectual games and refined physical activity. Both *weiqi* and *touhu* grew in popularity among scholars while they enjoyed luxurious feasts and idle talk. *Weiqi*, supported by the emperors, grew popular in all social classes. Contests were frequently arranged for well-known players and games were recorded to provide entertainment. Public appraisals were made, sometimes of as many as several hundred contestants, and players were divided into nine grades, according to level of performance, no doubt like today's gradings in the martial arts.

The division between the military and the scholars and their respective attitudes to physical activity is confirmed by Wu (1975), who has described how archery contests during this period served only military purposes. In the preface to a military archery tract, it claims:

> As literary men call themselves scholars, so we should call ourselves military men. On account of this division, later, scholars . . . will all be womanish.

According to Wu, this division, similar to the division between courtly life and monastic life in the West, may have accounted for centuries of Chinese attitudes towards physical fitness, and in turn have affected attitudes towards competition and preparation for physical challenge. Spectatorism grew in popularity at the expense of participation, and the pursuit of pleasure for its own sake, artistic and literary dilettantism, and the religious fervour which characterized the period, led to a sublimation of the physical.

THE ARISTOCRATIC EMPIRES: THE SUI, TANG AND FIVE DYNASTIES PERIOD (AD 581–960)

Introduction

This period was a time of transition from the medieval to the modern world, particularly in East Asia. The empires of the Sui (AD 581–617) and the Tang (AD 618–907) were based on the strongly sinicized empires of the Western Wei (AD 535–557) and Northern Chou (AD 557–581), and were regarded as generally Chinese, as opposed to the barbaric kingdoms and empires which ruled during the fourth to sixth centuries. The reunion of Yangtse China with North China gave the new empires an opening to the sea, a tropical zone and territories in South East Asia. During the Tang dynasty, major administrative reformation was carried out, and the Empire was divided into ten regions under the control of ministers of administration, finance and justice. Academies and higher education institutions were set up in the two capitals, Chiang-an and Loyang, and schools were established in the prefectures and sub-prefectures. Major public works were carried out, including canals and granaries, and the two capital cities were rebuilt on a grandiose scale circa AD 600.

In military life, the military successes of this period were substantial, with expansions into Turkey, Cambodia, Korea and India amongst others. The core of the armies was aristocratic. The aristocrats' taste for military affairs, love of horses and action grew out of prolonged association, and the influence of the horse and its armed riders was substantial during the Tang dynasty; 5,000 horses in AD 618 had grown to 700,000 by the middle of the seventh century, and regulations governing the militias insisted that soldiers provide their own horses. During the seventh and eighth centuries, the northern aristocracy had a passion for horses, and polo, doubtless imported from Iran, was extremely popular in Chiang-an.

Over the next two centuries, a series of political upheavals, internal rebellions and military defeats marked a general retreat from the period of expansion. Administrative changes led to exploitation of the poorer peoples, and independent regional military authorities, famines and bands of robbers led to the decline and eventual fall of the Tang. The Five Dynasties period ensued, Chiang-an lay in ruins and Loyang was depopulated by the tenth century. In cultural terms, the Sui and Tang dynasties were renowned for Buddhist studies and poetry. In the seventh and eighth centuries, China had welcomed foreign influences, but thereafter, as an ebbing of military fortune began in the middle of the eighth century, China withdrew once again into itself, became hostile to foreign cultures and returned to a classical Chinese tradition. During the Tang, the upper classes were enamoured of barbarian influences – dances, music, games, cuisine, clothes, houses. Chiang-an became the meeting place of the peoples of Asia, and this invasion of cultures could not fail to affect the sensibilities of the age and enrich the Tang civilization.

Physical activity in the military

The Tang emperors considered riding and archery to be important attributes, and in the *Original Record of Emperor Taizong*, in the *Book of Tang* it claims:

> In September AD 622, the emperor summoned all his bodyguards and horsemen to learn shooting in the courtyard of Shien Teh Palace. There were hundreds of people learning archery in front of the Emperor each day. Bows, swords, cloth and silk were awarded to those who could hit the target.

During the same reign, certain posts were assigned to those skilled in archery, and tests for both military and civilian selection were conducted by the Ministry of National Defence and the Ministry of Education respectively. Tests included weightlifting and load carrying, and soldiers had to be able to lift a huge city gate bolt five times, and carry five *Lu* or decalitres of rice on their back for a distance of thirty paces. Similar tests formed part of the *wuju* system of selection under Empress Wu Zetian (AD 690–705), and stature and physique became important criteria for selection.

The influence of the horse and its armed riders during the Tang dynasty has already been noted, and the link between horsemanship, exercise and the military was reflected in *jiju* or the game of polo. The Tang armies used polo as a means of military training, much as the Han armies had played football. All prefectural governors had standard polo grounds for training military horsemen, and the playing of polo formed one of the important ceremonies for reviewing troops.

Civilian recreations

The sport of polo quickly entered civilian and social life. The game was favoured by all sixteen Tang emperors, some of whom were excellent players. The Emperor Zhongzong built two polo grounds at his palace near Xian, many high officials had their own grounds, and even the scholars used the annual polo match at the Moonlantern Palace as one of three activities to celebrate success in imperial examinations. Poems were written on the sport, centres were established to breed horses for the sport, and a large number of artefacts testify to its popularity, encouraged in several regions by the spread of trade and emphasis on the horse.

The game was one of the most technically advanced of sports at this stage. Polo fields were 1,000 paces long by 100 paces wide, with level surfaces, often treated with oil to prevent dust flying. Matches were played with equal but sometimes indefinite numbers of players, with one or two goals, and points were scored for driving the ball into the goal(s). Twenty-four red flags were placed around the field at the start of a match. They were awarded for the scoring of a goal, and a match was won by the team having the most flags at the end of a given period of time. Playing equipment was sophisticated, the ball was of hard wood or bone, and wooden mallets had crescent shaped heads.

There was massive spectator interest in the sport, playing techniques and skills reached a high level and, in January AD 821, a match was played in Tokyo before a banquet between a team of envoys from Bohai and a team representing the Emperor of Japan. This may well prove to be the first truly international sport event, and it so captivated the interest of the Emperor that he recorded it in verse:

> Mallets are raised like so many crescent moons in the sky.
> While the ball darts to and fro like a meteor.
> The players hit right and left before the goalmouth,
> Amidst thundering claps of the horses' hoofs on the ground.
> The spectators cheer and beat their drums at each goal,
> Never having enough of the spectacular sight.

Liu Lingling (1993) has provided evidence of the sport being played by women in this period throughout China. According to historical records, Li Shimin, the Tang's second emperor, ordered fifty maids in the imperial palace to form polo teams, and eunuchs were recruited as coaches. Wu Xetian, then a maid, but later the sixth monarch in the dynasty and the sole empress in Chinese history, was made captain of the team. Liu describes a match held in August 633, when Wu Xetian led her team to perform for the Emperor.

> Amid the sound of music and drums, the team, divided into two groups, rode into the court. The players were all dressed in men's clothes. One group was in red satin and their hair was decorated with red flowers. The other group wore green satin and green flowers, and they all wore white boots. They made three circuits around the court before starting the performance, paying homage to the spectators. Finally they came up to the Emperor, dismounting and shouting 'Long live the Emperor' three times. After that, the match began and proceeded with the beat of hoofs, the crack of sticks against balls, and applause from the spectators. The result was that the red team, led by Wu Xetian, beat the green team 2–1.
>
> (1993: 48–50)

A variation on polo (*jiju*) was *luju*, in which a form of polo was played on donkeys, often by women and children who found the donkey less violent, smaller and more manageable than the horse. The activity was popular during the Tang and Song dynasties. Many literati believed polo should be proscribed, in view of its violence, but its popularity among the emperors and its value as a form of military training helped preserve its popularity. By the time of the Southern Song dynasty (AD 1127–1279), it had declined as a form of training, but remained popular as a palace entertainment and recreation until the early Qing dynasty in the 1600s. During the Tang dynasty, extensive literature, particularly poetry, and a large number of pictorial representations appear, attesting to its popularity.

Another ball game, which had almost vanished during the period AD 265–589, was revived successfully during the Tang dynasty. Football (*cuju*) had changed its nature dramatically from the form introduced in the Han dynasty. Sasajima (1975) has recorded the changes which took place from 91 BC, when it was first mentioned in *Shi-ji*, the oldest existent Chinese text, to its evolution by the time of the Tang dynasty. In the early stages, goals were scored by kicking the ball into a hole in the ground within a designated playing area (third to seventh century AD). The next development was football played by one to nine players, within or outside a designated area, whose purpose was to keep the ball in the air. Two kicks were allowed per player, after which the ball was passed. Rules were adopted and this form was in evidence from the second century AD up to the nineteenth century. Further modifications saw the emergence of two goals, one at each end of the field, and the use of air-filled balls, and finally the form with only one goal in the middle of the field like modern volleyball (twelfth to eighteenth century AD).

The game was popular with court officials, soldiers, children of the rich and even scholars. Baoding Zhiyan records that, in AD 806, all candidates who passed the court examination gathered at the palace and played football. In AD 877, a number of scholars are reported to have held a contest on a makeshift pitch, and Liu Tan, who was awarded the title of *Jinshi*, or advanced scholar, displayed superb football skills, to the amazement of military onlookers.

A number of other ball games are reported from this period. The game of *buda qin* (ball striking on foot), also known as woodenball, was popular and was played by children and shepherds. The game developed later into ball-beating and was similar to golf or field hockey, and its refinements will be described in the next chapter. Another prevalent form of social recreation was wrestling, which was popular during festivals and fairs. Wu (1975) has reported that during the Ghosts Festival, the people held wrestling or tumbling-down contests. Because these became so popular and began to incorporate wagers, there were those who sought their proscription. Wrestling was also popular as an entertainment at court, and wrestling teams often gave demonstrations. A celebrated wrestler, Meng Wanying, 'ever-victorious', wrestled undefeated for several decades and, in special training sessions, passed his skills on to young wrestlers. Emperors themselves wrestled and success in wrestling was often a means to career and social mobility.

Dance forms grew in variety and popularity. As Chiang-an became the meeting place for the peoples of Asia, the consequent invasion of cultures could not fail to affect and impress native tradition. The dances and music of Central Asia and India found favour, in particular the dances from Turfan, Kashgar, Bukhara and Kucha. The Tang and Five Dynasties period has been referred to as the golden age of dance, but despite popularity and variety, there is evidence that dancing as a form of social intercourse, particularly after the drinking of wine, declined.

Miscellaneous recorded recreations included the use of the swing by concubines and girls attached to palaces as a form of relaxation and physical pleasure. Tug-of-war continued to be popular, kite flying grew in popularity and kites were built in the forms of birds, butterflies, animals, insects and even human beings. Some kites incorporated bamboo flutes and became known as wind harps. In Northern China, skis made of wood were available for hunting and recreation. Board games, particularly *weiqi* (chess), developed further, and there was an explosion of interest in acrobatics, which enjoyed immense popularity both at court and in public places. There were exchanges of acrobats between China and India in AD 710. According to Zheng Chuhai's *Anecdotes of Emperor Xuan Zong* every banquet included performances of somersaults, balancing, rope-walking and wrestling, and pictorial representations from various periods attest to the levels of skill achieved.

One of the remarkable factors to emerge from a study of sport in Ancient China is the almost universal acceptance through time of the right and desirability of women to take exercise, particularly in royal circles. There were, obviously, restrictions, but as already identified and further confirmed by Tan (1987), games enjoyed by women were in vogue, such as swing, kites, shuttlecock, throwing balls, kicking balls, shooting arrows, throwing arrows, *buda, weiqi* and polo. Nobles and many local officials allowed their maids to indulge these activities in their residences. Tan further records that:

> In the Tang and Song dynasties, a special team of maids was formed in the Imperial palace, who learned dances accompanied by music, hitting balls and other games in a special school, and on big occasions and festivals performed such activities as treading balls, playing polo and dancing for the Emperor and nobles.
>
> (1987: 94)

These activities developed from generation to generation, by means of custom, convention and imitation, but, according to Tan, declined after the thirteenth century.

Health and exercise

In terms of activities associated with general exercise for health, the emperors of the Sui and the Tang continued to support previous work. The emphasis was still on longevity, and famous doctors were invited to give lectures on exercise and health. Books and essays were published, including one by the court doctor Chao Yuanfang, entitled *A Discussion of the Origin of Different Diseases*, which included 300 examples of *daoyin* exercises and also exercises to imitate the actions of animals. According to the System of a Hundred Official Posts in the *Book of Suli*, it is recorded that special posts associated with hygiene and medicine were established, and titles of honour were conferred upon doctors, masseurs and other therapists. Many specialized in *daoyin* and massage and gave instruction to younger exponents. According to Ba (1987b: 42), Sun Simiao (c. 581–682), a celebrated physician and expert on health, advocated that, despite adaptation to a changing natural environment, citizens should seek to retain tranquillity and mental control. This could be achieved by the development of energy and the practice of *daoyin*.

Summary

The transition of Chinese society from medieval to modern times during this period was reflected in sport and physical recreation. Forms of physical and mental activity became more refined. Tests for military selection, for example, included measurable components. Polo emerged as a universal sport with regulated boundaries and targets, *cuju* evolved from a form of military training to an activity easily participated in and popular amongst the military, courtiers, scholars, women and children. Other ball games emerged which were to be the forerunners of later, more sophisticated international sports, and which could be played equally by the court or the populace.

Forms of simple recreation emerged, in particular the swing and kite-flying, which would have long-term influences on leisure and pleasure, particularly for children. The acceptance and promotion of activities for women further reflected the social maturity and tolerance of this society. Wrestling enhanced its popularity at court and became increasingly part of folk festivals and occasions. Foreign influences on forms of dance and acrobatics were evident, leading to increased variety, and chess grew increasingly sophisticated. The comparative prosperity and stability of the Sui and Tang dynasties (581–907) allowed these activities to flourish, but frequent wars between warlords seeking to establish independent feudal dynasties during the Five Dynasties (907–960) were to result in a decline of some of the activities so popular at this time.

REFERENCES

Ancient Chinese texts

Not all of the texts referred to are available in English. Those available are:

Shang Shu (Book of History) (1960) ed. and trans. by J. Legge, *The Book of Historical Documents*, Hong Kong: Hong Kong University Press.

Shi Ji (Historical Records) (1961) ed. and trans. by B. Watson, *Records of the Grand Historian of China*, 2 vols, New York: Columbia University Press.

Shi Jing (Book of Songs) (1960) ed. and trans. by J. Legge, *The Chinese Classics*, Hong Kong: Hong Kong University Press.

Other texts which may be of value to readers and researchers are:

Han Shu (History of the Western Han dynasty) (1938, 1944, 1955) ed. and trans. H.H. Dubs, *The History of the Former Han Dynasty*, 3 vols, Baltimore: Waverley Press.

Li Ji (Book of Rites) (1967) ed. and trans. by J. Legge, *The Book of Rites*, 2 vols, New York: University Books.

Secondary sources

Ba Shan (1987a) 'An outline of sports history', *China Sports*, 19 (1): 47–8.

Ba Shan (1987b) 'An outline of sports history', *China Sports*, 19 (3): 47–8.

Gernet, J. (1982) *A History of Chinese Civilization*, Cambridge: Cambridge University Press.

Gramet, M. (1932) *Festivals and Songs of Ancient China*, London: George Routledge & Sons.

Liu Lingling (1993) 'Women's polo in Ancient China', *China Sports*, September, 27 (9): 48–50.

Radice, B. (1979) *Confucius: The Analects*, London: Penguin.

Ren Hai (1988) 'A comparative analysis of Ancient Greek and Chinese sport', Thesis, University of Alberta, Canada.

Sasajima Kohsuke (1975) 'Ancient sports and games brought into Japan in ancient times and their Japanisation', Proceedings of the Asian and Pacific Congress on Health, Physical Education and Recreation, Taipei, ROC.

Tan Hua (1987) 'Movement and sport in Chinese women's life, yesterday, today and tomorrow', Proceedings of the Congress on Women's Movement and Sport, volume 1, Jyvaskyla, Finland.

Wu Weng-chung (1975) *Selections of Historical Literature and Illustrations of Physical Activities in Chinese Culture*, Taiwan, ROC: Hanwen Bookstore.

Zhou Xikuan (1991) 'China: sports activities of the ancient and modern times', *Canadian Journal of Sport History*, 22 (2), December: 68–82.

Chapter 3

The emergence of modern sport
960–1840

Mike Speak

A NEW WORLD: THE SONG, LIAO AND JIN DYNASTIES (AD 960–1279) AND THE SOPHISTICATION OF SPORT

Introduction

Gernet (1982: 300) suggests that not a single aspect of political, economic or social life remained untouched by change during this period. The transition from a semi-mediaeval society under the Tang to a new world, whose basic characteristics reflect the China of modern times, was apparent in political attitudes, class relations, urban and rural societies, the military and the economy. During the eleventh century, the state's need for civil servants, the spread of education, the growth of agricultural production and the subsequent increase in incomes from land all led to an increase in the number of wealthy families. Armies were no longer conscripted, but mercenary, and the governing class had considerably expanded. In the rural districts, the wealthy families provided the guards (*Kung shu*) or archers to ensure order, and many from the rural districts were recruited into the mercenary army.

There also appeared during the Song period large commercial centres, heavily populated, with a diversified class of small and large merchants. K'ai-feng, capital of the Five Dynasties, and also the Northern Song, was the first example of an urban agglomeration where commerce and entertainment became predominant. From 1063, following the abandonment of a general city curfew, places of entertainment (*Wa-Ksu*) were greatly expanded in Hangchow, and remained open until dawn. In all classes apparently there was a tendency to form associations of people from the same region which helps to explain the spread of individual cultures. All manufactures expanded rapidly, a network of navigable canals was established and the economic expansion was fed by the evolution of a wealthy urban bourgeoisie who began to enjoy the luxuries formerly only available to imperial palaces. It was not coincidental that architecture, landscaping, dress, cooking, ceramics, weaving and products affecting daily life made such rapid progress during the eleventh to thirteenth centuries.

Economic, technical and social change was accompanied by a return to the classical tradition, the end of Buddhist domination and a return to a concept of man in a fully comprehensible world, represented by a practicality evident in experiment, invention, ideas and their application. There was a major change, equally, in attitudes towards physical effort and the pursuit of skilful athletic activities. Gernet summarizes the situation as follows:

> Whereas in the 7th and 8th centuries, an aristocracy in which there was a good deal of 'barbarian' blood had imposed its love of violent games (polo, riding, hunting), the governing class of the 11th–13th centuries, consisting of rich, educated families usually living in an urban environment on the income from their estates, despised physical effort and wished to stand aloof from the traditions of the steppe and from popular amusements. The profession of arms, so highly regarded at the beginning of the Tang age, had lost its prestige ever since the armies had consisted of mercenaries recruited from the dregs of society.
>
> The intellectual, contemplative, learned, sometimes even esoteric aspect of arts and letters among the Chinese upper classes asserted itself in the Song period and was to remain dominant under the Ming and Ching dynasties, in spite of reactions tending towards a return to practical knowledge and physical activities in original and isolated thinkers in the 17th C. Henceforth, the lettered Chinese, apart from a few exceptions, was to be a pure intellectual who thought that games of skill and athletic competitions were things for the lower classes. This deeply rooted contempt in the governing classes for physical effort and aptitude was to persist to our own day; sports were re-introduced into China only in fairly recent years, under the influence of the Anglo-Saxon countries. From the Song period onwards, only learned literature, painting, calligraphy, the collection of books and works of art, and the designing of gardens found favour with the educated classes.
>
> (1982: 331)

Yet this attitude could not influence the need or provision in the new urban centres for popular entertainment. The towns of the Song period, especially the capitals – Kai-feng, Hangchow, Peking – became permanent centres of entertainment. Amusement districts, separate from those where actors and musicians reigned supreme, served as a stage for professional showmen – storytellers, mime artists, puppeteers, animal trainers, specialists in shadow theatre, animal imitators and presumably acrobats – and became centres of popular leisure and entertainment.

Military influences

The Chinese world of the eleventh to thirteenth centuries saw remarkable progress in military techniques, which remained unaffected by the attitudes of the governing classes and intelligentsia. The emergence of gunpowder, whose formula was reported in 1044, some 241 years before it was mentioned in the West, was to have a considerable influence on the physical preparation of the military in later periods.

A military academy was set up to train Song officers, in which 200–300 students trained over a three-year period. Examinations covered military history and strategy, the analects of loyalty, filial piety, kindness and love, but also practical tests in archery, riding and weightlifting. There is evidence according to Wu (1975: 43) that the emperors were heavily committed to military progress. Sung Tai Chung (AD 967) restored the shooting ceremony, Jen Chung (AD 1022) examined warriors in riding and shooting, Sheng Chung (AD 1008) held shooting meets and feasts and Kao Chung of the Southern Song (AD 1127) established a law whereby common people could obtain official positions by learning shooting. In the move to mercenary armies, soldiers were chosen after a series of tests of physical aptitude – running, jumping, skill in shooting, eyesight – and classified according to height, the tallest being posted to crack units.

Social recreations

Ba Shan (1987b: 37–8) claims, in contradiction to Gernet, that from the Song to the Yuan dynasties (AD 960–1368) a growth in health-oriented activities and physical recreations followed in the wake of economic success and urban development. Distinctions must obviously be drawn between the recreations of the court and those of ordinary folk, but there is evidence of universal interest and even participation.

Many of the popular activities continued from earlier periods. Dance continued to follow the basic rules and forms established by the Tang, although modifications were made to both the Gentle and the Violent Dances. *Touhu* was revised by Simaguang, new, complicated rules devised involving nine people in judging, marking and organizing ceremonials and playing music for every two players. Fairness and etiquette were emphasized. Shuttlecock became a popular activity, especially for children, who also played hide and seek, *pa*-hitting (a game like 'peggy' in the West) and a variety of games and activities vividly recorded in a genre of paintings called *Ying-histu* (paintings of children at play).

Wrestling continued to be popular and became commonplace in the streets and lanes, and public performances by women made their appearance. Skating in northern climes grew popular, but bull fighting which had originated in the Qin dynasty (221–206 BC), and become popular under the Han, now began to decline, possibly to prevent valuable livestock being destroyed, but possibly as a result of society's interest in increasingly sophisticated forms of entertainment. Dragon boat racing continued in popularity during this period and was very common in the Song capital of Kaifeng, where races took place on Jinming Lake. Long-distance or cross-country running was also a popular activity, and those who displayed prowess were selected as couriers to carry military information.

Health and exercise

The tendency towards realism and the concept of man in a comprehensible world was reflected in patterns of exercise and health. The mystery and folklore which had governed earlier forms of exercise and which often sought 'esoteric recipes for longevity' (Ba 1987b: 37) disappeared, and exponents began to investigate and develop more practical forms of exercise, based on actual physiological principles. There were still those, however, who advocated unrealistic forms of breathing and exercise. Chen Ro, or Chen Shi-i as he was described by Emperor Tai-Chung (AD 967), lay in bed for more than 100 days practising breathing, and adopted a 24-exercise routine of quiet sitting with exercise over a twelve-month period.

More realistic and practical however were the ideas contained in *Bao Sheng Yau* (Lu Essentials of Maintaining Health) by a Song Taoist priest, Pu Chuguan, who reflected that in the case of a healthy person, the blood circulates likes flowing water. He designed simple exercises for limbs, trunk and head which could be carried out at any place and at any time. The period also saw the introduction of *Ba Duan Jin* or Exercises in Eight Forms which are still in vogue today, and popular for effectiveness in health maintenance. The systems varied according to the influence of northern, hard actions, or southern, soft actions. These exercises were aimed at mobilizing, digestion, strength, elimination of disease, circulation and kidney efficiency.

Another form of activity associated with health was the practice of sunbathing. Until its recent association with skin cancer, sunbathing, particularly in the West, was regarded as a healthy practice, associated with beaches, swimming and self esteem. Ba Shan (1987c: 45) records how it has been described in the work of Bai Juyi (AD 772–846), a Tang poet whose poem 'Sunbathing' describes its relaxing and therapeutic effects, of Zhou Bangyan (AD 1056–1121) a poet of the Northern Song whose description of sunbathing in winter likened it to the drinking of wine, and Zhou Mi (1232–98). In his *Notes on the Southern Dynasty*, it claims 'sunlight is no doubt conducive to good health, as it can give a sudden boost to a person's vital energy'. The ancient Chinese, without scientific evidence in support, were not in favour of exposure to the hottest of the sun's rays, and traditionally bathed the back which, according to Chinese medicine, provided the main channels for the circulation of vital energy, blood and nutrients and key acupuncture points.

Sport forms and growing sophistication

One of the signs of growing sophistication in the field of sport was the use of the new art of printing which resulted in more and better texts on sporting forms, rules and regulations and techniques which, although in existence, had not been recorded in detail before the Song dynasty.

Another proof of the emergence of organized sport was the formation of sports associations. The emergence of *Xiangpu* (wrestling) societies, with their own rules and regulations and archery societies, with strict entry requirements, reflects the growing sophistication of society and sport. Archery was as popular in civilian life as it was necessary in the military and, in what must be one of the earliest pieces of research into sports participation, Shu Shi (AD 1037–1101) surveyed participation in Hebei's Dingshou and Baoshu, and discovered the existence of 588 archery societies with a membership of 31,411 people, or nearly 15 per cent of the population.

Further evidence of sophistication in sport is provided in the *History of the Song Dynasty* which records that Emperor Taizong ordered his officials to draw up definite rules for polo. Standard sizes for playing area and goals were adopted, players of each team wore different colours and umpires and referees took charge.

The best example of the emergence of sport, as opposed to recreation, is provided by the classic text *Wanjing* (1282) which contains the most detailed regulations covering an activity which we would now call golf. There was an earlier reference to woodenball, wherein a ball was struck with a stick, which developed over time into *chiuwan* (hitting the pellet), in which players using clubs made of wood and bamboo competed over a terrain by hitting a solid wooden ball into holes. Details of the game which provide evidence of its golf nature are of interest to the sports historian.

Chiuwan, an ancient form of golf

The course or field of play

The course consisted of tees and holes, which could be as close as ten feet or as far apart as 100 paces, but there was no absolute limit. Holes tended to be in hollows, were marked with coloured flags, and locations were changed regularly. Players and spectators were not allowed to approach within five feet of holes to prevent cheating.

The equipment

Clubs were made of wood coated with animal 'muscles' and glue and had a bamboo handle. Clubs were of different length to suit the height of players, and different shapes. Players could select a club on arrival, but it could not be changed during the course of a game. The balls were made of hard wood for durability, were proportional to the size of club used and were kept in a leather bag.

The players

The number of players could vary and different numbers were differently described. There was a big game (9–10), a middle game (7–8) a small game (5–6), a group (3–4) and a couple (2). When numbers were even, players formed couples and groups, but when odd, no groups were formed.

The playing system

Players gathered at the tee and the partner with the longest drive teed off. When the ball stopped, its location was marked. The next player then hit the ball where it lay but was not allowed to use a tee, and so on until the hole was reached. Once a ball rolled into the hole, the hole was won and no more shots were allowed.

The result

Players collected counters before the start of a game and, according presumably to the number of holes won, counters were given for holes won, accumulated and at the end of the game the players with most counters were the winners. Prizes were available donated by the players, and ranged from valuable items offered by the wealthy to cheap articles offered by poorer players. Ties apparently were possible.

The text also describes in great detail the techniques of striking the ball, and lists at least twenty-one rules and regulations mainly covering technical matters but some concerned with etiquette (see Wu 1975: 62–8). The text also covers attitudes, selection of partners, correctness of action, the value of harmony, how to recognize the characters of different players and deal with proud players – laying stress on fairness and morality in sport. The game, it was also claimed, helped players relax, recuperate health and become cheerful, and the similarities with the modern game of golf are remarkable.

Summary

The period described above made its impact felt on the field of physical activity. The growth of towns, wealth and spread of education provided a need for forms of entertainment during increasing leisure time. Gernet's view that the governing classes despised physical effort may have been true for the literati and intelligentsia, but there is sufficient evidence of a range of activities enjoyed by the court and the people during this period to dismiss it as a valid perception of the whole society. It is true that the literati rejected these physical expressions of leisure interest, but they themselves continued to enjoy *touhu* and *weiqi* and, as in any society, exceptions in both directions was probably existed.

In the field of health and exercise, new, more rational forms were devised, ball games continued in popularity and significant new sports like *chiuwan*, a forerunner of golf, emerged. The growing sophistication of the society is reflected in three main ways in the development of sporting forms: first in the growing sophistication of rules and regulations in such activities as polo, *chiuwan*, *xiangpu* and *buda* ball; second in the increasing number of texts available on sporting activities, a subject worthy of documentation in its own right; and third in the formation of special societies in archery, *xiangpu* and *cuju*.

THE YUAN (AD 1271–1368) AND MING (AD 1368–1644) DYNASTIES

Introduction

The general impression left by a survey of China in the eleventh to thirteenth centuries is one of an amazing economic and intellectual upsurge, and a comparison with the West leaves Europe backward in almost every respect – trade, technology, scientific knowledge, political organization and the arts. Marco Polo's surprise, according to Gernet, at what he discovered was not simulated. The Ming dynasty was preceded by a Mongol invasion which relied for its success on a combination of the warrior tradition and military expertise. The Kingdom of the Western Liao was destroyed by Genghis Khan in AD 1218, alliances between the Song and the Mongols had finally destroyed the Chin by AD 1234, and the whole of North China fell under the Mongols. It took them another forty years to gain possession of the Yangtse and the Southern provinces. They had however a very undeveloped administrative system. Territories were divided into private domains, and the situation was summarized by Liu Pingchung (AD 1216–74), an unfrocked buddhist monk who was summoned to the Kublai's court at Karakorum in AD 1249. He presented a long memorandum on policy and administration, quoting the famous Han saying 'one can conquer the world on horseback; one cannot govern it on horseback'.

The Yuan dynasty of the Mongols had inherited a China in full economic expansion, from which they were to profit, but the indiscipline of the Mongol nobility, the corruption of civil and local authorities in the provinces and the growing hostility of the Chinese masses, fuelled by harsh and insensitive actions and supported by the establishment and growth of secret societies, was to culminate in its collapse by AD 1355. During the period a number of

envoys, merchants and missionaries made inroads into China, including the
Venetian Marco Polo. The Ming dynasty (AD 1368–1644) consisted of three
clearly defined periods. The Hung-wu (AD 1368–98) and Yung-le (AD 1403–24)
periods saw economic reconstruction, new and original institutions and
diplomatic and military expansion. The late fifteenth century and early
sixteenth century were periods of withdrawal and defence, before the third
period, from AD 1520 onwards, saw a further Renaissance, marked by a whole
series of economic, social and intellectual changes.

The founder of the Ming dynasty, who adopted the name of Hung-wu
(1328–98) was the son of a goldwasher who had become a monk in 1344,
then a rebel leader who between 1365 and 1367 eliminated rivals and established the Ming dynasty in 1368 at Nanking. By 1387, the whole of China
was re-unified. A massive effort at reconstruction was undertaken between
1370 and 1398 to repair the ruination and destruction of the Mongol period.
Irrigation, the restoration of land, the construction of reservoirs, repopula-
tion of devastated areas and reafforestation were all contributions to repair
the agrarian economy and form the basis of both the Ming and Ching
empires' reliance on agriculture. The Ming period saw the emergence of
the functional division of the working population into peasant, soldier or
craftsman who were dependent on three main ministries: finance, army and
public works. Hung-wu's background gave him an instinctive distrust of the
literati and intelligentsia and impelled him to control the government and
civil service by recruiting and promoting officials from the lower classes. This
tendency to centralize power in the hands of the emperor, govern by limited,
restricted and secret councils, isolating imperial authority and developing
secret police permeated the Ming dynasty and the climate of distrust it engen-
dered grew worse with time. In AD 1421, the Ming dynasty transferred its seat
of government to Peking from Nanking. Gradually, the early functional division of the population disintegrated and social mobility on the part of much
of the population created major change from the start of the sixteenth
century. The lowest strata of peasantry moved to the towns, seeking employment in small business and handicrafts or as servants for rich families.

There was considerable technical progress during the period, obvious in the
number of technical treatises which appeared, particularly in weaving, publishing and ceramics. New machines for agricultural processes and the introduction of new crops and soil improvement led to massive progress and, by the
sixteenth century, regional economic specialization had emerged to service a
population which had grown from 70 million at the start of the period to 130
million at the end. Technical progress was accompanied as it had been in
earlier epochs by social change: the rise of a proletariat and urban middle
class, the evolution of a class of important merchants and businessmen and
the transformation of rural life, influenced by the habits of the towns. Social
progress was in turn accompanied by a remarkable development in artistic
culture, in particular the theatre, the novel and a semi-learned, semi-popular

culture of an urban middle class eager for entertainment and education. There was a proliferation of schools and centres of study endowed with libraries and a revival of interest in many branches of practical knowledge: agronomy, military techniques, hydraulics, astronomy, mathematics, etc. Amongst the works published on medicine (hygiene, dietetics, acupuncture and moxibustion) special mention should be made of the treatise on botany and pharmacopoeia by Li Shih-chen (AD 1518–98), the *Pen-tiao Kang Mu* completed after sixteen years research and containing notes on 1,000 animals and 1,000 plants with medicinal uses. The literature of leisure was addressed to an urban public anxious for diversion, but whose lack of classical education required literature closer to the spoken language.

Military influences and the emergence of the martial arts

At the outset of this period, the Yuan dynasty of the Mongols had inherited a wealthy, well-organized empire. Their victories were achieved by military vigour and prowess, and examples have been recorded by Marco Polo (Latham 1958):

> They are stout fighters, excelling in courage and hardihood. They are of all men in the world the best able to endure exertion and hardship and the least costly to maintain and therefore the best adapted for conquering territory and overthrowing kingdoms . . . Their weapons are bows and swords and clubs; but they rely mainly on their bows for they are excellent archers.
>
> (1958: 99)

He describes not only the quality of archers, but also their quantity. One of their tactics was to feign flight, during which: 'When they are fleeing at top speed, they twist round with their bows and let fly their arrows to such good purpose that they kill the horses of the enemy and the riders too' (1958: 101). He further describes how Kublai Khan went into battle, 'his troops marshalled in thirty squadrons of 10,000 mounted archers each, grouped in 3 divisions' (1958: 116).

Zhong Bian (1987: 17–19) further described how Polo served in the court of Kublai Khan for seventeen years and travelled extensively. His *Travels* offer several insights into the leisure lives of the court and the Yuan dynasty and, as already indicated, their prowess as warriors. Their skill in archery in particular was praised and explained. 'Their arms consist of bows and iron maces and in some instances spears, but the first named is the weapon at which they are most expert, being accustomed, from childhood, to use it in their sports' (1987: 39). Another skill of the Tartars which is referred to by Polo was their ability to ride and train horses. He noted that 'the men are trained to remain on horseback for two days and two nights without dismounting, and to sleep in that position whilst their horses graze' (1987: 39).

One final illustration from the *Travels* emphasizes the physical nature of the Mongols. Kaidu, one of the Mongol kings, had a daughter Aiyaruk who was so strong that she was able to defeat all comers in combat. She refused marriage until she found a nobleman who could beat her in combat, and had the message broadcast. If defeated she would marry, if she won she would gain 100 horses. It is claimed that she acquired more than 10,000 horses by this means. In AD 1280, she was challenged by a son of King Pumar, who was not only young and handsome, but also of a wealthy and respected family, so much so that Kaidu her father, urged her privately to lose – which she refused outright. The outcome was defeat, mortification and shame for the prince, and deep sorrow in the palace (see Latham 1958: 317–19).

Wrestling was a popular activity among the Mongols. Li Xiaofei (1991) has indicated that, in AD 1209, a sports meet was held at the Oldos grassland, in what is now Inner Mongolia, in celebration of the coronation of Genghis Khan. There is evidence that the emperor used wrestling as one of the tests to recruit and promote officers. The brother of the emperor, Puligudai, one day defeated an arrogant champion named Bok, and there is the suggestion that on his death, one of his cervical vertebrae was retained as a divine artefact, so large was the hole in it that a man's fist could enter. Bok, as a form of sport wrestling, has survived to this day in Mongolia and was in 1991 included in the Fourth National Games for Minority People.

There is little evidence in the literature to suggest that forms of military training during the Ming dynasty were very different from those of the Song. One of the martial arts which developed during this period was the art of boxing which, in its Shaolin form, grew from eighteen actions to seventy-two and later to 170. The development, however, was apparently accompanied by fighting, troublemaking and general indiscipline on the part of its exponents, so much so that its masters were forced to produce ten regulations to control exponents. Summarized, they instructed:

1   The main purpose of boxing is for health and strength, and it should be practised morning and evening, without suspension.
2   Boxing is used for self-defence, not for aggression. Bear in mind the Buddhist principles of pity and kindness. Those who violate this principle will be punished.
3   Disciples should respect masters and elders, resist pride and show conformity, care and prudence.
4   Show kindness and gentleness to colleagues.
5   Bear insults and do not attempt to show off boxing skills to non-religious people in the community.
6   Do not compete with other Shaolin boxers, but learn the code signs of recognition, which indicate you belong to the same sect.

7 Do not drink wine or eat meat – forbidden by Buddhism and likely to lead to unconsciousness.

8 Do not enter into contact with women. This is a strict rule.

9 Do not teach boxing to non-religious people, it could be harmful. You may teach it to a person of good character, who has no previous record of roughness, cruelty and ill-temper, but he must observe the rules carefully.

10 Refrain from being arrogant, covetous and boastful, which has already destroyed some exponents and harmed others.

The 170 actions devised by Pai Yu-fung were collected into five major forms or styles of boxing. They were represented by Dragon (spirit) for relaxation, quiet and liveliness of action, Tiger (bones) for exercising all body parts, Leopard (strength) incorporating jumping, fists clenched and fast rising and falling actions, Snake (breathing), softness and activity of body, and finally Crane (energy) for steady actions with the emphasis on concentration. Detailed explanations are given in a text *The Secrets of Shao-Lin Boxing* but they are extremely abstract. These forms of boxing were used for military training. During the Ming dynasty, there emerged two schools of boxing philosophy, described as the 'inner' and 'outer' schools. The former stressed the defensive aspects of boxing whereas the 'outer' school taught aggressive aspects.

The development of various styles of martial arts during the Ming dynasty was accompanied by texts on boxing and martial arts, Yu Daiyou's *Book of the Sword*, Cheng Zoi-gyou's *Method of Shaolin's Spear* and Qi Jiguang's *Jixiao Xinshu* for military training. Some Confucian scholars such as Gu tinglin, Huang lizhou and Yan xixhai, practised martial arts, advocating a more practical approach to education, reading, writing, boxing, the arts, as opposed to a theory of inactive study.

Although boxing's traditions and practices developed during the Ming dynasty, society at large despised it. However, within the military, it was included in the examination system for officers. In AD 1457, before the examination, the government ordered officials to seek out those versed in boxing, fencing and strategy. They were examined by provincial governors and then sent to the Ministry of Military Affairs for the standard examination.

Social recreations

Marco Polo records some of the leisure interests of the Mongol leaders, including their passion for palaces and parkland. 'At this end [of the city] another wall encloses and encircles fully 16 miles of parkland' (Latham 1958: 108), stacked with game for the pleasures of hunting and falconry. Within the palaces, entertainment was often provided. 'When they have fed and the tables are removed, a great troupe of acrobats and other entertainers comes into the hall and performs remarkable feats of various kinds. And they all afford great amusement and entertainment in the Khan's presence, and the guests show their enjoyment by peals of laughter' (Latham 1958: 137). Polo also reveals how the Great Khan invited a troupe of jugglers and acrobats in AD 1277, supported by a leader and troops, to go and conquer the province of Mien (Burma). This was successfully done. Zhong Bian (1987) describes the hunting parties of Kublai Khan, which were often held during the three months hunting season from March to May. They were mammoth events, often to the East, involving tens of thousands of people. The main aim was recreation and the maintenance of physical fitness, but they also served as a review of the armed forces.

The *Travels* provide information on the lifestyle of women at court at the time. Polo describes the emperor's leisure during the Southern Song dynasty and narrates:

> the emperor amused himself in the company of his damsels, some in carriages and some on horseback, and no male was allowed to take part in these parties. The damsels were skilled in the art of coursing their hounds in pursuit of antelopes, deer, stags, hares and rabbits. When fatigued with these exercises, they retired into the groves on the banks of the lake, threw off their clothes, jumped into the water and swam joyously about in the nude.

The *Travels* also give an insight into the interest in general health of the people in Hangzhou in East China. Polo observed that the people, often servants, took daily baths at public cold baths. The men and women who frequented them always bathed in cold water, and it was their practice to so bathe daily, especially before meals. In the bathing establishments were rooms providing warm water for visitors who could not tolerate the cold water. The *Travels* also reveal how long-distance runners became couriers in the Khan's postal service, running at full speed for a distance of more than 3 miles. Post was carried at a speed of ten normal days in a day and a night, and clerks at each post station noted the start and finish time of each runner.

Summary

There is extensive pictorial evidence to suggest that a variety of sophisticated forms of recreational and sporting activity continued throughout the period. The painting series *Pleasures of Emperor Xuan Zong* depicts *buda* ball which was a favourite game of young people in many cities, archery, *cuju*, *chiuwan* and *touhu*. The traditional Chinese painting of *Beauties* by Du Jin portrays a number of recreational activities enjoyed by women, including *chiuwan* and *cuju* (football).

During the Ming dynasty, the levels of skill in chess and board games were raised and several instructional manuals produced. *Cuju* continued its evolution, and could be played by one to ten people without a goal, aiming to keep the ball in the air by kicking, or use of shoulders, abdomen or back, similar to shuttlecock. Another form followed the rules of the Song dynasty with a goal in the middle of the play area and players divided into two teams. Some emperors prohibited the game, but according to Wenli Yehuopian, most generals, high officials and emperors during the Ming dynasty enjoyed *cuju*. Emperor Xuangong even castrated a soldier who was a good player so that he could play in court as a eunuch. *Chiuwan*, which had been popular amongst high officials during the Song dynasty, became more widespread during the Ming, and very popular with the lower classes. *Wanjing* (The Classic of Ball Games) was reprinted during the Ming dynasty, and confirmed the popularity of *chiuwan*.

THE QING DYNASTY (AD 1644–1840) AND THE MANCHU'S EMPHASIS ON ACTIVE MAN

Introduction

The later stages of the Ming empire makes it relatively easy to understand how the Manchu had little difficulty in seizing power. Gernet (1982) has recorded a scenario of general anarchy, collapse of public finances, central government panic reinforced by the suicide of the Emperor Chang Hsienchung, the weakness of the armies stationed to defend the capital, division amongst the Chinese, and complicity which the Manchus found in parts of the population.

The people who in 1635 became known as the Manchus were descended from the tribes of north and north-east China who founded the Chin empire (AD 1115–1234). By 1644 they had acquired the military capacity, political cohesion, administrative organization and strategic bases to seize power in China. They settled in China like a race of overlords, aiming to reign over a population of slaves, much as their Mongol forebears had done, but their early harsh treatment of the labour force was forced to give way later to a more moderate treatment and climate. The Southern Ming had been unable to resist the Manchu onslaught. After early oppression, however, the emperors Kiang-hsi (AD 1661–1722), Yungcheng (AD 1723–36) and Chien-lung (AD 1736–96) showed enough adaptation, openmindedness and intelligence to earn the title of enlightened despots.

By their study of classical works and Chinese culture they won over the educated classes and sponsored the writing of the *History of the Ming*, a compilation of catalogues of paintings and calligraphy, dictionaries and anthology of the Tang poets, providing an opportunity for the literati to display their talents. They revived the concept of a neo-Confucian empire, which not only extended over a large part of the continent of Asia, but saw, of all countries in the world, the greatest increase in population, wealth and territory. By 1759, the empire covered 11 million square kilometres, compared with the 9.7 million of today's PRC. The conditions of internal peace, improved agriculture and general prosperity led to the growth of China's population from 143 million in AD 1741 to 360 million in AD 1812. Europe's growth in the same period was from 144 million in AD 1750 to 193 million by AD 1800. China dominated the continent, had uncontested power and moral order, and the period saw an upsurge in agriculture, manufacturing and commerce.

There was a veritable revolution in agriculture. Vegetables and fruit came to be part of ordinary people's diet, and pigs, poultry and fish provided from fish farming were all common dietary elements. The Chinese peasant in the mid-eighteenth century was generally better off than his French equivalent. He was better educated, the result of numerous public and private schools which provided a sound education. Some of the great literati of the eighteenth century were of humble origin. Technical progress kept pace, and great strides were made in the textile, porcelain, furniture, paper and steel industries, and foreign trade developed substantially.

The scientific and literary life of the nation was to flourish equally. The general tendency of the second half of the century was to criticize the intellectual traditions of the Ming age and return to the concrete. Gernet nominates Yen Yuan (1635–1704) as one of the harshest critics of neo-Confucian traditions who rejected classical culture as false in its principles and harmful in its consequences. According to Gernet:

> His researches into antiquity led him to the conviction that ancient culture had been essentially practical in nature; it made room for archery, chariot-driving and the science of numbers. Yen Yuan rehabilitated physical effort and manual dexterity. He wished to replace the bookish education that produced only timorous, introverted individuals, unsuited to action and incapable of taking decisions, with a training that would call on the whole man and give a proper place to practical skills. In 1696 Yen Yuan became head of an academy in Hopei and included in the timetable military training, strategy, archery, riding, boxing, mechanics, mathematics, astronomy and history.
>
> (1982: 502–5)

Yen Yuan was however an exception, practically unknown to his counterparts.

Gradually, as Manchu rule became more entrenched, Chinese patriotism, hatred of the Manchu and attachment to the Ming faded. Examinations were restarted to restock political and administrative personnel, private academies were restored and their control formed the habits of a general system of education. There was a reaction against popular literature, however, which stifled works of entertainment. The official *History of the Ming Dynasty* (Ming Sheh) was completed between 1679 and 1735, and contains 366 chapters. Whatever judgement is passed, however, on the political and social systems of eighteenth century China, power and culture were the privilege of a mere fraction of the population, but that privilege did not depend alone on the privilege of birth or social class.

Military influences

To strengthen its influence, the Qing government set up a system which combined political administration with military affairs. The examination system which was revived applied to military and civilian officers alike, and even civilian candidates were tested in their ability to shoot from horseback. The army comprised garrisons of the Eight Banners stationed in Beijing and its vicinity, as well as in certain strategic points throughout the country. The units flew banners in eight different colours, led a Spartan way of life receiving vigorous military training from early childhood, and were known as the bannermen. There were drill grounds in many residential areas, and Xie Yunxin (1991) describes how local able-bodied male residents were required to undertake early morning exercise and participate in fencing, archery and horse-riding.

> Even between spells of concentrated military training, they would take up a variety of civilian sports and games in the courtyards surrounded by houses on four sides, or in open spaces near the compounds, all for the purpose of building physical strength.
>
> (1991: 45)

Emperor Dao Guang claimed that the most fundamental skill for the bannermen was archery on horseback. From Nurhachi, who defeated all his foes and steadily expanded his power and influence, to Fu Lim who led the Manchu forces into North China and established himself as Emperor Shum Shi of the Qing dynasty, victory had depended on the expertise of horseback archers. When the Manchu rulers settled in Beijing, they regarded the annual Mulanquimi – a comprehensive autumn military festival featuring archery on horseback – as part of the heritage they should uphold and carry forward. Following the enthronement of Emperor Qing Long, he re-introduced the autumn military festival in AD 1782 and maintained the custom throughout his reign.

Xie Yunxin (1991) describes the most popular sport amongst the bannermen as exercises with the padlock, made of stone with an iron bar for the grip, and weighing between three and thirty catties (1–45 kg). Exercises were of three types – swinging it in circular paths, lifting it overhead with one or both arms, and tossing and catching it repeatedly. Competitions were held in each category based on the weight of the padlock, either between barracks or between banners, or as a regular feature of large-scale military sports meetings sponsored by the imperial court. Winners were often promoted or received higher wages. The Qing dynasty also considered wrestling as an important training activity. The emperor K'ang Hsi was an accomplished wrestler and set up a special camp to recruit and train outstanding wrestlers. In Xinjiang, the Mongols had a regular wrestling contest for youths during the mid-autumn festival. There were five separate ranks, prizes were awarded, and those who could defeat ten people were put into the top rank.

One of the most interesting and spectacular developments in sport during the Qing dynasty was the progress made in ice sports. It is suggested that such sports enjoyed popular success, but the absence of records means that evidence is often confined to activities organized by the court or the army. It is reported that Nurhachi (1559–1626), father of K'ang Hsi, the first Qing emperor, conducted skate training among his troops. On entering Central China, he made it a custom to review the Eight Banners on ice. This must have become a tradition, since during the reign of Ch'ien-Lung (1736–96) the government encouraged the spirits of the soldiers by organizing ice-sports. In the footnotes of a royal poem, one such occasion is described:

> The ice of Tai Yi Pool was very thick every winter, and the Eight Banners and Three Banners armies of the royal court were ordered to practise ice-sports. The skaters were divided into groups and threw a coloured ball at a target on a flagged door. The emperor inspects the result and awards prizes according to merit . . . The skating ceremony is a tradition in our nation. The skaters line up, and wear coloured clothes and shoes with teeth.
>
> (see Wu 1975: 69)

There are further references to ice-sports in *Dijing Suishiji* (Seasonal Records of the Capital). During the reign of Chien-Lung, it is recorded by Pan rongsheng that:

> In front of the Five-Dragon Pavilions, the water in the middle sea froze into ice in winter. The emperor ordered the manufacture of wooden beds, beneath each of which two steel bars were inlaid. One bed carrying three or four persons was pulled by people with ropes. It ran as fast as flying and is called 'Pulling Bed' . . . There were iron teeth on the soles of the shoes worn by the pullers. They made the pullers slide on the ice as quickly as lightning. It was called skating. The quickest would get prizes.
>
> (Wu 1975: 68)

Further evidence of the nature of skates is available in *Seasonal Records of the Capital*.

Skating shoes are made of iron. In the middle of each there is a leather lace, to fasten the iron shoe to the leather shoe. As soon as the player stood up, the shoe went onward at once without stopping. The skilful players are like dragon flies touching the surface of the water, or the purple swallows flying over the waves.

(Wu 1975: 69)

During the Qing dynasty, ice sport meetings were held every year in the Tai Yi Pool (presently the Beihai Park and Zhongnanhai in Beijing) during the winter solstice. There were several further forms of sport on ice at the time, traditionally watched by the emperor. There was the class race, in which 1,000 soldiers stationed by a banner a mile from the royal sledge skated as fast as possible to reach the sledge. The emperor's bodyguards caught them as they arrived and prizes were awarded. Another game was called ball seizing, in which soldiers dressed in different coloured costumes would line up facing each other. A guard would kick a ball into the middle and soldiers would rush to acquire possession and throw it to teammates. A third game was called ball shooting by winding dragons in which a procession of about 400 skaters curved around the ice like a dragon. The procession was made up of small groups of three, led by a skater with a small flag followed by two companions carrying a bow and arrows. Close to the royal seat was a flag door, on which two balls were suspended, a high one called the sky ball, and a lower one called the earth ball. Those successful at hitting the targets won prizes. Figure skating also formed part of these occasions, during which skaters performed difficult routines on the ice. The ice inspection of the Eight Banners by the emperor was an annual affair, undertaken on different days, with prizes awarded according to classes. Gradually, as the Qing dynasty reached its close, these royal games disappeared.

Poems were written about skating, and there are suggestions that Emperor Qinglong and Queen Mother Gixi used to watch the skating in Beihai, Yilan-kang and Qingxiaolou in the Forbidden City as a ceremonial activity. There is also evidence of the utility of skating. According to Pingjin gulao, skaters in Tianjin during the time of Emperor Guangxu would act as postmen, and could reduce the normal delivery time to Hebei of half a month to a single day. *Tuochuang* was also popular, an activity where individuals towed sledges carrying three or four people for picnics in the country on sunny days.

Physical activity, which had long been closely associated with military preparation, took many forms. During the Yuan dynasty, government contests had been abolished, as military officers inherited their posts from their fathers, but contests were revived during the Qing. Only those who had passed a local government examination could participate in the universal contest, from which candidates were selected to take the Imperial Examination. This consisted of practical and theoretical elements, and only those who succeeded in the practical examinations could progress to the theory examinations. Wu Weng-chung (1975: 49–50) describes the content of the examinations, and gives present-day archers some idea of the demands.

The practical component consisted of four elements:

1   Shooting on foot at a target 150 paces away with a bow weighing 10 catties and with ten bamboo arrows. Successful candidates had to hit the target once in the local contest, twice in the universal contest and three times in the imperial to gain a class A grade.
2   Shooting from horseback at two small targets five inches high placed fifty paces apart within a course of 150 paces. Shots had to be fired twice during each run of the horse, which consisted of four runs in the local and twice in the imperial. Successful candidates had to score two hits in each contest.
3   Long distance shooting at a clay wall 220 paces distant. Three shots only were allowed, of which one hit was acceptable.
4   Spearing on horseback at four wooden figures each three Chinese feet tall with a five inch target on the head, and thirty paces apart. One hit in a run over 150 paces was acceptable.

The theoretical questions consisted of ten questions on Shun-tze's strategy, and successful candidates were allocated to classes 1, 2 and 3 depending on their success rate.

Martial arts and the influence of Shaolin

Physical training was not only encouraged for the military, but came also to be associated with forms of nationalism. Those loyal to the Ming dynasty who saw a need to restore it laid great emphasis on physical training. A number of scholars, among them Ku Ting-Lin (AD 1613–82) and Wang Chuan-shan (AD 1619–92) encouraged boxing. Their writings reveal sadness at the enfeeblement of the nation, and detestation of the Manchurian invasion. Other scholars, like Huang Li-chow (1610–95) and Yen Shi-chai (1635–1704) advocated practical elements in the curriculum, including boxing and the martial arts. Yen's philosophy was based on the view that inactivity was ruinous to the body. He considered courage to be the highest virtue, and practised archery daily in the garden with his disciples. He considered physical toil beneficial for the muscles, bones, respiratory and circulatory systems, but his view that exercise can contribute to a strong individual, family, nation and even world was not generally acceptable at the time. Despite his efforts, the old ways and distaste for physical effort in general society could not accommodate 'activity theory'. One of Yen's disciples, a scholar named Li Shu-Ku (1619–1733), attempted to promote his activity philosophy, and criticized the notion of scholars who had little experience of the real world and whose only knowledge was from the classics. He ascribed the failure of the Sung and Ming dynasties to this weakness.

P'ng and Donn (1979: 14) describe the influence of boxing as a martial art, and the impact of the Shaolin monks. As the Fukien Shaolin temple's fame spread, exponents of the combative arts began to converge on it. The Qing government had reason to be grateful to Shaolin when, during the reign of Emperor K'ang Hsi in 1672, 108 monks volunteered for military service against marauding bands on China's western borders. The monks' skill and heroism expelled the invaders, but a short time afterwards it was discovered that the Fukien monks were actually rebels who aimed to restore the Ming government by popular uprising. The Qing ordered the destruction of the monastery and the massacre of its occupants, but five monks escaped, were joined by others and eventually fought the Manchu at Hebei. It may be logical to assume that monks from both Shaolin temples, at Honan and Fukien, participated in political and combative activity against the Manchus, right up to the Boxer Rebellion at the start of the twentieth century.

Brownell (1991) confirms that muscular Buddhism preceded muscular Christianity by at least 1,200 years, and cites the importance of the Shaolin temples in support of political causes. Brownell claims that the dispersal of monks from Shaolin and their teaching of Shaolin arts (*Kung-fu*) caused the Qing to enact strict bans on the people practising *Kung-fu* and weapons practice. There is a suggestion that all of China's secret societies were linked to Shaolin, and led rebellions against the Manchus, but also that the spread of martial arts was also linked to high levels of violence in local communities. This was the case apparently in Guandong and Fujian, where in most villages, *guan* or small halls were established for the practice of *Kung-fu*. The skills were necessary, it is claimed, for family feuds, battles between villages where disputes over water lines were regular, in the cities where *Kung-fu* masters were hired by trade guilds to teach their workers, form protection units and resist bullying and corruption, or to protect merchants in cross-country journeys. Large groups of skilled martial arts experts were also used against invaders and, in 1841, 10,000 villagers attacked the British troops in Guandong, killing 200 soldiers.

Brownell points to a discrepancy in the view held of martial arts. On the one hand, there are those who see the arts imbued with philosophical, meditative practices typical of the non-aggressive Chinese character. This was necessary, since outside the imperialist forces, Buddhist or Taoist temples were the only places where their practice was officially tolerated. The view from the other end of the social scale was of a society characterized by endemic physical violence, in which martial arts were necessary to survive.

Social recreation

Hunting activities during the Qing followed the pattern of previous dynasties, although Xie Yunxin (1991: 46) has recorded the emergence of falconry as a past-time among a newly emerged Manchu leisured class. The Manchus also revealed a fondness for keeping birds as pets, some for their birdsong and others for the beauty of their plumage. During the Qing dynasty, this privilege was first confined only to the nobles of the Eight Banners, who would flaunt their caged birds in public places, often accompanied by a large retinue. Later, the practice was adopted by many citizens and is currently a common sight. Of greater significance, however, was the establishment by Emperor Qing-Long (1735–96) of five major and numerous smaller hunting grounds.

Although primarily established for the pleasure of hunting, expeditions also served the purpose of consolidating Manchu rule, safeguarding border areas and maintaining national unity. The autumn hunting tours, known as *mulanquimi*, also involved local chiefs and senior officers to encourage unity of purpose. The most massive hunting exercises had the character of military manoeuvres. Tian Ma (1991: 41–2) describes how during the reign of Kang-Xi (1661–1722) the emperor and senior officials would visit a castle and hunt daily, accompanied by 70,000 horsemen and 3,000 archers. A circle with a diameter of 1.5km around a mountain was drawn by the positions of the archers, all moved forward together and large numbers of animals were trapped and killed in this way.

Kang-Xi was a keen huntsman and had learned riding and archery as a child from a guard called Muergen. In old age, he estimated he had killed 135 tigers, twenty bears, twenty-five leopards, ten lynxes, fourteen David's deer, ninety-six wolves, 132 boars and hundreds of deer. He ruled that all children of imperial families and the Eight Banners officers must learn archery on horseback and, after they reached the age of 10, they would have to undergo an annual test examined by the crown prince and chief ministers. During the test, the crown prince would shoot first. Emperor Ching-Long followed the example of Kang-Xi. In fact, he was commended as a 12-year-old by Kang-Xi and awarded a yellow vest for accuracy when he hit the bulls-eye with all five arrows in a contest. He followed the practice of Kang-Xi in improving military and diplomatic skills by the annual *mulanquimi*, which he staged forty-one times in his sixty-one year reign. There is also evidence, from the painting, *Banquets at a Frontier Fortress*, during the reign of Qian Loy (1735–96), that wrestling activities also formed part of these occasions, and continued evidence of weightlifting competitions, which during the Qing dynasty consisted of lifting stone barbells classified under three categories, 200 *jin*, 250 *jin* and 300 *jin*.

Summary

The impact of the Qing dynasty had been in a continuation of the exercises and skills emanating from the military, a sophistication of forms of boxing which were to have an impact not only on political events, but later on the lives of ordinary people, and no small contribution to the development of ice sports. The attitude of the Manchus to physical exercise and skilful pursuits, particularly horseriding and archery, was very positive. Their inclusion of archery and riding in public examinations bore evidence of their stress on the active man, but their anxieties about the political implications of the ordinary man exercising and shooting led to abolition on grounds of national defence. The influence of Shaolin and its muscular Buddhists is worthy of further study in the historical search for links between exercise, sport and religion.

RECREATION AND SPORT IN ANCIENT CHINA: SOME OBSERVATIONS

Chapters 2 and 3 have attempted to outline the main strands of physical activity, recreation and sport within ancient Chinese civilizations. The range of geographic, climatic, political and socio-economic influences has been vast over a broad time scale, and activity has been influenced by many different cultural groups. What emerges, however, from this pioneering survey are some fascinating strands which merit further detailed and analytical study.

Gernet's observation, referred to at the outset, that 'the West, which has borrowed from China right down to our day without realising it, is far from recognising its sizeable debt to her', is supported strongly in the field of sport. We have noted the development and sophistication of forms of archery, wrestling, weightlifting, football, hockey, golf and polo and which quite separately from any development in the western world enjoined advanced skills, rules and regulations and behavioural characteristics sufficient to classify them as sports in a modern sense. Other activities, such as board games, dance, acrobatics, tug-of-war, kite-flying, swings and dragon boat racing have made a massive impact on the leisure and pleasure of citizens throughout the world without really becoming world championship sports, and martial arts, in a variety of forms, are now practised throughout a range of civilizations.

There is evidence that the link between religion and exercise was established in China and the East long before the crusades and some 1,300 years before muscular Christianity became a popular concept in Victorian England. In its later stages, religion became associated with the defence of the motherland as Shaolin monks and exponents of their arts sought to restore the Ming dynasty and were key players in the Boxer Rebellion in the twentieth century.

The influence of the military in the development of Chinese sports and challenges was all-important. Many of the athletic activities practised during the whole of the period under observation derived from the military: horsemanship, archery, running, hurdles, throwing, jumping, martial arts, charioteering, wrestling, tug-of-war, football, weightlifting, polo, ice skating, boxing, all owed their development and eventual spread into the civil community to their military origins. The military were also responsible for tests of physical ability and capacity which became part of the examination system in schools, academies and government service.

The contribution of Chinese forms of exercise and knowledge of health procedures and practices has in recent years come under severe scrutiny from the medical profession and exercise scientists in the West. There is a need for intensive study in this field to ascertain what lessons might be learned from Chinese practices which stretch back in time more than 4,000 years. The Chinese health philosophy stressed longevity, good health and serenity of mind and, throughout its history, proponents of exercise for health have stressed breathing, harmony of movement and consciousness as quintessential. There has been little emphasis throughout the period on musculature, strength and vigour, and an affinity with nature in all its forms has been stressed. Chinese physicians throughout history have recommended gentle, non-vigorous exercise so that the harmony of breathing, movement and mood could be achieved. Specialists have been employed throughout Chinese civilization to serve the emperors and society in medicine, hygiene, massage and exercise.

Evidence has suggested that the dispersal of population within China's vast agricultural base has not been conducive over the millennia to regular large gatherings of people. However, wherever opportunities arose, citizens and villagers came together in festive pleasure. Such occasions were often the scene for *Jiao Di* games, during the Han dynasty, incorporating music, acrobatics, dancing and magic. Other activities on these holiday occasions were feats of strength, horse-riding, pole-climbing together with shuttlecock, kite-flying, lion and dragon dances.

During the Sui, Tang and Five Dynasties period, polo, whether *jiju* or *luju*, was popular, as were football, hockey and golf, which was played even by herdsmen. Wrestling was often part of the entertainment during festivals and fairs and gambling was associated with it. Archery varied as a popular recreation, but by the time of the Song dynasty there is evidence that in Dingshou and Baoshu, 588 archery societies had enrolled 31,411 members or a seventh of the population. Bullfighting has a long history of popularity, but the earlier practices of man against bull eventually changed to bull against bull. Board games, particularly forms of chess, were popular throughout the periods under scrutiny, and hunting was practised in a number of different ways at different social levels.

Three areas of special interest merit further study. First, it is surprising what evidence exists for the presence of women in sport throughout the long period under scrutiny. In most early societies there is evidence of female involvement in dance, but in the Chinese civilization as early as the sixteenth to eleventh centuries BC, there are reports of women swimming, fishing and boating. There is pictorial evidence of women using the swing, and during the period of the Aristocratic Empires women played both polo (*jiju*) and *luju* on donkeys. Teams were formed and eunuchs appointed as coaches, and the game remained popular with women until the early Qing dynasty. There is evidence of participation by the leading females in the nation, in particular by Wu Wetian in AD 633 who was captain of a team which entertained the emperor, and who later became Empress herself. Poetry was written about the game by women themselves. Tan Hua (1987) has further confirmed female participation in throwing balls, football, golf, shuttlecock, archery, polo, *buda*, *weiqi*, *touhu*, kites and swings. Some were highly talented, in particular Hu Chongua who became Empress Dowager in AD 515 and whose skill as an archer surpassed most of her officials and of course Aiyurak, daughter of the Mongol King Kandu, who acquired more than 10,000 horses by defeating suitors in unarmed wrestling combat. There was positive encouragement, particularly within royal and courtly circles, for females to enjoy recreation, and many of the illustrations reveal the extent of their participation, including wrestling (AD 220–80) and during the Song (AD 960–1368).

Second, there is evidence which suggests that, outside of the military, there was a lack of emphasis on pure competition, and more interest in etiquette and good behaviour which were supportive of a harmonious, patriarchal social structure. Many activities throughout the period concentrated on the cultivation of virtue as a priority and on the process rather than the outcome. In archery and *touhu* for example, participants were required to demonstrate moral virtue in addition to skill, so that winner and loser equally could gain respect. Zhou (1991: 71) has indeed suggested that, because of the special emphasis placed on moral education and ethics in traditional Chinese society, ancient Chinese sport was overburdened with moral principles. During the time of Confucius, ritual shooting in archery served to confirm the social order and the virtue of the archer – propriety, good character, filial duty and love of learning. As archery was substituted by *touhu*, it grew to adopt an even more complex system of rules and behaviour, incorporating lessons in virtuous behaviour, character development and social skills. Within the activity were also encouraged notions of respect for rank and elders, deference, reverence and purity. During the Song dynasties, AD 960–1368, the importance of fairness and etiquette was emphasized in the rules.

The game of football also encouraged an acceptance of good behaviour and, as early as AD 100, the poet Li You during the Han Dynasty wrote:

Keep away from partiality
Maintain fairness and peace
Don't complain of others' faults
Such is the matter of *cuju*
If all this is necessary for *cuju*
How much more for the business of life.

This may be the first reference to the notion of sporting behaviour reflecting or influencing behaviour in society at large. In the class text *Wanjing*, completed in 1282 on *chiuwan* or golf, sections deal with the etiquette of the game, and include advice on players' attitudes, selection of partners, correctness of action and how to deal with proud players. The emphasis is on fairness and morality in sport. The monks of Shaolin, who practised boxing, were also mindful of its moral value, and stressed kindness, pity, gentleness, care, prudence, respect for masters and elders and the need to refrain from arrogance and boastfulness.

The third area of interest which merits further study is the publication of texts on sport, recreation and exercise. A starting point would obviously be a comprehensive bibliography on relevant texts. We know that *Nei Jing* (Internal Medicine) as early as the Warring States period (475–221 BC) provided a theoretical basis for physical exercise, and during the same period according to Ren Hai (1988) reliable literary evidence began to appear about the nature of *Dao Yin*, exercise and breathing. Tao Hou-jung (AD 452–536), in a book entitled *Records on Ways to Keep Fit and Prolong Life*, reviewed the work of predecessors and introduced a range of health maintenance theories and practices, together with six different forms of *daoyin*. During the Sui and Tang dynasties a number of essays and books on health and exercise were published, including one by the court doctor Chao Yuanfang, which included 300 examples of *daoyin* exercises. During the Song dynasty, further practical and realistic ideas on exercise and health were produced in *Bao Sheng Yao Hu* (Essentials of Maintaining Health). The concept of blood circulation was explored, and exercises designed for different parts of the body.

There is also evidence of early texts for specific activities. *Shenyi* (The Definition of Shooting) during the time of Confucius was an early example and during the Zhou (eleventh century to 771 BC) detailed rules were drawn up to govern the practice of *touhu*. In *Han Shu* (History of the Western Han Dynasty) (206 BC–AD 24), there are thirty-eight chapters on sword skills. During the same period, Pan Gu (AD 32–92) has recorded six texts on hand fighting, which in turn referred to 199 works of thirteen different schools on training hands and feet. From the previous chapters, it is obvious that many texts have references to forms of sport, but it is the specialist texts which are of interest to the sport historian. During the Yuan dynasty (AD 1271–1368) the new art of printing resulted in the emergence of more books on sport, especially on the rules and methods of play, which had not been recorded in detail before the Song dynasty (AD 960–1279). *Wanjing*, a classic text on *chiuwan*, or golf, was completed in 1282, and contained detailed regulations on the nature of play, techniques and etiquette. *Wanjing* was reprinted during the Ming dynasty (AD 1368–1644).

These three strands are of special importance in the study of sport history in China and merit fuller treatment in the future. There are other aspects of interest, particularly the influence of the military on the development of sporting activities, the attitude towards competition on the part of the Chinese, and the very real need to harmonize evidence of activities with the social, economic and political backgrounds of the societies they served.

At the end of the Qing dynasty, wholesale changes were brought about by the influence of western incursion. In 1842, the Treaty Ports were opened to foreigners, Christian priests poured into China, foreigners brought their sports and customs to China, but it was to be much later before these activities would be practised wholesale by Chinese people.

REFERENCES

Ba Shan (1987c) 'Sunbathing in ancient times', *China Sports*, 19 (12): 45.

Ba Shan (1987b) 'An outline of sports history', *China Sports*, 19 (3): 47–8.

Brownell, S. (1991) 'The changing relationship between sport and the state in the People's Republic of China', in Fernand Landry, Marc Landry and Magdelaine Yertes (eds) *Sport: The Third Millennium*, Proceedings of the National Symposium, Sainte-Foy: Les Presses de l'Université Laval.

Gernet, J. (1982) *A History of Chinese Civilization*, Cambridge: Cambridge University Press.

Latham, R. (1958) *Marco Polo: The Travels*, London: Penguin.

P'ng, C.K. and Donn, F.D. (1979) *Shaolin, An Introduction to Lohan Fighting Techniques*, Tokyo: C.E. Tuttle.

Ren Hai (1988) 'A comparative Analysis of Ancient Greek and Chinese Sport', thesis, University of Alberta, Canada.

Tan Hua (1987) 'Movement and sport in Chinese women's lives, yesterday, today and tomorrow', Proceedings of the Congress on Women's Movement and Sport, vol. 1, Jyvaskyla, Finland.

Tian Ma (1991) 'Hunting as a sport in the Qing dynasty', *China Sports*, 22 (3): 40–2.

Wu Weng-chung (1975) *Selections of Historical Literature and Illustrations of Physical Activities in Chinese Culture*, Taiwan, ROC: Hanwen Bookstore.

Xie Yunxin (1991) 'The Manchu's sports life', *China Sports*, 23 (8): 45–7.

Zhong Bian (1987) 'Sports in Ancient China as described by Marco Polo's travels', *China Sports*, 19 (3).

Li Xiaofei (1991) 'Bok: the Mongolian style wrestling', *China Sports*, 23 (2): 36–8.

Zhou Xikuan (1991) 'China: sports activities of the ancient and modern times', *Canadian Journal of Sport History*, 22 (2), December: 68–82.

Chapter 4

China in the modern world
1840–1949

Mike Speak

RECESSION, DECAY AND THE INTRUSION OF THE WEST (1840–75)

Social, economic and political background

The first half of the nineteenth century in China had seen a worsening of both social and economic climates, in which rash expenditure, corruption in the ruling elite and the military, continuous growth in the population, and over-extension of empire were eventually to lead to massive social upheaval and recession. According to Gernet:

> the political and administrative system, the techniques of production and commercial practices . . . had become inadequate in an Empire which controlled vast territories and whose population seems to have more than doubled in a century.
>
> (1982: 531)

Financial weakness was exacerbated by the trade in opium which, despite vetoes, involved corruption at every level of society, serious political, social and moral consequences, and a massive outflow of capital.

According to Schirokauer (1991: 266), 'the encroachment of the foreign powers, serious as it was, constituted only one of the threats facing the Qing dynasty'. The population had increased to 430 million by 1850 without any comparable rise in productivity or resources. The neglect of public works, the uneven distribution of land and the opium crisis left many in despair, and famine, poverty and corruption often gave rise to banditry and coercion.

The Tai Ping rebellion from 1850 to 1864 aimed at a revolutionary programme of political, economic and social reform, incorporating egalitarianism in all its forms, common ownership of land and production, monogamy and regular Christian services. Opium, tobacco, alcohol, gambling, prostitution, sexual misconduct and foot-binding were all prohibited. Hatred of the Manchus and the coalition of anti-Manchu secret societies provided a focus for the rebellion, but despite massive support, it was eventually put down. The Bannermen and other central forces had been powerless to stop the insurgency, and it was left to strong, regional, well-disciplined armies with some support from western powers after the 'generous' treaties of 1860 to suppress the revolt and restore the Qing.

The weaknesses indicated above facilitated intrusions into China by foreign powers, particularly those from the West. China was forced to compromise itself in the aftermath of civil war, a need for foreign capital, military and scientific expertise, and necessary industrial development. The sheer size of China was to make rapid development difficult, and there were those in society, both traditionalists and progressives, who sought to resist foreign influence. Backwardness was exemplified in the crushing defeats of the Chinese army and navy in the Opium Wars and later by the Japanese in 1894.

One of the most significant elements in the development of sport in China was obviously the influence of western powers, some of whose cultures already embraced a variety of developed and developing forms of sport. The Treaty of Nanjing (1842), which ended the first Opium War, ceded Hong Kong to Britain, opened the ports of Amoy, Shanghai, Fuzhou, Ningbo and Canton to foreign traders, and gave consular jurisdiction and concessions to western powers which allowed them to establish political, economic and cultural footholds in China. Later treaties allowed churches and hospitals to be established in the treaty ports, and the French to propagate Catholicism. By the Treaty of Tianjin (1858) and the Conventions of Beijing (1860) following further skirmishes between the western powers and China, eleven new treaty ports were opened, rights to travel in the interior granted, foreign envoys allowed to reside in Beijing, and missionaries allowed to buy land and erect buildings in all parts of China. These were all to have some significance for the eventual spread of sport.

THE INTRODUCTION OF WESTERN PHYSICAL EDUCATION AND MODERN SPORT

One of the most engrossing pleasures for the sport historian is to dip into personal accounts of people living in a particular community at a given point in time. The question of cultural or even racial bias has to be balanced against government, official statements and stated policy. Somewhere in between may lie the truth!

Before the introduction of new, western sports, the Chinese had enjoyed a long tradition of games, play activities and popular festivals. Many of these have been described in preceding chapters, but it may be helpful to consider the views of contemporaries as to those activities in evidence during this particular period. Hunter (1911) and many other authors of the period refer to processions and the racing of dragon-boats, and Werner (1919) refers to activities from the past which were still alive, either associated with festivals or activities in their own right: archery, chess, shuttlecock, kite-flying and walking on stilts. He also comments on the recreations of the Manchus, who

> do not seem to have introduced many new games, though their emperors were fond of sport. Most of the ancient forms of recreation continue to be in use, but the significant fact to be observed is that generally they have given up most of the more manly sports formerly practised. In open spaces could be seen men lifting poles headed with heavy stones, or playing the old foot-shuttlecock, or flying kites . . . The games of children, contrary to the impression which would be made on a super-ficial observer, are numerous and varied, and tend to develop strength, skill, quickness of action, the parental instinct, sagacity and accuracy.
>
> (Werner 1919: 51–2)

There is little doubt that those activities practised as part of festival, cer-emonial or folk-occasions continued to be part of the fabric of life, particu-larly in rural areas. The influence of the westerner, however, was beginning to make itself felt, particularly in the cities, among the wealthier Chinese, and in the educational and social institutions of a changing China. Ch'en (1979: 122) describes how, even in the earliest missionary schools, 'the boys and girls learnt to play Chinese and foreign games'. Brownell (1995) claims that Chinese people are still coming to terms with the clash of cultures that characterized the encounter with the West.

Correspondents of the day reveal how sports were quickly established by foreigners within the security of the treaty ports and the reasons behind their institution. Hunter (1911) in *Bits of Old China* confirms that in 1837 the younger members of the thirteen factories set up the Canton Regatta Club, and organized races, much to the consternation of the local Chinese respon-sible for foreigners, since their experiences of races on the water involved the use of oars and boat-hooks, and the Chinese term for competing with boats was *tow-sam-pan*, literally 'fighting boats'.

Crew some time later, in his book *Foreign Devils in the Flowery Kingdom* (1940), explains the process and the reasons for such apparent preoccupation with leisure and sport:

> So far as amusements were concerned, the foreigners were left to their own resources . . . They had the choice of growing morbid and melan-choly through boredom and loneliness, or organising games, tourna-ments and parties which would help them pass the time between the infrequent calls of ships bringing new faces and letters from home . . .
>
> The organisation of sports and establishment of multitudinous clubs followed . . . There was only a handful of foreigners in Canton before they built some small boats and organised yacht races, much to the

confusion of the Chinese officials, who couldn't see any fun in a boat race not accompanied by the beating of drums, like the dragon-boat races.

(1940: 208–307)

He continues by describing some of the activities available to the international community:

I believe the Shanghai Baseball Club is older than any similar organisation in America, for it was in existence before Lincoln was elected President . . . Sports were organised along 'hong' (company) lines, and jockeys, golfers, bowlers, cricketers and oarsmen competed for the glory of the 'hong' just as college athletes compete for the Alma Mater . . . Dozens of clubs connected with some sporting or athletic event flourished; clubs devoted to baseball, cricket, lawn bowls, bowling, billiards, golf, polo, hockey, rowing, swimming etc. But the most important of all the Shanghai organisations was the Race Club.

(1940: 298–307)

Percival (1889: 8–12), in his *Land of the Dragon*, describes how the Shanghai Yacht and Boat Clubs' annual regattas in the spring and autumn saw the 'Scotch, German and English crews pulling for their laurels'. There were also three lawn tennis clubs 'and most of the private houses have beautifully kept lawns attached, with from two to four nets, and three small boys to each net for running after the balls'. He also refers to the rifle butts, with practice from 6 am to 9 am, and to matches with men from Hong Kong. Perhaps his most telling comment is that 'Many young and wealthy Chinese, from various parts of the interior, look upon Shanghai as Europeans look upon Paris or London'.

Although Shanghai was the model for other treaty ports, each in turn had its own leisure and sporting provision. Tientsin, according to Feuerwerker (1976), had eight tennis clubs, swimming, hockey, cricket and golf clubs, and the race course with a fine new grandstand to replace the older structure burned by the Boxers. At Hankow, he describes how the British, French, Russian, German and Japanese concessions stretched along the Yangtze River for miles, and how each afternoon the foreign community gathered at the Race Club for tea, followed by tennis or golf. Hankow's eighteen-hole golf course was the best in Asia and the club house contained games rooms and a swimming pool.

Werner (1928), in somewhat more critical vein, draws attention to what he sees as excess:

Not only to social intercourse but to sport also is too much time devoted. This might be excusable when survival depended on physical efficiency . . . but the progress of civilisation in the future will depend more on mental and moral development . . . longevity does not necessarily depend on indulgence in athletic games.

(1928: 713)

However, the combination of large available leisure time, cheap servants and an excellent climate, together with a need for both social and commercial intercourse, ensured that Old China Hands, from all foreign parts, indulged in and thrived on their sport and recreation. The model for sporting development was available in the treaty ports and we shall note its influence following the establishment of the Republic, but Werner (1919) indicates that the absorption process was already underway before the turn of the century:

> During the last score of years or so, the Chinese have shown an inclination to adopt Western sports and games, but not generally or independently, and chiefly in connection with schools, colleges and clubs, owned or conducted by, or in association with foreigners. Here they may be seen acquitting themselves admirably at tennis, football, baseball and other manly outdoor sports, and proving that a race popularly supposed to be able to 'do without exercise' can take up such comparatively violent forms of it without apparently suffering any injury. And it is to be noted that those who are doing so are largely recruits from the families of the literary class, whose 'burning of the midnight oil' for many centuries has rendered them, as a class, anaemic and wanting in physical stamina.

(1919: 105)

Ch'en (1979: 216–17) commenting on Shanghai at the end of the nineteenth century, explains how the Chinese, quickly 'took up betting at race meetings, organised their own clubs, and how 'pool rooms and bowling alleys for Chinese clients first opened in 1881'.

THE SELF-SUFFICIENCY MOVEMENT AND THE END OF THE OLD ORDER (1875–1912)

Social, economic and political background

The Qing empire had come close to extinction, and the consequences of innumerable rebellions, culminating in the Tai Ping, were loss of wealth, a loss of life unparalleled in modern history and estimated by Gernet (1982) at between 20 and 30 million, and a recognition of the need for change. The agrarian economy became a priority, followed by a need to re-establish and develop commerce and industry. The rebellions had seriously weakened

China's resolve and highlighted the weakness of the Bannermen and central forces. The commanders of the new regional armies, through their contact with western powers, had become strongly persuaded of the need to modernize both industry and the military.

According to Hughes (1937), the concept of self-strengthening grew through the 1860s, but proponents remained conscious of the fact that 'behind the technical achievements which seemed to make the West so strong, there lay a Western culture which was worth consideration' (1937: 36). This view was supported by a steady increase in the education of Chinese abroad, in the USA, Europe and Japan.

A territorial dispute over Korea in 1894, which ended in the defeat of China by Japan, followed by the punitive Treaty of Shimonesekin 1896, resulted in foreign powers seizing further initiative and the leasing – almost colonizing – of additional territories: Wei-Hai-Wei to England, Kwangchow to France, Tsingtao to Germany and Dairen to Russia. This persuaded some Chinese that, if China was not to be 'carved up like a melon', urgent reform was necessary. A rising in the South organized by Sun Yat-sen was put down, attempts at reform by the young emperor were thwarted by the Empress Dowager and her advisers, and an insignificant secret society called the I-Ho-Tuan (known in the West as the Boxers on account of their interest in the martial arts) suddenly assumed alarming proportions.

Brownell (1995) explains how the spread throughout the countryside of peasant uprisings, anti-Qing rebellions and secret societies was associated with the spread of martial arts training in village martial arts halls. The Qing attempted to outlaw martial arts training but this proved impossible. Eventually, the Boxers were given imperial support and, in 1900, orders were issued from Peking to provincial governors that foreigners were to be executed. Over the next few weeks, it has been estimated that 200 missionaries, 30,000 Catholic and 2,000 Protestant Chinese were killed. Many governors refused to obey the instructions, the Powers intervened and an international force took Peking. Brownell (1991: 287) explains how the Boxer Rebellion was the last stand of *kung fu* as a technique of warfare, and the defeat of the Boxers at the hands of westerners armed with modern military technology relegated the martial art 'to the symbolic realm along with other sports'. Peace was concluded by the signing of the 'Protocol' on 9 September 1901. The terms of the agreement were harsh, and an indemnity of £67,500,000 was demanded. Beneficial reforms included a radical reform of the state examination system and the establishment of a Ministry of Education in 1902. The USA devoted half of its allotted indemnity to provide opportunities for Chinese to study in American universities.

In 1909, the Emperor Kuang Hsu died, followed shortly afterwards by the Empress Dowager. The provinces declared their independence, in October 1911 the troops mutinied and, in February 1912, the child emperor resigned the throne. The revolutionary leaders assembled in Nanking declared Dr Sun Yat Sen President of the Republic of China, and China hoped to appear before the world as a new, democratic nation.

The modernization of education, physical education and sport

Before 1902, Chinese education was very much a local affair, with the exception of the state examination system for public office. The underlying principle was the development of personality and the training of moral character. The steady growth of the missionary movement after 1860 produced an increase not only in the number of schools, but in the quality and breadth of education available. The education of girls was not really accommodated until 1902, but the defeat of China by Japan hastened the demand for a broader education. The pace of education can be assessed from the growth of schools; in 1905 there were 4,222 schools with just 102,767 scholars. By 1911, 52,650 modern schools were educating 1,625,534 students.

A change of policy towards foreign intrusion favoured the development of physical education in schools, and the British, German and Swedish systems of gymnastics were introduced and eventually adopted by the police and the armed forces. Programmes were introduced in the Nanjing Military College in 1875, in Tianjin's Naval Academy in 1881 and in the Hubei Military Academy in 1895.

Students returning from universities and colleges in America and Europe also brought back an awareness of, and sometimes an interest in, physical activity and sport. Ch'en (1979: 158) suggests that 'the generation of returned students of the 1870s broke away from the Confucian restraints by learning to sing and engage in sports', but according to Hackensmith (1966: 273) the major influences on the acceptance of physical education and sport in schools at this time were the missionary schools and the YMCA. It was here that western sports such as athletics, baseball, basketball, gymnastics, table-tennis, tennis and volleyball were introduced to children, and Chai and Chai (1969) indicate that modern sport helped to break down traditional Chinese society, which thitherto had been based on Confucian principles. Indeed, Zhou Xikuan (1991: 72) claims that the confrontation of traditional Chinese activities and new western sports became a main theme of physical education in China. He also points out that, in the cities, schools tended to adopt western sports, but in rural areas it was the traditional sports activities which dominated and even grew more popular. At the Museum of Chinese Sport History in the Olympic Stadium in Beijing, considerable attention is paid to both forms.

In 1902, following reorganization of the education system, many 'western' subjects were introduced into the curriculum and, in 1905, physical education became a required subject. Legislation required three to five hours each week of exercise in elementary schools, and the same later for middle and normal schools. However, Rizak (1989), citing Glassford and Clumpner, suggests that for the majority of Chinese this was a theoretical provision, since only 5 per cent of children attended school. 'For those few of the Chinese upper classes given the opportunity to attend schools, the government moved to imitate Western methods', 1989: 103).

Problems facing the introduction of modern PE and sport in China

Brownell (1995), however, draws attention to some of the problems facing the acceptance of western physical education, and particularly sport, on the part of the Chinese. Both military drill or gymnastics and sport entailed elements directly counter to the dominant Qing concept of culture, which was shaped by intellectual ideals. Men of culture wore long gowns with long sleeves to signify they were not involved in physical labour. When Chinese students first took up western sports at missionary schools, they wore long gowns. Hughes (1937: 176) claims that, 'Athletics have their way in China today, but 25 years ago, it was an effort for a schoolboy to shed his long gown to take part in a game of football'.

In the scholar-official view of the world, sports were an activity for the lower classes. Brownell also draws attention to the cultural significance of the 'queue' or long pigtail, required of all men by imperial decree, and its incompatibility with modern sport. At the first National Games, high jumper Sun Baoxin twice dislodged the bar with his queue. A western official advised him to 'cut it off', which he did, returning next day to win with a jump of 5' 5.25" (Kolatch 1972: 12–13).

For women, bound feet constituted an obstacle to sport participation. Reformers argued that western women were able to produce stronger off-spring, since they were able to practise callisthenics. Because of the pre-valence of foot-binding, lack of opportunity for girls to attend school and the organization of sport by westerners who did not particularly encourage female participation in sport, it was not until the late 1920s that Chinese women took part in significant numbers (Brownell 1995: 39–43).

Another factor in resistance was the attitude of parents. Except in small circles, sports were not encouraged. If the parents had experienced sport, some encouragement was possible, but generally, sport and its teachers were looked down on. Equally unacceptable was the 'medals and trophyism' aspect of competitive sport.

There was also a further, more elementary reason for resistance to the new sports. Bonavia (1989: 62) suggests that the Euro–American ideal of violent sport as an integral part of moral training and formation of character was quite alien to the traditional Chinese ethic.

There was also pressure, given the political situation of the day, for schools to include military exercises and for compulsory national service at the expense of sport. Hsu (1975: 127) states that, in 1911, the education authorities of various provinces 'advocated that all pupils be given strict and intense training to make them brave and loyal to the country'. The military in their proposals for national military education, put forward in 1911 and 1915, strongly emphasized gymnastics and Chinese martial arts to inculcate diligence, obedience, endurance, morale and national consciousness, characteristics which reformers claimed could be generated by the new sports.

The growth of competitive sport

Hughes (1937) describes the impact made by western educators at this time:

> The YMCAs and YWCAs also began work at this time, along definitely educational lines, at first slowly, and then, after the foundation of the Republic, with immense speed of expansion. They drew their foreign staffs almost exclusively from America and this brought into the country a body of keen, alert young University graduates, all conscious of the need for healthy minds in healthy bodies, and the superlative values of democratic institutions.
>
> (1937: 169)

Clumpner and Pendleton (1981) indicate that athletics appeared at St John's University in Shanghai in 1890 and basketball at Tianjin YMCA in 1896. The YMCA was instrumental not only in establishing recreation programmes, but also for laying the foundation for China's national athletics programme and training instructors and sports administrators in Shanghai and Tientsin. A series of provincial and national championships were pioneered by the YMCA under the direction of Max J. Exner from Shanghai, which culminated in the sending of a Chinese team to the Far Eastern Games in 1913. Ch'en (1979) comments:

> The YMCAs' . . . leading role in promoting organised sports were particularly pronounced successes. The first soccer match in Tientsin, 1904, was between the YMCA and Western soldiers. By the 1920s, soccer was a popular sport among the Chinese. Without the assistance of the YMCA, especially that of Dr. Exner, it was doubtful whether the first Chinese National Games of 1910 could ever have been staged. Thereafter, the physical appearance of Chinese campuses changed with the addition of sports grounds, signifying a changed attitude.
>
> (1979: 134)

Gu Shiquan, in Knuttgen (1990: 63), indicates that, from 1899, regular sports meets were held between St John's College and the Nanyang Public School and that the first All China Colleges and Schools Sports League Games were held in 1910. He further comments that:

> The Western influence in athletics eventually went so far that China's athletics world became dominated by foreigners. Sports organisers, coaches and referees at athletic competitions were all foreigners; regional and national sports organisations were established and managed by foreigners; and foreign priests handled the preparations and arrangements for the Far East Games. Even the heads of the physical education departments at Chinese Colleges and the leaders of Chinese sports teams sent abroad were foreigners. It was an American who made a speech on behalf of China at the opening ceremony of the 6th Far East Games in 1923.
>
> (1990: 17)

The implication was certainly that it was unacceptable for the long-term future of Chinese sport for this situation to continue. The influence of the YMCA, however, was exerted not only in colleges and schools, but also through city associations, which came to have great club buildings in which day and night schools were carried on. Hughes (1937: 169) praises the work of the young staff members: 'Since these young, energetic men and women came as helpers and not competitors, they were very popular and, in the matter of physical training and games, were instrumental in arousing the interest of students.' He also makes the telling point that, since facilities were paid for by Chinese money, subscribed locally, they were considered by the Chinese as '*their* facilities hosting *their* programmes'.

POST-IMPERIAL CHINA AND THE ESTABLISHMENT OF THE REPUBLIC 1912–49

Social, economic and political background

The downfall of the Qing government had been a consequence of several factors: the defeat by Japan in 1894, the aftermath of the Boxer Rebellion, waves of anti-Manchu and anti-monarchist feeling, growing patriotism in the provinces and a series of economic disasters which combined to produce disaffection of conservatives and modernists alike. The 'revolution' of 1911 and the almost unexpected success of the Republicans were, according to Gernet, merely 'an interlude in the break-up of political power in China' (1982: 17).

Although Sun Yat-sen had been elected president of the new Republic, he offered the presidency to Yuan Shih-k'ai, in the hope that his military strength could defend a powerless and penniless new regime. The government was transferred from Nanjing to Beijing, Yuan strengthened his personal influence and grip on power until 1916, but gradually came under pressure from disaffected provinces and Japan which, on the outbreak of the world war, seized railways, military bases and territories and took hold of Mongolia, Manchuria and Shantung.

After the war, China fell into the grip of independent military governors with their own resources and armies and christened 'warlords' by the western press. Their armies, with modern weapons and transport at their disposal, exploited and pillaged the country, and China was thrown into turmoil. At the same time, China was having to stave off competing foreign nations and their economic, political and military demands.

By 1927, the situation had stabilized somewhat with the establishment in Nanjing of the Kuomintang Nationalist Party under the command of Chiang Kai-shek. The foreign nations with Chinese interests were ready to support the new regime since revolution could now be disregarded. The regime also attracted the support of property owners, the banks and the commercial middle class, guaranteeing financial stability, and the one party system ensured control of the government, civil service, the army and the political police. Unification made rapid progress and China began to win back some of the concessions made by the Manchu government. Little effort was made, however, in the countryside, and the majority of the population continued to live in abject poverty.

The Chinese Communist Party, founded in 1921, soon won the support of the peasant unions and rural soviets. The ultimate goal was the triumph of the rural world, which was seen as the victim of foreign capital and the Chinese bourgeoisie. The method was confrontation with the Nationalists from 1927 to 1937 and, more importantly in the long run, the patriotic struggle against the Japanese invader from 1937. Japan had invaded and occupied the north-east territories of China in 1931–2. These lands of 40 million people with good ports, coal mines and the best rail network in East Asia increased Japan's economic and industrial strength at the expense of China's, and gave Japan an excellent strategic base for a future invasion of China.

Japan invaded in July 1937, bombed Shanghai in August and the Kuomintang withdrew to Hankow and then Chungking. The Nationalist government found itself deprived of its main sources of revenue, cut off from the great economic metropolis of Shanghai and the banking and international circles who had offered so much support. There was little support from the West until Japan attacked the American fleet at Pearl Harbor in 1941. The Communists appeared to be the only ones offering resistance to the Japanese, but were themselves being hounded by the Nationalists.

Following the end of the Second World War, during which the Chinese, under pressure from the USA, had accepted the principle of a united front against the Japanese, the Communists gradually overcame the Nationalists, until, by 1949, their armies took Beijing and Tientsin, were in Shanghai in May, Canton in October and Chungking in November to end a bitter civil war. The Nationalists sought refuge in Taiwan whilst the People's Republic of China was proclaimed on 1 October 1949, to open a new chapter in the history of China which was to have remarkable repercussions for sport, in different ways and at different junctures, before the new millennium.

PE and sport in the service of the Republic

Physical education had become a required school subject in 1905 and teachers' courses to support the new programme were launched at Nanjing Teachers' College (1916), the National Peking Normal University (1917), Gingling Girls' College in Nanjing, Soochow University and several private institutions. Abby Mayhew of the University of Wisconsin, who went to China in 1912 to set up the YWCA programme, established a Physical Training School for Chinese Women in Shanghai, since girls were now to be included in all programmes.

The democratization of education in China was to gain massive impetus from the work of distinguished visitors from the West, particularly Professor John Dewey and Paul Monroe of Columbia University, who went to China in 1919, and Bertrand Russell of Cambridge University in 1920. In the field of physical activity, distinguished specialists were also at work, and Van Dalen and Bennett (1971: 622) refer to the work of Dr C.H. McCloy, who left the USA for China in 1913, promoted physical education and sport through his work for the Chinese National Council of the YMCA, as director of a physical education school in Nanjing (1921–6), as editor of the *Chinese Journal of Physical Education and Hygiene* (1922–4) and as author of several books published in Chinese. Gradually, the influences of German and Japanese 'drill' systems declined and were replaced by American-style physical education, with the individual the focus.

Brownell (1995: 46) indicates that physical education in nineteenth century Europe and sport more recently throughout the world were a way of linking the individual with the nation-state. In China, 'it developed alongside efforts to turn a dynastic realm into a modern nation-state according to the political ideas of the time'. Riordan (1991) also suggests that many developing states stress the idea of physical culture in the interest of both the individual and the state. He draws attention to Mao's classic support in 1917, when he claimed:

> Physical culture is the complement of virtue and wisdom. In terms of priorities, it is the body that contains knowledge, and knowledge is the seat of virtue. So it follows that first attention should be given to a child's physical needs; there is time later to cultivate morality and wisdom.
>
> (1991: 52–3)

Kanin (1978: 264) opined that Mao saw sport as a tool for ideological education and national rejuvenation – the national spirit would be awakened by means of strenuous physical activity. He hoped to strengthen China 'by taking Western forms and giving them Chinese content'. He was unable to put his views into practice until much later, but was always a strong proponent of the value of physical activity.

The Kuomintang, no less than Mao, saw the value of a strong, centralized programme to assist China to develop a strong spirit of national unity which, according to Semotiuk (1974), would enable her to emerge as a modern state capable of defending her sovereignty. Zhou (1991) points out that during this period, three regimes were operating in China: the dominant Kuomintang, the People's Regime of the Chinese Communist Party and the Puppet Regime in Manchukuo. They all favoured the promotion of sport and physical activity, but with different philosophies on goals and ideology.

The 1920s had seen the formation of the Chinese Communist Party, and increasing criticism of the western presence in China by both Nationalists and Communists. According to Brownell (1995: 48) 'sports came to be identified with the culture of the treaty-port bourgeoisie who were viewed as Chinese–Western hybrids'. Communist revolutionaries criticized both western and Nationalist sports for their obsession with trophies and medals but used sport themselves to recruit young people, improve the fitness and morale of soldiers and celebrate significant occasions. Gu Shiquan in Knuttgen (1990) describes in some detail the importance of sport in the revolutionary bases and the Red Army, which even organized sport activities during the Long March (1990: 18–20).

Nationalistic fervour had accompanied the establishment of the Republic, and there was widespread agreement that sports served the good of the state. As with education and the earlier debate on the relative merits of gymnastics or sport, there was now a good deal of debate over whether traditional activities or the new sports were more productive. Brownell (1991) explains how kung fu was reshaped to fit the western model with the inauguration of a newly-named 'national martial art' – guoshu – as a competitive sport in 1928. In the 1930s, a conflict arose between those who supported guoshu and proponents of western sports, traditionalists arguing in favour of the martial art as a means of strengthening the race and the nation, reformers claiming that traditional methods were ineffective. Traditional activities however, were particularly popular on festive occasions, among the working classes and within the secret societies. Gu Shiquan in Knuttgen (1990) claims that the Northern Warlords government (1912–27) considered forms of wushu to be compulsory in schools and institutions in China and that, until 1940, they remained integral components of many physical education courses.

In 1929, the National government enacted the Physical Education Law, establishing a National Committee for PE within the Ministry of Education. Krotee and Wang Jin (1988) indicate that this formalized many of the influences operating within the new Republic and that it reflected the growing importance of physical activity for the state. They cite two extracts from the law which reflect its socio-cultural significance:

Article 1:   The main purpose of physical education programmes in the Republic of China is the development of a sound body and a sense of justice and fair play, with a view to training the people to be able to defend themselves and the nation.

Article 2:   All Chinese, regardless of sex and age, shall be given proper physical training, which shall be carried out in families, schools and public organisations under the supervision of parents, teachers and officers so as to achieve a balanced and rapid development of physical education.

According to Lui (1932), supervisors of PE were appointed and programmes organized systematically throughout the country. Programmes in the elementary schools consisted of gymnastics, drill and games, but in the secondary schools Swedish gymnastics was supplemented by athletics, baseball, basketball, soccer and swimming, although Clumpner and Pendleton (1978) suggest that sport was mainly an extra-curricular activity. Facility provision was gradually made, but despite a proliferation of schools and teachers, according to Hughes (1937: 175) 'there was no strong government to implement the plans of the Ministry of Education in Beijing. Very little progress was made with the training of teachers or improvement of teaching methods. Ideas such as practical science teaching, handwork and physical training were adopted in theory on instructions from HQ'.

The traditionalists, as in 1911 and 1915, and against a background of serious political events and threats to national security, tried to ensure that military training was part and parcel of physical education. Hsu (1975) cites Article 7 of the 1929 Aims and Principles of Education of the Republic of China as evidence of a perceived need.

For school education of all levels and social education, national physical education must be universally emphasised. For high schools and college education, military training must be sufficiently applied. The purpose of developing physical education is to enhance national physical strength, to culture sound spirit and to foster regular habits of life for our nationals.

(1975: 131)

Sport administration, national and international competition

In an attempt to ensure the smooth development of modern Chinese sport, Wu and Que in Knuttgen (1990) describe how the All China Sports Promotion Association was formed in Nanjing in 1924. Its tasks were: to conduct exchanges on sport issues with other nations; to draw up rules for various amateur sports; to organize regional soccer matches; and to host the Far East Games in China. Zhou (1991) describes how, in addition to the establishment of a Guiding Commission of Physical Education in Nanjing in 1927 and the issuing of National Sports Regulations in 1929, the government also established a Sports Committee in 1932 under the Ministry of Education to be responsible for guidance and supervision. In addition, the first national physical education conference was convened in 1932, and the government assumed responsibility through the China National Athletic Association for the sponsorship of the 4th to 10th National Athletic Meets (Pendleton 1984). Van Dalen and Bennett (1971) indicate that official regulations to establish playgrounds were promulgated in 1939 and, in 1942, the Ministry of Education authorized the formation of provincial and municipal PE committees.

Sewell (1933) in *The Land and Life of China* records how many of the young Chinese at this time were taking to the new sports at the expense of more traditional play activities. Shuttlecock, kite-flying, shadow boxing and lion dancing were still practised, but:

> these old sports were strangely out of favour at the school . . . Chinese boys and girls have taken up new games with zest – football, volleyball, basketball, and to a certain extent baseball, but especially tennis. Athletic contests, running, jumping, throwing, are also popular. Every school has its sports day, and there are large gatherings in the district and in the province. Every successful competitor hopes to be chosen for the National Track Meet or the Far Eastern Olympic Games where China, Japan, the Philippine Islands and other lands in the East compete with each other.
>
> (1933: 106–7)

Whatever the strengths and weaknesses of the education system and its promotion of sport, at least physical activity was part of the new education, and children were being introduced either formally or informally to sporting forms, particularly in the schools.

Outside the education system, new 'National Games' organized mainly by the YMCA in 1910 in Nanjing and 1914 in Beijing helped to change the perception of sport in the minds of the Chinese. Brownell (1995) records that these games were watched by over 60,000 spectators in all, partly due to the novelty of sport to most Chinese. The format of the sports meet included such practices as parading behind the school flag, listening to speeches, raising the national flag and singing the national anthem, now standard practice in many Asian countries. They no doubt gave a sense of occasion to the meet, which Brownell claims 'quickly made its way into public life' (19: 42).

After the war, the third National Games were held at Wuchang, Hubei in 1924 with the Republican government building on the YMCA tradition, but attempting to use the sports to support the development of the nation-state. They were the first games organized exclusively by the Chinese, the scale was unprecedented with attendances of 40–50,000 for each of the three days, and the inclusion of three exhibition events for women. Hackensmith records that 'athletes representing schools, colleges, clubs, merchants, clerks and labourers competed in athletics, soccer, baseball and tennis' (1966: 274). There were also regional, provincial and municipal games but all games were to come to an end in 1937 when war with Japan was declared.

Sports facilities were constructed in major cities, and in 1930, the government supported the All-China National meet at Hangchow, which hosted over 1,000 athletes, of whom 200 were women. Women's participation in sport in China, as previously indicated, was affected by the practice of foot-binding, the small number of girls attending missionary schools and the organization of sport mainly by westerners whose attitudes were not generally in favour of female sport competition. Although women's first entry in the National Games was in 1924 with basketball, softball and volleyball, it was not until the late 1920s that significant numbers of women participated in sport (see Brownell (1995: 43–4).

A massive impetus was given to the development of sport in China and the Far East by the inauguration of the Far Eastern Olympic Games. China sent forty athletes to the first meet in Manila in 1913, 200 to the games in Shanghai in 1915, and competed regularly until 1934 when the Games were dissolved over the political issue of whether or not Manchukuo should be affiliated. Japan tried to enter athletes from Manchukuo as a separate team, but China refused to allow this challenge to its integrity.

Clumpner and Pendleton find it hard to assess the significance of the Far Eastern Games, but claim that 'they did encourage participation in sport, indirectly caused the government to promulgate laws on PE and convene conferences, and may also have contributed to enhancing national pride among the Chinese' (1981: 108). They draw attention also to a further factor in the emergence of sport – the consolidation of a national Chinese government. From 1928 to 1949, the Kuomintang, despite a troubled political climate which was hardly conducive to a fully-fledged national development of sport, did enact the 1929 law and, according to Zhu (1936), establish weekly allocations of time for PE, morning exercise and after-school recreation and military training. Semotiuk (1974) confirms the view that the Kuomintang accorded physical training, particularly of a militaristic nature, high priority during their rule. Part of the 1929 law stated: 'The young men and women of the Chinese Republic have a responsibility to be the recipients of physical education, and parents or guardians have the responsibility of enforcing it.'

However, Clumpner and Pendleton add that, despite these measures, 'by the time the Communist Party came to power in 1949, the vast majority of Chinese had never stepped into a classroom, much less participated in physical education and sport' (1981: 109). Kanin (1978) further points out that although Chiang Kai-shek and the Kuomintang took an active part in the spread of western sport, the Japanese invasion came before national sport could prepare national defence and 'the Kuomintang never could complete its plan to use sport to advance national unity' (1978: 263)

On the international front, China joined the International Olympic Committee in 1923 but did not attend a meeting of the Olympic body until 1928. It had been invited to take part in the Olympic Games of 1896 in Athens, but the Qing government apparently did not entertain the invitation. By 1920, the IOC had formally recognized the Far East Sports Association and China sent an athlete, Li Changchun, to the Games in Los Angeles in 1932 as a diplomatic gesture to forestall Japan's attempt to send participants under the name of Manchuria (see Hsu 1995). Chiang Kai-shek soon recognized that the Olympics were an increasingly important 'political forum' (Kanin 1978: 264), recruited a German coach to train the Chinese team and the delegation to the Berlin Olympics of 1936 totalled 107.

This was the acme of the Kuomintang presence in international sport and only seven athletes attended the London Olympics in 1948. As Riordan (1991: 85) points out however, no medals were achieved during this period. Wu and Que in Knuttgen (1990: 51) indicate that the quality of performance in Chinese sport at this time was low, and claim that the designation of China as the 'sick man of Asia' was related to 'China's backward physical culture and sports and her accompanying failure in international sport competitions'. In 1936, a German newspaper carried a cartoon depicting several Chinese searching for Olympic medals beside a large goose egg, symbolizing zero, and it was not until 1984 that China won its first Olympic gold medal.

SUMMARY

The period 1840 to 1949 saw China move from a totally introspective dynasty, with an unrealistic belief in its own power and importance, to a member of the international community of nations. Its sheer size and its inherent conservatism operated against it being able to modernize as rapidly as other Far Eastern powers, but a series of military defeats at the hands of western powers and Japan, together with its observation of the industrial and scientific superiority of foreign states in the treaty ports and concessions, forced it to see the necessity for change and modernization. The Qing dynasty gave way to the Republic of China in 1912, and a Nationalist government, supported by international and Chinese bourgeois interests, steered a path through the 1930s and 1940s, but the invasions by Japan and the securing of massive popular support from patriots and the rural population, led to the declaration of a Communist People's Republic of China in 1949.

In the field of sport, the early influences of the missionary schools were reinforced by the establishment of sporting cultures in the treaty ports and the gradual absorption of sport by the Chinese bourgeoisie. Under the new Republic, support for western forms of physical education was tempered by a belief in some quarters of the need for military training and the superiority of the indigenous Chinese martial arts. The influence of western education- ists and in particular the work of the YMCA in promoting sport, estab- lishing associations, training sports administrators and coaches, and in organizing municipal, regional and national Games, cannot be underesti- mated in the modernization of Chinese sport.

Under the Republic, the Chinese gradually, but deliberately took over the organization of these Games and, through experience with the Far East Olympic Games, were able to register with the IOC and send representatives to the Olympics themselves. The speed with which the Nationalists were able to use sport to enhance the concept of a new, modern Chinese nation-state was hampered by the extreme political, economic and military circumstances of the period, but progress in laws on sport, programmes in schools, at least in theory, the training of PE and sport teachers, the establishment of national sports associations, the organization in Chinese, by Chinese, of national and regional sports meets and their popularity amongst the population at large, the construction of large sports facilities particularly in the major cities, and the opening of competitive sport to females, were all indications of the value which the Nationalists placed on sport, in the service of either the nation- state or individual fulfilment.

Their political opponents, the Communists, were also convinced of the value of physical health, fitness and sport, and the declaration of the People's Republic of China in 1949 was to usher in a period of sport development which, in its contrasts over the subsequent fifty years, will probably never be matched in any society.

REFERENCES

Bonavia, D. (1989) *The Chinese: A Portrait*, London: Penguin Books.
Brownell, S. (1995) *Training the Body for China: Sports in the Moral Order of the People's Republic*, Chicago: University of Chicago Press.

Brownell, S. (1991) 'The changing relationship between sport and the state in the People's Republic of China', in Fernand Landry, Marc Landry and Magdelaine Yertes (eds) *Sport: The Third Millennium*, Proceedings of the National Symposium, Sainte-Foy: Les Presses de l'Université Laval.

Ch'en, Jerome (1979) *China and the West: Society and Culture 1815–1937*, London: Hutchinson.

Chai, C. and Chai, W. (1969) *The Changing of Society in China*, New York: New American Library.

Clumpner, R.A. and Pendleton, B.B. (1981) 'The People's Republic of China,' in James Riordan (ed.) *Sport under Communism*. London: G Hurst

Crew, C. (1940) *Foreign Devils in the Flowery Kingdom*, New York and London: Harper & Bros.

Feuerwerker, A. (1976) *The Foreign Establishment in China in the Early Twentieth Century*, Ann Arbor: Center for Chinese Studies, University of Michigan.

Gernet, J. (1982) *A History of Chinese Civilization*, Cambridge: Cambridge University Press.

Hackensmith, C.W. (1966) *History of Physical Education*, New York: Harper & Row.

Hsu Yi-hsiung (1975) 'Formation of the philosophy of Chinese physical education on national military education in the early twentieth century', APCHPER Proceedings, Taipei, ROC, August.

Hughes, E.R. (1937) *The Invasion of China by the Western World*, London: Adam and Charles Black.

Hunter, W.C. (1911) *Bits of Old China*, Shanghai: Kelly & Walsh.

Kanin, D.B. (1978) 'Ideology and diplomacy: the dimensions of Chinese political sport', in B. Lowe, D.B. Kanin and A. Strenk (eds) *Sport and International Relations*, Champaign, Illinois: Stipes.

Kolatch, J. (1972) *Sport: Politics and Ideology of China*, Middle Village, New York: Jonathan David.

Knuttgen, Howard G. *et al.* (1990) *Sport in China*, Champaign, Illinois: Human Kinetics.

Krotee, M.L. and Wong Jin (1988) 'A comparative study of the People's Republic of China and the United States in regard to the sociocultural process concerning the role of physical education and sport in national development', paper presented to the ICSPES Conference, Hong Kong, 26 August 1988.

Lui, S. (1932) 'The PE movement in China', *Journal of Health and Physical Education*, 3(4), April: 17–21.

Pendleton, B. (1984) '"The two Chinas": Imbroglio in international sport', in ICHPER Sport and Politics, *Proceedings of the 26th ICHPER World Congress*, 1983, Israel: Wingate.

Percival, W.S. (1889) *The Land of the Dragon*, London: Hurst & Blackett.

Riordan, J. (1991) *Sport, Politics and Communism*, Manchester: Manchester University Press.

Rizak, G. (1989) 'Sport in the People's Republic of China', in F.A. Wagner (ed.) *Sport in Asia and Africa*, Boston: Greenwood Press.

Schirokauer, C. (1991) *A Brief History of Chinese Civilisation*, Orlando: Harcourt Brace & Co.

Semotiuk, D. (1974) 'Some historical interpretations of physical culture in China', paper presented at the North American Society for Sport History, London, Ontario, Canada, 11 May.

Sewell, W.G. (1945) [1933] *The Land and Life of China*, 3rd edn, London: Edinburgh House Press.

Van Dalen, D.B. and Bennett, B.L. (1971) *A World History of Physical Education*, 2nd edn, Englewood Cliffs, New Jersey: Prentice Hall.

Werner, E.T.C. (1928) *Autumn Leaves*, Shanghai: Kelly & Walsh.

Werner, E.T.C. (1919) *China of the Chinese*, London: Sir Isaac Pitman & Sons.

Zhou Xikuan (1991) 'China: sports activities of the ancient and modern times', *Canadian Journal of Sport History*, 22 (2), December: 68–82.

Zhu Ming-yi (1936) 'Physical culture', *The Chinese Yearbook 1935–1936*, Shanghai.

Chapter 5

Sport and physical education in school and university

Robin Jones

Although it might be expected that the Chinese education system is homogeneous, there is considerable diversity within and between the different parts. Both physical education in schools and universities and sport in special schools and institutes are considered in this chapter.

Education in modern China suffered a significant setback during the Cultural Revolution (1966–76) when a whole generation of young people lost years of opportunity. During the same period, sport also suffered because the young people who would have become the sports stars of the future were also prevented from developing their talent. Coaches and administrators of sport also lost their futures to the dogma of the time and the whole physical education movement came to a virtual standstill. The years since the Cultural Revolution have seen education become an important part of the government's reforms. The Chinese Communist Party's Central Committee in May 1995 said: 'A vital factor for the success of our cause lies in the availability of skilled people, which requires the vigorous development of education as economic growth allows.'[1]

At state level, physical education in schools and universities is governed by regulations drawn up in 1995, and signed by President Jiang Zemin.[2] These regulations identify crucial areas where schools are required to follow state policy and are important in setting out the way physical education is presented and taught (see Appendix at the end of this chapter). The hierarchical structure of the Chinese education system is apparent in the regulations and, although provincial autonomy has increased in recent years, schools are still obliged to conform to the national pattern. The system is carefully controlled by the government, and displays a surprising amount of selection.

THE OVERALL SCHOOL AND UNIVERSITY SYSTEM

Schools

As China surges forward economically and industrially, there is a pressing need for a trained labour force. Thus, for the last decade, the Chinese education system has been addressing the problem of training skilled people at all levels by creating specialist schools for various categories of students: key schools for academic students, technical and vocational schools for professional, administrative and clerical jobs, skilled trades and technical work; and special sports schools for the gifted. A consequence of this policy is that Chinese schools are selective in their intake of students, and there is considerable pressure on students (and their families) to 'make the grade'. Key schools are found in both the primary and secondary sectors of education; a school is designated 'key' on the basis of the quality of the teaching and its facilities, and about 15 to 20 per cent of schools meet these requirements. Figure 5.1 shows the general pattern of Chinese education.

For both key and non-key schools, six years of primary education is followed by three years of junior middle school, at which point further selection takes place for the transfer to either senior middle school or vocational school. At the age of 15, about 15 per cent of students leave junior middle school for direct entry into work. Of the remainder, about 40 per cent of students transfer to senior middle school for three years, whilst the other 60 per cent go to the vocational and technical schools (there are three or four variations of these schools, according to the particular trade, profession or clerical work on which they focus). Nine years compulsory education, i.e. primary, plus junior middle school, is the universal pattern in China, and this period covers two important transfer points. First, primary to either key or non-key junior middle school, at 12, and second, junior middle to either key or non-key senior middle school, at 15. Primary schools themselves may be key or non-key, so there is considerable differentiation and selection of students between the ages of 6 and 15.

From key middle schools, the transfer rate to senior middle schools is virtually 100 per cent. However, from non-key junior middle schools to senior non-key middle schools, the transfer rate is lower at around 60 per cent. In practice, there are relatively few students who transfer from a non-key school to a key school, but it is possible. The situation is confused also by some schools allowing fee paying students to bypass the examination system, even though this is discouraged by the government.

Following senior middle school or vocational school, students may then enter the work force, or take the State Examination for entrance into higher education.

Table 5.1 Kinds of key and non-key schools in China

primary, key	primary, non-key
junior middle, key	junior middle, non-key
senior middle, key	senior middle, non-key

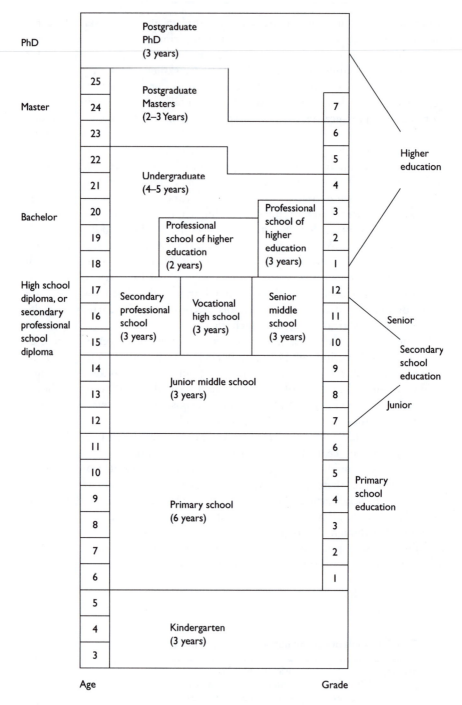

Figure 5.1 The Chinese education system

Table 5.2 Transfer rates from middle schools to universities, vocational schools and work (approximate figures)

From	To	%	Remainder to
Key, senior middle school	University	80	Work
Non-key, senior middle school	Senior vocational school	60	Work
Vocational school	Senior vocational school	60	Work

Universities

There are several different kinds of universities:

- General universities covering a broad spectrum of subjects
- Subject-specific universities, e.g. transport, medicine, sport
- Normal universities that are responsible for training teachers
- Special universities (a few) for ethnic minority groups in China
- Institutes of various kinds that cater, as in the universities, for different aspects (including sport)

Undergraduate courses are usually of four years' duration.

The Chinese Communist Party (CCP) is a structural part of the university system. Departments, besides having a head of department, also have a party leader whose task is to liaise with those students who are or who wish to become party members (usually around 10 per cent of the group). Alongside the work of the CCP, all new students at university are required to undergo two weeks of basic military training on arrival at university. The training, alike for men and women, is campus based and involves squad training, marching, weapon training, martial arts drills, parades and so on. There is no doubt that this is taken seriously by the leaders and the military instructors who organize the activity. It is seen as providing discipline and cohesion for the students, who respond readily to the instructions, even if, privately, some admit to disliking the requirement.

Communal life for students differs markedly from western university campus life. Dormitories for students are typical (six or eight undergraduates to a room, or three or four postgraduates), with tight institutional controls over such things as access for visitors. Student accommodation is cheap (about 10 yuan per month), but student grants of 80 yuan per month for undergraduates and 260 yuan per month for postgraduates are well below the cost of living. Even 260 yuan is barely sufficient to cover food and basic clothing, so undergraduates are usually heavily dependent on their families for additional funds. Luxurious student union buildings, pop concerts, discos, bars and a busy social life are not the pattern of Chinese student life!

Key primary and key middle schools may be attached to universities as part of the hierarchy of provision in Chinese education, helping to ensure that education is highly prized by families and leading to quite intense pressure on students at each level. As China moves away from the cosy security afforded by the system that guaranteed jobs for virtually everyone, at any cost, the 'prize' of education is much sought after. In a rather perverse way, this has allowed institutions to meet some of the cash shortfalls (created as the government pushes forward with the reforms) through schemes whereby places at middle schools and universities can be bought.

In 1995, 49.7 per cent of those middle school students taking the university entrance examination were enrolled at university. The same year also saw the introduction of a unified system of university fees (ranging from 1,000 yuan to 1,500 yuan per year) to try to prevent the universities charging higher fees to those students with low grades in the entrance examination. But in spite of discouragement by the government, it seems unlikely that schools and universities will abandon this established practice altogether; it is, after all, a source of additional revenue.

Physical education in the overall structure

Throughout the education system, physical education is compulsory for all students. In primary and middle schools, pupils have physical education lessons on two or three days each week, plus extra curricular activities on other days. Following senior middle school, university students during their four-year courses are required to include two hours sport a week in the first two years. For all ages from primary up to university or adult level (according to the sport), sports schools are part of the education system, and exist in addition to, but separate from, normal schools. Students combine a general curriculum with sports training. Institutes of Physical Education are the principal centres for the training of specialist teachers and coaches. Like universities, their courses follow on from senior middle school, and are of four years' duration. Both theoretical and practical work is covered and the final qualification is equivalent to a degree.

PRIMARY SCHOOLS

Children in China attend primary school from the age of 6 to 12 years, during which time their PE focuses largely on basic athletics, games and gymnastics. Transfer from middle school to primary school is controlled by examination; academic potential is the major factor in the selection process (Chinese and mathematics are central to these tests). Sports tests are also part of the physical education programme in primary schools, and from the age of 9, national age group norms are applicable across a range of activities. The National Sports Standards Tests, or age group norms, span all years from 9 to 19, covering primary, junior middle and senior middle school (see also Chapter 13). For most years, there are up to seventeen tests that, with some changes and modifications at different stages, continue throughout the span and, of course, boys and girls have different tables and standards. Students are tested on five or six of the seventeen, according to their abilities. Table 5.3 gives an example. These tests are routinely used by schools as part of the physical education programme, but they are also formally recognized when students transfer from one school to another, benefiting the physically able student and acting as a motivation for others. Minimum standards are required from everyone at primary and middle school. There may also be local variations of these tests that differ only slightly from the national standards.

In conjunction with the Sports Commission, middle schools may also be identified with a particular sport, according to their strengths (which may be a combination of facilities, PE teacher strengths and the decision of the Sports Commission) and the primary school pupils are then matched as far as possible (on the basis of their sporting potential) with the relevant middle school that specializes in the particular sport.

MIDDLE SCHOOLS

Middle schools, covering the ages 12 to 18, comprise the secondary stage of Chinese education; key middle schools cater for those students at the top end of the academic ability range.

At age 18, the end of senior middle school, students are eligible to take the State Examination for entrance into university. Every year, the state sets the marks that are needed for entrance and, according to their total marks,

Table 5.3 National age group standards – female, 9 years

Test	Points	100	75	50	25	5
50 metre sprint		8.5s	9.0s	9.5s	10.5s	11.3s
25m shuttles – m. in 10s		48m	46m	43m	38m	34m
4 × 10m shuttle		11.6s	12.7s	14.2s	15.7s	16.9s
8 × 50m shuttle		1m 33s	1m 48s	2.03s	2.18s	2m 30s
Skipping, 60secs		180	145	110	75	47
High jump		0.96m	0.85m	0.75m	0.65m	0.57m
Long jump		3.12m	2.72m	2.32m	1.92m	1.60m
Standing broad jump		1.76m	1.56m	1.36m	1.16m	1.0m
Shot put		6.0m	5.0m	4.0m	3.0m	2.20m
Softball throw		23m	18m	13m	8m	4m
Medicine ball throw, 2 hand		20m	15m	10m	5m	1m
Sit ups		44	34	24	14	6
Inclined chins		38	28	18	8	2
Press ups – 20 secs		14	12	9	7	5

Source: Chengdu (1997)

students are allocated a place at university. In this, sport has a place that is quite unlike that in Britain, because sporting ability is formally used in the selection process for university entrance. A gold medal in the Olympic Games gives access to any university in the subject choice of the student, whilst in lower competitions there is a well-defined range of sports perform-ances or rankings for which students are awarded a number of points in the State Examination, thus enhancing their chances of gaining a university place. To gain these rankings, students must achieve the required standard in an 'official' competition at city level or above (see Tables 5.4 and 5.5).

Between 500 and 600 points are usually required in the State Examinations for entry into the best universities. Therefore, the fact that performance in sports tests and sports competitions is recognized gives added status to the PE programme.

Up to the Cultural Revolution (1966–76), China operated a scheme of physical tests for students that was a close match with the GTO/PWD[3] scheme of the former Soviet Union. During the years after the Cultural Rev-olution this was replaced by a 'sports level for teenagers', or physical profi-ciency test (based mainly on running, jumping and throwing), and which is

Table 5.4 Points awarded for standards achieved in official competition

Sports ranking	Points awarded in State Examination
International standard	Direct access to university
National standard	Direct access to university
First ranking	Direct access to university. Only applies to certain sports, but includes track and field, swimming, soccer, volleyball, basketball, badminton, table tennis and wu shu
First to second ranking	Up to 200 points (but five years for the degree rather than the usual four)
Second ranking	30 points
Third ranking	20 points

Source: Chengdu (1995) Handbook of Middle School

Table 5.5 Middle school PE standards for 'graduation'. Minimum 45% required for 'Pass'. Distances in metres

Boys	45%	Max	Girls	45%	Max
100m	16.1	12.8	100m	18.7	15.4
1500m	6.34	5.17	800m	4.05	3.10
Shot	6.6	9.9	Shot	4.30	6.70
Long jump	3.98	4.86	Long jump	3.07	3.95
Chins	9	15	Standing broad jump	1.57	2.01
Throw medicine ball, 2kg	7.80	11.5	Throw medicine ball, 2kg	4.8	7.2

Source: Chengdu (1995) Handbook of Middle School

now part of the National Age Group Norms. At the end of senior middle school (age 18/19), when students are about to enter tertiary education (universities, institutes, senior vocational or technical colleges), they are required to have reached the minimum standard in these physical tests before being allowed to proceed. There is some inconsistency in saying that everyone must reach a certain physical standard, whilst also saying that there is a pass–fail threshold because it could imply that the fail level is so low as to be meaningless, or that the fail level is 'flexible and arbitrary'. As will be mentioned later, in practice there is some flexibility in applying the marks to the entrance examination; students are allowed (and expected) to take the physical proficiency aspects on more than one occasion so as to reach the overall pass standard for graduation from middle school, which is set at 45 per cent.

A further example of National Age Group Norms is given in Table 5.6.

It can be seen from the tables that fifty, thirty, or twenty points for first, second or third grade in sport can provide a significant boost to an overall score of perhaps 570 required in the State Entrance Examination for a top university. However, outstanding performance in sport may be recognized much further, and lower overall scores of around 350 may be accepted (with an extension of the length of the university course also possible).

The fact that students going to university have to continue with weekly PE for the first two years of their studies gives weight to the requirement for middle school students to reach a pass standard in PE, but there are

Table 5.6 National Age Group Norms, male, 18 years

Event	Points*	100	75	50	25	5
50 metres		6.4s	6.9s	7.4s	8.4s	9.2s
100 metres		12.5s	14.0s	15.5s	17.0s	18.2s
25m shuttle, m. in 10 sec		56m	54m	51m	46m	42m
4 × 10 metre shuttle		9.6s	10.7s	12.2s	13.7s	14.9s
1000 metres		3m 15s	3m 40s	4m 05s	4m 30s	4m 50s
1500 metres		5m 14s	5m 49s	6m 24s	6m 59s	7m 27s
25m shuttle, m. in 4 mins		960m	910m	860m	810m	770m
200 metres swimming		4m 00s	4m 25s	4m 50s	5m 15s	5m 35s
1500m, ice skating		3m 30s	5m 10s	6m 50s	8m 30s	9m 50s
High jump		1.42m	1.32m	1.22m	1.12m	1.04m
Long jump		4.97	4.57m	4.17m	3.77m	3.45m
Standing broad jump		2.65	2.45m	2.25m	2.05m	1.89m
Shot		10.20m	8.70m	7.20m	5.70m	4.50m
Medicine ball throw, 2 hands		11.90m	10.40m	8.90m	7.40m	6.20
Chins		16	14	11	6	2
Dips, parallel bar		19	17	14	9	5
Timed chin hang		96	76	56	36	20

Source: *National Age Group Norms*, 1989

Note
* Points for intermediate distances, times and scores are possible.

obviously students for whom PE is a trial rather than a tribulation! In contrast to some programmes of PE in other countries, Chinese schools do not offer students options in selecting their sports, but rather present a programme based on the general and specific requirements of the State Regulations, the decisions of the Provincial Sports Commission on the appropriate sports for their school and the lead given by the school principal and PE staff. Teachers are required to conform to the national rules for physical education, and students are 'in receipt' of the curriculum rather than being partners to it. Physical education is based on four components: health, fitness, the mastery of basic sports skills, and knowledge of the basic rules and techniques of sports. Use of the National Age Group Tests continues throughout the junior middle school in running, jumping and throwing and, at the end of junior middle school, the standards achieved become part of the student's academic profile, which is then used to decide whether a student continues into senior middle school. Because it is from senior middle school that university education follows, the junior middle to senior middle school transfer is critical. It is the determining point at which future careers are largely settled. The following tables give the standards for the physical tests which one key middle school uses for the junior to senior middle school transfer. The school has 3,300 students and sends around 90 per cent of its students to university each year, including five or six to sports institutes. Table 5.7 shows the details.

The standards in these tables were established and set by the Provincial Sports Commission and, in general, are slightly higher than those in the

Table 5.7 Standards for transfer from junior to senior middle school (age 15)

(a)	Boys: 1000 metres				Girls: 800 metres		
Points	Times	Points	Times	Points	Times	points	times
100	3.30	50	4.40	100	3.20	50	4.32
95	3.36	45	4.45	95	3.28	45	4.38
90	3.42	40	4.50	90	3.36	40	4.44
85	3.52	35	4.55	85	3.44	35	4.50
80	4.00	30	5.00	80	3.52	30	4.56
75	4.08	25	5.05	75	4.00	25	5.02
70	4.16	20	5.10	70	4.06	20	5.08
65	4.24	15	5.15	65	4.12	15	5.14
60	4.30	10	5.20	60	4.20	10	5.20
55	4.35	5	5.25	55	4.26	5	5.26

(b)	Boys: standing broad jump			Girls: standing broad jump			
Metres	Points	Metres	Points	Metres	Points	Metres	Points
2.60	100	1.94	53	2.10	100	1.64	54
2.57	98	1.91	50	2.08	98	1.61	51
2.54	96	1.88	47	2.06	96	1.58	48
2.51	94	1.85	44	2.04	94	1.55	45
2.48	92	1.82	41	2.02	92	1.52	42

Table 5.7 Continued

	Boys: standing broad jump				Girls: standing broad jump		
Metres	*Points*	*Metres*	*Points*	*Metres*	*Points*	*Metres*	*Points*
2.45	90	1.79	38	2.00	90	1.49	39
2.42	88	1.76	35	1.98	88	1.46	36
2.39	86	1.73	32	1.96	86	1.43	33
2.36	84	1.70	29	1.94	84	1.40	30
2.33	82	1.67	26	1.92	82	1.37	27
2.30	80	1.64	23	1.90	80	1.34	24
2.27	78	1.61	20	1.88	78	1.31	21
2.24	76	1.58	17	1.86	76	1.28	18
2.21	74	1.55	14	1.84	74	1.25	15
2.18	72	1.52	11	1.82	72	1.22	12
2.15	70	1.49	8	1.80	70	1.19	9
2.12	68	1.46	5	1.78	68	1.16	6
2.09	66	1.43	3	1.76	66	1.13	3
2.06	64	1.40	0	1.74	64	1.10	0
2.03	62			1.72	62		
2.00	59			1.70	60		
1.97	56			1.67	57		

(c)		Boys: shot put (3kg)				Girls: shot put (3kg)		
	Metres	*Points*	*Metres*	*Points*	*Metres*	*Points*	*Metres*	*Points*
	10.50	100	7.60	64	7.20	100	5.00	64
	10.40	99	7.40	61	7.10	99	4.80	61
	10.30	98	7.20	58	7.00	98	4.60	58
	10.20	97	7.00	55	6.90	97	4.40	55
	10.10	96	6.80	52	6.80	96	4.20	52
	10.00	95	6.60	49	6.70	95	4.00	49
	9.90	94	6.40	46	6.60	94	3.80	46
	9.80	93	6.20	43	6.50	93	3.60	43
	9.70	92	6.00	40	6.40	92	3.40	40
	9.60	91	5.80	36	6.30	91	3.20	36
	9.50	90	5.60	32	6.20	90	3.00	32
	9.40	89	5.40	28	6.10	89	2.80	28
	9.30	88	5.20	24	6.00	88	2.60	24
	9.20	87	5.00	20	5.90	87	2.40	20
	9.10	86	4.80	16	5.80	86	2.20	16
	9.00	85	4.60	12	5.70	85	2.00	12
	8.90	82	4.40	8	5.60	82	1.80	8
	8.60	79	4.20	4	5.50	79	1.64	4
	8.40	76	4.00	0	5.40	76	1.40	0
	8.20	73			5.30	73		
	8.00	70			5.20	70		
	7.80	67			5.10	67		

Source: Xindu, 1997

national standards lists. The minimum pass standard for the three activities is a cumulative total of eighteen points (as listed in the tables), the average for all students in the final year of junior middle school being about twenty-five. Usually two or three students achieve a maximum score of 300. A score of 100 points in any or each of the three physical activities is then translated as ten points in the transfer test from junior to senior middle school. In 1997 460 points were needed for the transfer at this particular school; thus a student who scored a maximum of 300 on the physical tests would be credited with thirty points out of the required 460 for the transfer test, i.e. a potential 6.5 per cent credit for good performance in physical tests.

In key middle schools, there is considerable emphasis on academic success and university education (which accounts for about 90 per cent of the students), but the importance attached to academic lessons has resulted, in the opinion of one PE teacher, in negative consequences for physical education in the middle schools and even in the primary schools. The PE teacher complained of lack of time for the subject, content that had become boring by its narrowness, teaching methods that suffered from large class sizes and mixed sex groups (he did not explain why this was detrimental and, in fact, not all middle schools teach mixed PE; one explanation may be the limitations of facilities and staff) and students who had little choice in their physical education and who were not streamed by physical ability. To understand this further, the organization of the other subjects should be explained.

Within key middle schools, students are grouped, according to their academic strengths, into the sciences or the humanities; their studies in middle school are divided into junior and senior blocks of three years. Those slightly weak in Chinese and mathematics may be restricted to junior middle school (unless they demonstrate progress) and thereafter they would transfer into vocational or technical schools. Students with demonstrable ability in Chinese and mathematics and the potential for university will continue into senior middle school, by which time they will have been grouped broadly into either science or arts/humanities, following a curriculum that has, in the 1990s, been largely influenced by the requirements of the State Examination for university entrance. Until 1998, the State Examination was relatively narrow, allowing virtually no choice of curriculum by the students (there is no psychology, sociology, sports studies or computer studies, for example) and consequently, even though a school may actually have taught a broader range of subjects and have an active physical education department, the strictures of the State Examination were dominant; it influenced the PE programme and student attitudes to the subject. A new pattern of State Examination is being introduced in 1999, referred to as the '3 plus X' system. Chinese, mathematics and English will form the core of this new system, plus 'X', one (or more) other subject(s) chosen by the school. The 'X' subjects will be divided into a section on arts and literature (politics, history and geography) and one on sciences (physics, chemistry and biology), thus giving some flexibility to individual schools. Also being introduced in 1999 is a new senior middle school curriculum that is no longer aimed exclusively at university entrance, and will allow students to choose certain courses.[4]

A view commonly expressed in China is that sport requires little intellect and this is underlined to some extent by the separation of schools into special sports schools, middle schools and key middle schools. Equally, there are schools where physical education, supported by the principal, is seen to contribute to the total education of the students. The 1999 changes to the curriculm and new examinations structure, together with a greater awareness of opportunities for professional sport, and a growing leisure market, might, therefore, herald a shift in this attitude of low respect for physical education. Table 5.8 shows the balance of the timetable at one key middle school.

A further element of selection has occurred in some key middle schools with the establishment of express streams for the academically able student, which reduces the normal six-year secondary programme by two years.

A key middle school particularly well equipped with facilities, including a fifty-metre, eight-lane outdoor swimming pool, a new 400-metre shale athletics track, a full size soccer pitch in the middle of the track, outdoor volleyball court and fitness equipment comprising parallel and horizontal bars, contrasts sharply with another key middle school that possesses no track, no field, and only marginal outdoor space for volleyball, basketball or general exercise.

For the well-equipped school, the PE curriculum, spanning three years junior and three years senior middle school, is based on five areas:

1   Swimming (few schools have their own swimming pool, so an eight-lane, fifty-metre pool is a luxury)
2   Track and field
3   Gymnastics
4   *Wushu*
5   Ball sports (table tennis, basketball, soccer and badminton).

Table 5.8 Overall content of a key middle school timetable

	Lessons per week
Mathematics	9
Chinese	8
English	8
History	5
Physics	5
Chemistry	5
Geography	3 (in grades 7, 8, 10 and 11; none in grades 9 and 12)
Music/art	1 (the same as geography)
Physical education	2 (plus extra curricular activities on three days)

Source: Xindu, 1997

Whilst teachers may exercise some choice over lesson content, students are not given options in their timetabled lessons. Each week, students have two, forty-five minute lessons, and daily extra curricular sport opportunities for about one hour (afternoon games). Informal inter-school competitions are held every month or so, but state regulations require annual competitions to be held for the schools in each area.

Although the precise pattern may vary from place to place, a typical weekly programme of PE in a middle school includes:

1   Mass exercise for the whole school, either at the start of the school day or at morning break. It is conducted, outdoors, by the PE staff, the students lining up in rows, perhaps in the centre of the running track, with amplified music to co-ordinate the timing of the exercises. A routine of swinging, stretching, stepping or jumping on the spot is undertaken by the students, in the limited space. The exercises last for about twenty minutes.

2   Routine eye exercises are required on three to five days per week. These are done in the classroom, again to music, supervised by the class teacher. The object of the exercises is to relieve eye stress by massaging the eyes and the surrounding tissue with the fingertips in a regular and prescribed manner. Students sit, with their elbows on the desks, their eyes closed and for around ten minutes gently massage their eyes.

3   The school day starts at 7.45 am with fifteen minutes of private reading (some schools use this time for exercises). Four lessons in the morning are split by an exercise break of about twenty minutes, and a two-and-a-half hour lunch break is followed by three afternoon lessons, again split by a twenty-minute break, which may be used for eye massage. Within this overall framework, junior 1 students have up to four timetabled PE lessons a week in a class of around fifty, whilst for the remaining five years of middle school the students have up to three PE lessons a week. The PE curriculum is based on: gymnastics, track and field, table tennis, badminton, soccer, volleyball, basketball, *wu shu*, swimming and dancing.

Schools have limited choice over which sports they can offer, and are also subject to the Sports Commission designating a particular sport to the school. The PE teachers see the aims of PE as:

  i)   to improve the general quality of PE for all
  ii) to produce excellence in performance for the able student
  iii) to teach sportsmanship, diligence, teamwork and co-operation
  iv) to train future PE teachers

School inspectors visit schools on an annual basis to monitor progress and standards. Key middle schools typically have up to 2,500 students and twelve to sixteen PE teachers.

4. There is a (selected) extra curricular sports programme where students can practise their sport to a much higher level than timetabled lessons. It is almost certain that the school will have better facilities in that sport. Membership of the 'clubs' demands regular commitment; they are not for the student who just wants a little recreative fun. Students may spend up to three hours a week in their sports training.

By the end of senior middle school, all students are expected to have reached the minimum standard in the relevant national age group tests. The tests allow everyone to reach the minimum standard with reasonable application. Students who are injured or sick must apply for exemption from the test by applying to the Sports Commission on the following form:

School: Name:	Male/Female	Grade/class: Age:
Reason for application for exemption from PE test:		Parent's signature:
School remarks:		Principal's signature:
Medical report:		Doctor's signature:
Education Commission remarks:		Signature/Stamp/Date:

Source: Xindu, Sichuan 1997

Whilst PE lessons may not have the same high status as, say, mathematics, PE is promoted in a positive and enthusiastic manner in the schools themselves. The following (from a middle school physical education notice board) shows how one school brings the question of standards to the attention of its students:

As students, you should:
1 Love communism, love the country, love physical education. Upgrade your standard of physical education for the glory of class and school.
2 Obey the school rules and take classes seriously.
3 Work hard towards the set goals. Take physical education seriously. Take an active part in all activities. Improve yourself and strive for outstanding standards.
4 Respect teachers, show care for your community, foster team spirit, dress properly, do not fight, do not use vulgarities, do not scold, do not sport strange hairstyles, enhance personal development.
5 Take sport and competition seriously, display sportsmanship and respect judges and opponents.

6   Work hard, observe good standards of hygiene, take care of equipment
    and public property.

(Beijing 1993)

The direct and all embracing message contained in the Chinese school rules
certainly leaves little room for misunderstanding if taken literally by the
students. But there is hardly any indication how some aspects should be
implemented or interpreted, such as care for the community or strange
hairstyles. There is an implied hierarchy of compliance that stresses the
subordinate relationship of the individual to the rest of the system – government, country, school, teacher, class, community, team, subject – with only
brief mention of 'self'. In this respect, therefore, the rules are very much a
reflection of the traditional ethic of Chinese society, Confucianism, where
'self' plays a subordinate role to 'others'. Although modern China under
Mao Zedong challenged the dominance of Confucian ethics in the new
society, eradication was neither possible nor (it may be argued) desirable.

Schools in China are allowed to seek additional school funding from
commercial activity such as manufacturing or trading, the income from
which may be used in a variety of ways, including sports facility development. Schemes that middle schools have initiated include the manufacture of
small laboratory equipment, the raising of chickens for the food market, a
taxi scheme, the building of small office and shop units for leasing, and a car
wash scheme. The schemes do not use student labour but are set up as
normal commercial ventures. Middle schools may also impose certain
charges on the students, adding further to the money raised locally for
education. In key schools, these charges are typically: accommodation fees
(boarders), up to 400 yuan for each five-month semester, depending on the
standard of accommodation; school lunches (all students), 150 yuan for each
five-month semester; school books/materials (all students), 80 yuan per
school year.

Boarding at key middle schools is not uncommon. Students share dormitories of up to ten to a room, each room with bunk beds, study tables,
shower and toilet.

BEYOND SCHOOL: THE TERTIARY LEVEL

There are three elements of sport and physical education in higher education.

General sports classes

Government regulations determine that students of all subjects in higher
education receive two hours of general sport per week during the first two
years of the four-year undergraduate course. Students are obliged to follow

the programme set by the sports department of the university. For universities with a student population of 10–12,000 this means catering for 5–6,000 students a week, and requires sports departments of forty to fifty staff. Essentially, such departments are service departments, providing practical classes for all students; the courses are not theoretical and, with a few exceptions, the staff have no major academic function (exceptions include specialist Institutes of Physical Education, and PE departments in Normal, i.e. teacher training universities). A university week comprises thirty or thirty-five time slots, so a staff of forty, working with groups of forty students twice a week (or one, two-hour slot), would mean a staff load of around eight hours per week. Sports facilities in universities generally include: outdoor volleyball and basketball courts, an athletics track (cinder) and central playing area, usually the football pitch. Tennis courts (shale), table tennis tables (concrete), outdoor badminton courts and fitness stations of parallel bars and single bars of various heights are also widely seen. Some universities also have indoor facilities for basketball and volleyball. The facilities are heavily used and, given that China has many other priorities that call on its resources, it is easy to understand the problems that universities face over facilities in the rapidly developing climate of high cost, hi-tech education.

Normal universities

Throughout China, there are about 200 universities charged with the specific task of training teachers. These universities are referred to as 'normal universities' or teachers' universities (*shi fan da xue*). In Shanghai, East China Normal University is one such university and, along with Beijing Normal University, North East Normal University (Jilin province), Central Eastern Normal University (Wuhan, Hubei province), South West Normal University, (Chongqing, now a municipality, but before 1997 part of Sichuan province) and Xian Normal University (Shaanxi province) belongs to the group of six teachers' universities that are funded directly by the State Education Commission (now Ministry of Education). In the majority of normal universities, only bachelors degrees are offered (which would include some curriculum physical education as a non-specialist course). Around 10 per cent of normal universities offer masters degrees in physical education (or at least some aspect of physical education), and in one, East China Normal, it is also possible to go on to PhD studies in sports psychology.

East China Normal University (ECNU) has more than 10,000 students across all subjects. Physical education on the campus comprises the department of PE (with 200 bachelor students, eight masters students and four PhD students in 1997), and the Sports Division, which deals with the service teaching of the students in all the departments of the university.

Although one of the six state-funded normal universities, ECNU, also receives some funding from the Shanghai government, but in 1997, the physical education department received only 60,000 yuan per year to run the teacher education programme, excluding staff salaries. This is less than 300 yuan per student and puts enormous pressure on the department to raise money by other means. A new sports hall, built on the campus for the Eighth Chinese National Games (Shanghai, October 1997), will provide greatly improved indoor sports facilities, after the Games, to augment the minimal indoor facilities already in use. Staff ratios for the PE department are generous, with forty staff comprising thirty-one lecturers and nine office staff. By comparison, the sports department, which provides the basic two hours a week sports programme for students in the other departments of the university, has forty-one staff.

Students in the physical education department follow a comprehensive curriculum to prepare them to teach in schools, including a period of school based teaching practice. Tables 5.9 and 5.10 give details of the course for PE majors at ECNU.

Table 5.9 Courses followed by physical education students at East China Normal University. Duration of course: four years

General courses	Basic, compulsory	Advanced, compulsory	Compulsory
Modern Chinese history	Anatomy	Sport physiology	Teaching practice, 5 weeks
English	Sport psychology	Sport biomechanics	Graduation thesis, 5,000 words
Moral education	General physiology	Sport drawing/ painting	Year I thesis, 5,000 words
Basic law	Intro. to PE theory	Sport history	
Philosophy	Sport health/ hygiene	Options	
Computing	Sport statistics	Track and field	
Military training	School sports	Basketball	
Education theory		Volleyball	
Educational technology		Soccer Gymnastics *Wushu* Artistic gymnastics Swimming Dance Basic gym/basic games Small ball Electives (see Table 5.10)	

Table 5.10 Elective courses for physical education students at East China Normal University. (Students elect four hours per week.) Sports science laboratory facilities are limited; biomechanics has no laboratory. The department has its own library

	Number of weeks	Hours per week	Total hours
Sport biomechanics	18	2	36
Sport training science	18	2	36
Exercise science	18	2	36
Track and field theory	18	2	36
Sport photography	18	2	36
Comparative PE	18	2	36
Sport management	18	2	36
Child development	18	2	36
Sport nutrition	18	2	36
Sport beauty science	18	2	36
Qigong	18	1	36
Body building	18	1	36
Weightlifting (men)	18	1	36
Soccer (women)	18	1	36
Physical health science	18	2	36
Sport English	18	2	36
Sport economics	18	2	36
Sport sociology	18	4	72
Sport Sc/research methods	18	2	36

On completion of their study at normal universities, students are expected to teach in schools. Unlike other universities, jobs for graduates in this sector are still guaranteed by the State; a new teacher could expect to have accommodation provided by the school as part of the job, even though this might only be a single room in a teachers' block, with shared facilities. Career advancement would also bring with it the opportunity for improved living accommodation, depending on the school and the limitations of cost and space afforded in different cities and areas of the country. However, the new economic climate of China is encouraging many young people, especially the educated, to seek greater rewards in the free market of trade, commerce and industry. For some students at teaching universities, this poses a dilemma. Their course commits them to teaching, but their career orientation may change during their four years training, and a decision not to teach is a costly one. Student teachers are bonded for three to five years after leaving university, and breaking the bond results in cash penalties of 15–30,000 yuan. Nonetheless, students do break the bond (relatively few in the case of physical education students) with the aid of family help, or personal savings from vacation work, for example. A new teacher is paid about 600 yuan per month (1997).

Specialist institutes of physical education

At tertiary level, sport and physical education in China can be followed to bachelor degree level in state and provincial institutes of physical education (degrees in physical education in China were first established in 1981).[5] China now has sixteen specialist institutes of physical education that between them produce the top echelon of teachers and coaches for sport. Six of these institutes – Beijing, Chengdu, Wuhan, Shanghai, Shenyang and Xian – were, until its closure, under the direct control of the State Physical Education and Sports Commission[6] (partly because they were established earlier than the provincial institutes and control from Beijing was the pattern at that time). Besides the specialist sports institutes, a further 217 sports departments in universities and colleges also help to train teachers for primary schools, middle schools, vocational institutes and colleges at various levels.

Above bachelor degree level the opportunities for higher degrees in physical education are more limited, the principal centre being the Beijing University of Physical Education (formerly 'Institute' until 1994 when it was upgraded to Beijing Sports University). Beijing and now Shanghai, offer doctoral programmes.

The Beijing University of Physical Education has a teaching staff of almost 500 and a student population of about 2,000 (approximately 1,900 undergraduates and 100 postgraduates)[7] who follow one of several courses – teacher education, coach education, sports science, adult education or sports management. An emerging field of study, sports management has been introduced in Beijing, first, because the sports system is moving towards market accountability and, second, because more opportunities now exist, with the five-day working week, for individuals to plan their own leisure time. Sports leaders have realized there is a growing leisure industry in China that requires trained managers, and Beijing University of Physical Education plans to meet the demand.

Government reforms to universities, known as Project 211, aim to identify the top 100 universities in China and develop them to the highest possible standard by the start of the twenty-first century. Project 211 includes Beijing Sports University, but does not include the remaining sports institutes, leaving the potential for them to become marginalized. There has been no obvious move to upgrade other institutes to university status.

Chengdu Institute of Physical Education is the major sports institute in south-west China. Its 2,200 full-time students are supplemented by 800 part-time students and serviced by 700 staff including 100 professors and associate professors, 250 lecturers and 350 management and clerical staff. The institute now insists that staff obtain a masters degree, although one-third of them already have masters or doctoral degrees. Chengdu is entitled to award bachelors degrees to the undergraduates, and masters degrees to the forty full-time masters students. The ratio of men to women is about 4:1 (more women fail the fitness test).

Funding has undergone radical change. In 1997, Chengdu Institute of Physical Education received about 5,500 yuan per student per year (a marked contrast with the 300 yuan per student at East China Normal University). In the early 1990s, this was sufficient for the full twelve months, but by 1997, would only cover nine months' funding. The shortfall is being met by student fees of 1,000 yuan per year (1997), but within the scheme, students from low income backgrounds can get reductions in the form of scholarships, loans or part-time campus jobs.[8]

The study programme at Chengdu comprises four major courses:

1   Sport education. Students following this course become teachers in middle schools.
2   Sport coaching. Students following this course become coaches in special sports schools (at various levels).
3   *Wushu*. Students in this course become coaches, as above.
4   Chinese medicine. This is not a general medical course, but one related specifically to osteopathy. Students become sports doctors to sports teams, work in hospitals and rehabilitation, and research institutes for sport.

Courses 1, 2, and 3 are each of four years' duration, covering a conventional pattern of work, but course 4, Chinese medicine, sits rather uncomfortably within the portfolio of courses. The inclusion of sports medicine/osteopathy originated because of the skills and interests of one individual at the time the institute was being established. In this respect, Chengdu is untypical.

In 1997, the intake of students for the four courses was:

	Number	*Minimum entry requirement*
Sport education	310 (=52%)	330 in the state examination
Sport and training	90 (=16%)	State exam plus practical test
Wushu	90 (=16%)	State exam plus practical test
Chinese medicine	90 (=16%)	490 in the state examination.

A number of common courses are taken by all students: foreign language, philosophy, theory of education, psychology, sports theory, computing, and statistics. The sport education course comprises 4,000 hours spread over four years and includes forty compulsory courses and thirty optional courses. (See also the curriculum of East China Normal University for the type of curriculum content for teacher training.)

Each week comprises twenty-eight to thirty timetable hours (including two to four hours free), six teaching hours per day and a five-day week. The working day is from 8 a.m. to 12 noon, and from 2 p.m. to 6 p.m. and a typical teaching load for staff is twelve hours a week. Theory courses take place in the mornings and practical courses in the afternoon, with occasional evening lectures; and some students take additional courses at other universities in the evenings.

Students are assessed by coursework (including an extended essay) and examination, with practical work counting for up to 60 per cent of the final mark, depending on the module. The Office of Teaching Affairs is responsible for choosing the actual examination paper from a selection of up to ten papers submitted by the lecturing staff. Re-sits are allowed after three days and again after one year; students who continue to fail would then not receive a diploma, but may have a chance to be recommended to a school by the institute. The institute also offers a three-year correspondence course in sport education or sport coaching, for either a bachelors degree or a certificate of graduation.

Special sports schools

During the years following the founding of the PRC in 1949, China developed a sports system that was largely modelled on that of the former Soviet Union. Although not an active member of the IOC in the early years, China did have national teams that competed against other Communist countries, as well as being at the top in international table tennis. Sports schools were established at national and provincial level, for those with high sporting potential. In the early decades, the sports schools were concerned primarily with sports performance; the athlete's welfare and future was in the hands of the state, and there was little need (if any) to be concerned about the long-term implications of full-time commitment to sport. At the end of their competitive careers, athletes could be absorbed into state industries, college or university study, or sports administration. Unsuccessful athletes returned to their former schools or position, and had to 'pick up the pieces' from there. By comparison with Britain's approach in the 1960s and 1970s, Chinese athletes were given far more state support to enable them to reach a high level and, as with other Communist countries, were often accused by the West of being professionals under the guise of being state amateurs.

There are several links in the chain leading to the sports school, each link becoming progressively more specific to the sport. In the early phase, special sports classes are held in the normal schools for students with sporting potential. Not all schools have special sports classes, but those that do are able to develop this potential by having well-qualified teachers in the sport (the regulations allow the school to appoint extra staff for this purpose) and the opportunity to practise the sport at the school sports club. Sports profiles are kept of students' abilities which, if a student goes on to sports school, accompany him or her and become more detailed. The profile (in the form of a booklet), includes the information given in Table 5.11, together with

Table 5.11 Fitness test record for students at special sports schools

Name	Sex	Date of birth
Bone age	X Ray number	Address
Father's name	Occupation	Telephone number
Mother's name	Occupation	Telephone number
Date selected	Year	Date left
Original school	Standard	Going to
Coach's remarks		

Source: Chengdu 1991

detailed anthropometric and morphological measurements, competition and training results and a section for student remarks.

Given the size of China's population, there is an almost inevitable shortage of trained PE teachers and coaches, but one advantage of the system is that resources can be targeted. Thus, even though there may not be enough well-qualified primary PE teachers in the schools, the pupils at the schools may also attend the spare time sports schools where sound basic coaching is available and where sporting talent may develop. 'Taster' sessions are also held at the sports school in the evenings and during school holidays; these sessions are not free, and parents have to pay quite substantial fees for the coaching. For example, during the summer months of 1995 in Chengdu, Sichuan, a two-week course of swimming lessons cost 80 yuan (one hour a day six days per week), or about 6 yuan per lesson[9] (cheaper than casual use of the pool at 8 yuan per hour). Other sports were also available on a similar basis – tennis, table tennis, skating (artificial ice), and soccer.[10]

Sports boarding schools, of which China has about 100, provide full-time sports training in parallel with full-time schooling, for potential members of the provincial team or higher. The twin 'full-time' description is not a misnomer because the students follow a fully planned programme of sports training and education that leaves them little time for themselves. It is a rigorous schedule, where success in competition is the main criterion for remaining at the sports school and where failure, or lack of progress, results in students returning to their normal school. There is no doubt that academic progress is less of a priority than sporting progress and there is thus an inherent risk attached to attendance at the sports school if, as is inevitable for many, sporting success does not follow.

One such sports boarding school is located at the Sichuan Sports Skills College, in Chengdu. During the late 1970s and early 1980s, in the province of Sichuan, signs of government reform were beginning to show. In 1986, the Sichuan Sports Working Team, with the approval of the State Education Commission, became the Sichuan Sports Skills College. Previously, the Sports

Working Team catered solely for sports training and performance, but the Sports Skills College took on an educative role, and ten years later it is one of the key sports institutions in south-west China, combining high level sports training with conventional schooling, vocational courses and adult education for its athletes. The college now accepts responsibility for preparing athletes not only for competition, but also for their post-competitive careers. The guarantee of a job in the state sports sector no longer holds, and athletes are trained in vocational skills as well as sports skills. The reasoning for this is clear: the state is asking athletes to train and compete for the province or country, but increasingly there is competition for the 'loyalty' of athletes in the new climate of an open market. The insecurity of a sporting career, without the insurance of education or other training, is reducing the pool of young athletes (and their families) who are prepared to risk their future in sport. Sichuan Sports Skills College is trying to ensure that athletes are employable after their competitive years. At the seventh Chinese National Games in 1993, Sichuan entered a team of over 400 athletes which, for the majority, represented not only the pinnacle of their sporting careers, but also the end (because the next games were four years away, and a new crop of young athletes would take over). This highlights one of the potential problems of the reforms. It is a recognized problem, and throughout China, ten provinces or municipalities have now set up a similar system to that in Sichuan (cities in brackets): Sichuan (Chengdu), Shaanxi (Xian), Beijing, Shanghai, Zhejiang (Hangzhou), Guangdong (Guangzhou), Liaoning (Shenyang), Heilongjiang (Harbin), Hunan (Changsha) and Jiangsu (Nanjing). These ten institutes offer courses up to higher education level, along with special vocational training, designed to ensure that athletes are not disadvantaged by devoting a large part of their young lives to sport. Other provinces operate up to middle school only, and have yet to develop higher or adult education.

Government Document Number 6, 1996, specifically covers people retiring from competitive sport:

1   athletes must have job training
2   those athletes reaching the highest levels will receive the most extensive training
3   the programme will be reviewed annually
4   athletes may arrange their own jobs or accept an offer from the state
5   an advice bureau will be set up
6   athletes will receive interim payment from the state whilst they are seeking employment.

Under the general heading 'Service to the State', these regulations bring sport into line with the conditions applying to the armed forces.

The change, in 1996, to a five-day working week, carried implications for the sports institutes. It was accepted that the training of athletes may not fit into a conventional five-day pattern, and an extension to five-and-a-half days was allowed. School age athletes at the Sports Skills College follow a 'half day school, half day training' pattern, whilst older athletes have two half-days and one evening for education and the rest for sports training. Additionally, for all athletes, Saturday morning training takes place.

Comprising six departments – track and field, swimming, weightlifting, small ball (badminton, table tennis, and tennis), big ball (soccer, basketball, and volleyball) and gymnastics – the Sports Skills College has about 1,400 athletes-in-training, coaches, teachers and support staff. The departments are spread over three major campuses in separate parts of the city, each with its own accommodation for the students and (some) of the staff.

The track and field campus has two indoor, synthetic, 100-metre long training houses for both sprint events and field events, a synthetic 400-metre track and a cinder 400-metre track. The main campus includes swimming and diving (50-metre pool and separate diving pool), gymnastics (men's hall, women's hall, sport acrobatics hall and artistic gymnastics hall), table tennis (two halls with about thirty tables), badminton (six courts), tennis (twelve outdoor shale and synthetic courts and indoor hall under construction), basketball (one hall), volleyball (one hall), and soccer (field and surrounding track). The third campus houses facilities for those post-competitive athletes on sports coaching and sports administration courses along with boxing, weightlifting, judo and *wushu*.

Sports science and sports science research institutes

Throughout China is a network of provincial sports science research institutes. Research implies the search for and discovery of new knowledge, but the priorities of the research programmes in China are more related to the performance of individual athletes, and the achievement of their potential, than to the discovery of knowledge yet to be applied to athletic performance. In other words, the research institute's function would perhaps be better understood as sports science support for athletes and coaches, monitoring of training and competition through basic testing, and providing feedback to coaches, than pure research.

For those provinces with small research budgets, the sports science research institutes are limited in their ability to conduct sophisticated research. Without well-equipped laboratories, sports science research is unlikely to yield results at the highest level, and this in turn militates against the institutes with smaller budgets, and there is not much evidence that shortfalls in research budgets are being met by commercial sponsorship, in the way that competitive sport is attracting sponsorship (e.g. soccer). Sports science may not be keeping pace with the reforms; or at least, there is uneven development throughout the country.

CONCLUDING REMARKS

The basic aim of Chinese physical education of providing one hour of physical activity for all students every day is a noble one and gives a strong message to successive generations about the importance the government attaches to sport. At the same time, it is equally clear that the government is powerfully committed to promoting high level sports performance with its network of provincial sports schools and, indeed, the normal schools themselves are the start of this commitment.

By the end of 1995, China's 'Nationwide Health Plan' had been announced, aiming to broaden the whole base of participation in sporting activity (see Chapter 13). One of the changes this will bring about is a greater concern for mass sport,[11] which will be far less likely to happen if the Chinese economy does not continue to grow. As it is, the potential effect on schools could be considerable, by ensuring that physical education is fully recognized and developed. By 1998, the State Sports Commission had been closed, and its replacement will adopt more of an administrative role, with less direct involvement in sports provision, as the new sports management structure develops. The consequences of this for physical education in schools and universities are yet to emerge. Although soccer and tennis have made considerable progress in the last five years in the sports schools, there are few normal schools with good facilities in these two sports. The decline in support for non-Olympic sports is unlikely to affect the school curriculum, which is already dominated by Olympic and international sports, with the notable exception of *wushu*.

NOTES

1 Party Central Committee, *Reform of China's Educational Structure*, Foreign Languages Press, Beijng, 1985, p. 1.
2 State Education Commission and State Physical Culture and Sports Commission, 1990 'Regulations Governing School Physical Education' (signed by Li Tie Yin, SEC and Wu Shao Zu, PCSC). Translation from the original, Chengdu, 1995. See Appendix 1 for full text.
3 GTO/PWD, 'Gotov k trudu i oborone' (Prepared for work and defence), was the fitness scheme introduced by the former Soviet Union in the early 1930s and continued, with modifications, until the collapse of the USSR. See J. Riordan, *Sport Under Communism*, London: C. Hurst and Co, 1978, for a full account.
4 Reported in *China Daily,* 10 January 1998, p. 2.
5 Liu Zhi Min and Yang Wei Dong, 'The Comparison between Physical Education Departments of the Comprehensive Universities in China and Britain', paper presented at the Asian Conference on Comparative Physical Education, Shanghai, December 1994.
6 The expectation is that the six national institutes will remain under the new sports office, which itself is under the State Council.
7 F.H. Fu, 'A Comparison of the National and Provincial Institutes of Physical

Culture in the People's Republic of China', in Wilcox, R.C. (ed.) *Sport in the Global Village*, Washington: Fitness Information Technology, 1994, pp. 395–402.

8 Details from an interview with Dai Ke Hai – Dean of Student Management and Teaching Affairs Office, Chengdu Institute of Physical Education, 1997.

9 Bearing in mind that a monthly salary of up to 600 yuan would cover many of the service industry jobs from shop assistant to supervisor in a factory unit or similar, a tuition fee of 80 yuan is substantial. On the other hand, there is also an increasing number of parents who either jointly or singly earn sufficient to pay the fee with little hardship.

10 The fee for the other sports varied. The tennis fee was 10 yuan per hour; skating a little more.

11 Author's discussions with leaders of Sichuan Sports Commission, August 1995.

APPENDIX

Outline health plan for sport and physical education in the People's Republic of China

President's Order (PRC) Number 55, Jiang Zemin, 29 August 1995.
On August 29 1995, at the 8th National People's Representative Meeting (and 15th sub-committee meeting), regulations were passed, and have been in use since 1 October 1995.

Chapter I Introduction

1   These regulations are intended to develop sporting standards and opportunities in accordance with socialist principles.

2   Sport is to be developed to enhance physical fitness, by raising levels of activity and promoting all kinds of sport.

3   The improved management of sport and the support of businesses, society and people should be encouraged, for the contribution sport makes to the nation's economic, military and social development.

4   The national sports committe will be responsible for managing the nation's sport, assisted by other departments in their own particular fields. Provincial governments are also authorized to carry out this duty.

5   Sport for young people is promoted for their physical and mental health.

6   Minority groups will be supported in the development of sport and sport leaders.

7   Sports science and sports research will be promoted for the improvement of sport.

8   Organizations that contribute to sport will be supported.

9   International sport is encouraged, based on principles of independence, equality, mutual respect and the maintenance of national authority and dignity.

Chapter 2 Sport for all

10 Participation in sport for all citizens will be encouraged, respecting amateur and voluntary values based on cultural, scientific and civilized principles.

11 The National Fitness Plan will be implemented and a classification system for sports instructors will be introduced to aid the promotion of sport for all.

12 Sport for all should be supported by local governments; each city and county should have a sport for all committee.

13 The government and its departments should promote many kinds of sport and competition.

14 Different trades and labour organizations should organize their own specific sports.

15 Traditional sports will be encouraged.

16 The sporting needs of the elderly and disabled should be provided for by local governments.

Chapter 3 School physical education

17 PE should be included in the school curriculum for the moral, intellectual and physical development of the students.

18 PE is compulsory in schools. Physical performance should be evaluated alongside academic performance, and schools should make special provision for students with illness or disability.

19 Daily PE should be guaranteed, and schools should aim to reach the national PE training standards.

20 Schools should organize a varied programme of Extra Curricular Sports Activities and should, additionally, organize an annual sports competition.

21 Schools should employ qualified PE teachers and provide good professional conditions and pay, according to national guidelines.

22 Schools should follow national guidelines for the provision of sports facilities, which may be used for other purposes too.

23 Student's health should be subject to regular checks by the school and local health departments.

Chapter 4 Competitive sport

24 Competitive sport is promoted. Athletes are encouraged to improve their sports skills and to gain honour for the country.

25 The development of amateur sport will be encouraged to foster elite athletes.

26 Rules, drawn up by the Sports Commission, should direct the selection of athletes and teams according to principles of equity and achievement.

27 Methods of training and management should follow strict scientific rules and athletes should be educated in nationalism, socialism, morality and discipline.

28 Athletes should be entitled to jobs and education.

29 Every sports association should register its athletes, and only registered athletes are eligible to take part in competition, through the Sports Commission.

30 Athletes', coaches' and referees' professional skills should be classified at national, provincial, city and township level.

31 Sports competitions should be classified. The National Games should be managed by the national Sports Commission, or relevant department; national championships in each sport should be managed by their own national sports organization; local competitions should be organized by local organizations.

32 A system for checking and approving national records should be established, to be recognized by the Sports Commission

33 Conflicts and disagreements in sports competitions will be resolved by a sports judges department, under the regulations and control of the Sports Commission.

34 Sports competitions should follow principles of equity and fairness. Organizers, athletes, coaches and referees should not cheat. Drug doping and other methods should not be used and drug detecting organizations should have rigorous procedures. Gambling in sports competitions is not allowed by organizations or individuals.

35 Symbols such as names, flags and mascots must abide by national rules at important competitions in China.

Chapter 5 Sports organizations

36 Sport for all organizations are encouraged to promote sport development.

37 Sports organizations should be encouraged to co-ordinate the effort of athletes and officials and help them reach their targets.

38 The Chinese Olympic Committee is responsible for promoting the Olympic Games in China, and for representing China in Olympic affairs.

39 Sports science organizations and sports scientists should promote sports technology.

40 National Governing Bodies are responsible for their own sports, and should represent China in the international organization of their sport.

Chapter 6 Sport and legislation

41 Local government, above town level, is responsible for the budget for local sport. Sport facility construction should be in accordance with the

national plan, and increases to the budget should depend on national economic factors.

42 Business companies and sports organizations should be encouraged to raise finance and to sponsor sport.

43 National sports should be financially well managed.

44 Sports and competitions organized above town level are subject to national laws.

45 Local government above town level should follow national laws over the use of public sports facilities. Public sports facilities should be part of city planning for construction and ground utilization. City plans for business areas, schools, streets and residential areas should incorporate sports facilities. Districts and towns should gradually develop adequate sports facilities, depending on economic development.

46 Public sports facilities should promote sport for all. Students, the elderly and disabled, should have full access to public facilities. This may increase the rate of use of public sports facilities. Neither organizations nor individuals may occupy or damage public sports facilities. In some specific situations, sports facilities may be temporarily occupied, if approved by the sports and construction departments. They must be returned on time. If the city wishes to change the use of sports facilities, they must provide alternative sports facilities in advance.

47 Equipment and facilities used in national and international sports competitions should be approved by the national Sports Commission.

48 Sports institutions should foster professional training, educational courses, coaching, scientific research and management in sport.

Chapter 7 Legal obligations

49 Any cheating in sports competitions will be punished according to the law. People in charge of sport and sports organizers in national sport departments are subject to the law and take responsibility for the actions of others.

50 Illegal doping in sport will be punished according to the rules. People in charge will also be held responsible.

51 Sports departments should assist the police in the prevention of gambling. People found guilty of criminal cheating and gambling may be gaoled.

52 Any person mis-using or damaging public sports facilities should be ordered by the sports authorities to return and repair the facility in a prescribed time, according to the law. If the offender disobeys safety laws, the police should punish accordingly.

53 Anyone creating trouble at sports competitions or disobeying public order laws should be apprehended and banned. People disobeying safety rules may be gaoled.

54 Anyone abusing national sports finances will be required to return the money in a prescribed time. Sports organizers will be accountable and criminal behaviour may lead to gaol.

Chapter 8 Appendix

55 The army should promote and develop sport. The Central Military Commission is responsible for army sports law and also for following these national laws.
56 These laws come into operation on 1 October 1995.

Later in the regulations booklet, Wu Shao Zu, Head of the Sports Commission (until its closure in March 1998) explains the need to improve:

1 Sports management, sports facilities for public use, scientific training and research.
2 The need for coaches and athletes to be committed to success for China.
3 The importance of sports science support for this success.

He comments further that sports competition has grown, but cheating and the problem of drugs are evident and laws are therefore needed. Three strict rules for doping should be applied:

1 A strict ban on drugs
2 Strict drugs testing to be carried out
3 Strict management and enforcement of drug laws.

Chapter 6

Elite sport

Dennis Whitby

Sport in old (pre-1949) China existed for the wealthy, and the poor health of the Chinese people in general resulted in the country being described as 'the sick man of Asia'. Only one athlete competed in the 1932 Olympic Games and, although athletes competed in the 1936 and 1948 Games, they did so with little distinction. Only one swimmer competed in the 1952 Games; the football and basketball teams arrived too late.

The founding of the People's Republic of China in 1949 brought fundamental changes to sport. The government started to pay attention to the health of the general population and promoted sports development. The Party Central Committee issued a directive entitled 'strengthening work in physical culture and sport for the people'. Chairman Mao Zedong wrote the inscription 'promote physical culture; build up the people's health'.

A centralized sports administration system, based on the pattern of the Soviet Union, was established. Regular programmes of physical training were introduced in army units, communes, factories, offices and schools; institutes of physical education were established, research was initiated and sports facilities were constructed or renovated. In 1959, Rong Guotuan became the first Chinese athlete to win a world championship (in table tennis) and, by 1966, Chinese athletes were excelling in sports such as archery, badminton, shooting, swimming, table tennis, volleyball and weightlifting.

During the Cultural Revolution of 1966–76, however, the development of sport in China was brought to a standstill. From 1966 until 1970, there was a total absence of competition. From 1971, international competition was resumed, but only involving countries of similar political ideologies, such as Cambodia, North Korea and Vietnam. Images of China during the Revolution are of enforced conformity to ideology, intensity, isolation, fanaticism and the 'thoughts of Mao'. Athletes were persecuted, sports organizations were immobilized and facilities were wrecked.

From 1956 until 1976, China boycotted the Olympic Games, refusing to compete side-by-side with Formosa (Taiwan). Instead, China competed in the anti-American and communist-inspired Games of the New Emerging Forces (GANEFO), held in Jakarta, Indonesia in 1964.

Sport was seen mainly as a means of promoting political ideology. Two daily ten-minute sessions of collective gymnastics were required of everyone; schoolchildren received one hour of sports and physical education each day. Massive competitions were organized and a network was established for the selection and training of top athletes. But isolation brought stagnation and the gap between Chinese and world standards in sport widened.

The Cultural Revolution ended in 1976 with the fall of the 'Gang of Four'. Since then, changes have been rapid. In 1978, China's leaders announced the 'Four Modernizations' programme, covering industry, agriculture, defence, and science and technology. The following year, the country's 'open-door' policy was introduced. Since then, great strides have been made in all aspects of society, including sport.

China was readmitted to the Olympic movement in 1980. Although the US-led boycott (supported by China) prevented the athletes who had gained selection from competing in the Olympic Games in Moscow that year, progress in a number of sports during the next three years was rapid. Third in the team event in the World Gymnastics Championships in Moscow in 1981, the men's gymnastics team won the title at the next World Championships in Romania in 1983 and took second place at the Los Angeles 1984 Olympic Games. The women's team, second in the team event in Moscow in 1981, took third place behind Romania and the United States in Los Angeles. China's gymnasts won a total of nine individual medals in Los Angeles – five of them gold.

The Chinese women's volleyball team, after winning the World Cup title in Japan in 1981, took first place a year later at the World Championships in Peru. In Los Angeles, they won the gold medal. Chinese women's basketball also developed quickly. The national team was placed third at the World Championships in Brazil in 1983 and won the bronze medal at the 1984 Olympic Games. The Chinese women's handball team took the bronze in Los Angeles.

International successes were also achieved in diving and weightlifting. Li Yihua won the springboard event at the Third World Cup Diving Championships in 1983 and medals were won by three different divers in Los Angeles. In the absence of most Eastern-aligned countries, Chinese weightlifters won gold medals. In three other sports – archery, fencing and shooting – China also proved that it could compete with the world's best. In 1984, Zhu Jianhua became the first Chinese track and field athlete to win a medal in the Olympic Games.

Altogether, China's team of 225 athletes, competing in sixteen of twenty-one sports, won fifteen gold, eight silver and nine bronze medals at the 1984 Olympic Games. Gold medals were won in women's diving, fencing and volleyball, men's weightlifting and both men's and women's gymnastics and shooting. The medal haul was obviously enhanced by the boycott of the Games by the Soviet Union and its allies.

By competing in the Games, China emphasized its political independence from Moscow; by competing with such success, China served notice that it planned to join the elite of international sport. The political sports slogan of the day – 'break out of Asia and advance on the world' – was vastly different to the 'friendship first, competition second' concept of Mao.

China's performances in the 1988 and 1992 Olympic Games, outlined below, reflect the effort that the country has made since 1984 to gain prominence at international level. China's failed bid to stage the 2000 Olympics by just two votes, however, was a major disappointment. Many politicians and human rights activists opposed Beijing's bid, suggesting that China did not deserve the honour until the country had improved its human rights record. China decided not to bid for the 2004 Games.

How have the results been achieved? From the practical point of view, they can be explained by the implementation of a comprehensive competitive programme and a parallel progressive programme of elite athlete development. Working together, the two programmes take the talented young athlete from the spare-time sports school to the central sports school, the provincial team and, finally, to the national team, while providing ample opportunities for competition.

MAJOR COMPETITIONS

Domestic competitions

China is divided, for administrative and other purposes, into twenty-two provinces, five autonomous regions and four municipalities – Beijing, Shanghai, Tianjin and Chongqing. Each province is divided into cities and counties. Cities are divided into districts. The goal of each city/district/county team is to excel at the provincial games; these are held every four years. At the 9th Guangdong Provincial Games in Zhaoqing in November 1994 (which the author attended), a total of 6,366 athletes represented twenty-one cities and districts in thirty different sports. The provincial games are used to identify athletes who will train with the provincial team in preparation for the National Games, held three years later.

The first four National Games were held in Beijing, in 1959, 1965, 1975 and 1979. The author witnessed the 5th National Games in Shanghai in 1983. In March of that year, more than 9,000 athletes competed in the preliminaries, representing their provinces, autonomous regions, municipalities, the People's Liberation Army and the Locomotive Sports Association in twenty-five different sports. In September, almost 4,000 athletes competed in the finals in Shanghai.

The National Games have since been held in Guangzhou (1987) and Beijing (1993, together with Chengdu and Sichuan). The 1993 National

Games witnessed remarkable performances by Mah Jun Ren's athletes (from Liaoning province), especially in the women's 1500 metres, 3,000 metres and 10,000 metres. The National Winter Games are also held every four years.

Any city or provincial physical culture and sports commission given the responsibility of organizing a major games uses the opportunity to upgrade its facilities. A new sports centre, consisting of a 60,000-seat stadium, an 8,000-seat gymnasium and a diving/swimming hall, was built for the 1987 Games in Guangzhou. The total cost of organizing the Games was Y300 million (US$3.4m).

Provincial sports officials judge their progress and standing in the country's sporting ranks, and are judged according to the team's placing at the National Games and the number of medals that are won. During the author's frequent visits to China to meet officials of various provincial organizations, the conversation has invariably turned to the number of medals won by provincial team athletes at the most recent National, Asian and Olympic Games. After the Olympic Games, success at the National Games is the major goal.

Liaoning is currently China's most successful sporting province. In the 1992 Olympic Games, Liaoning athletes won three gold, four silver and five bronze medals. At the 7th National Games in 1993, Liaoning won a total of sixty-four gold medals – including twenty-six in athletics and six in swimming – to win the team title. Guangdong (thirty-one gold medals), Shanghai (twenty-nine) and Beijing (twenty-one) filled the next three positions. As might be expected, the northern provinces of Jilin and Heilongjiang dominate the National Winter Games.

Liaoning's gold medal haul in track and field in 1993 tells an interesting story. The World Track and Field Championships were held in Stuttgart in August 1993, just one month before the National Games. Because a number of the country's top athletes were reluctant to compete in Stuttgart, preferring to compete for their provincial teams in the National Games, an agreement was reached whereby medals that were won at the World Championships would count in the final medal tally at the Games. This encouraged a number of top athletes to compete in Stuttgart. In addition, each world record at the National Games counted as a gold medal. Mah Jun Ren's athletes won a total of three gold medals in Stuttgart and, as noted above, set fourteen new world records in Beijing – hence the total of twenty-six gold medals won by Liaoning athletes in track and field!

In 1985, the 1st National Junior Games were organized in Zhengzhou, the capital of Henan province, for athletes under the age of 20. The objective was to alternate the Junior Games with the National Games every two years. The author attended the Games to select some young track and field athletes to train with the national team in Beijing. Athletes competed for their provinces, autonomous regions or municipalities in seventeen different sports. The 2nd National Junior Games were held in Shenyang, Liaoning province, in 1989.

In 1988, the 1st National Urban Games were organized in Jinan, Shandong province. The 2nd National Urban Games were organized in 1991 in Tongshan, Hebei province. The Urban Games have now replaced the National Junior Games. It was felt that the financial burden for the second most important domestic competition should be shifted from the provinces to the cities which, particularly on the eastern seaboard, are benefiting financially from China's open-door policy.

The Urban Games are now held every four years. Some provinces are represented in the Games by more than one city. Indeed, the need to develop athletes away from the major training centre of each province was another reason for replacing the National Junior Games with the Urban Games. Three cities in Guangdong province – Guangzhou, Shenzhen and Zhuhai – competed in the thirteen-day 3rd National Urban Games held in Nanjing in November 1995.

Typical of such major games, thousands of schoolchildren and army personnel participated in the Opening Ceremony, held in the Wutaishan Stadium and featuring music and dances from the Yangtze River Delta. Such ceremonies require months of preparation and are obviously very expensive. The cost in Nanjing was Y3 million (US$340,000).

More than 3,300 athletes, representing forty-nine cities and regions, competed in eleven sports – basketball, diving, fencing, football, gymnastics, judo, rowing, shooting, swimming, table tennis and track and field. The upper age limit varied from sport to sport. Track and field was limited to athletes born in 1975. Each team could also enter two athletes born in 1973 and 1974 respectively. It turned out that these athletes won most of the medals! The oldest participants were 23 – in football and shooting.

Competitions in archery, badminton, volleyball, weightlifting and wrestling were held in other cities in the province of Jiangsu: Chenjiang, Wuxi, Changzhou, Yangzhou and Suzhou, respectively. Team honours went to the host city, with Guangzhou (Guangdong province), Dalian and Shenyang (both Liaoning province) taking the next three positions.

Every four years, the country's minorities, representing about 5 per cent of the population (66 million), compete for their provincial teams in the National Games of Minority Nationalities' Traditional Sports; only the country's majority Han Chinese (more than 90 per cent of the population) does not participate. The author attended the 5th Minority Games, held in Kunming, Yunnan province, in November 1995. A total of 3,300 athletes competed for their provinces, autonomous regions and municipalities. Athletes from fifty-five national minorities took part; the largest was the Hui nationality with 534 participants. Another spectacular opening ceremony, entitled 'Jointly Create the Glory' and involving 9,000 participants, was performed in the Tuo Dong Sports Stadium. The Games are more a demonstration of cultures and national unity than a sports event. The author observed five of the eleven contested sports: crossbow shooting, gateball, horse racing, shuttlecock and wrestling. In addition to the competition, there were demonstrations in more than 137 traditional sports.

Besides these major games, each sport organizes its own domestic programme of competition, including its national championships. Two such championships are organized in track and field each year – in June and October, the first a team competition, the second, individual. The difference is that team scores are kept only in the first competition.

International competitions

For those who move beyond the provincial team to train with, and represent, the Chinese national team, the competition goals are obviously different. China competes regularly in the Asian championships of many sports and the quadrennial East Asian Games. But it is the Asian Games and the Olympic Games which are of major importance to the national team. Top athletes in China follow two-year programmes of development in preparation for the Games.

China first competed in the Asian Games in Tehran in 1974, finishing in third position with thirty-three gold medals. Eight years later – in the 9th Games in New Delhi – China finally ended thirty-one years of domination by Japan and emerged as the chief sporting power of Asia. The Games attracted teams from thirty-three nations. China won sixty-one gold medals.

The 10th Asian Games were held in Seoul, South Korea, four years later. The competition was close, with China winning ninety-four gold medals, just one more than the host country. But China's athletes dominated the next Games in Beijing in 1990, winning 183 gold medals, and continued their domination in the 12th Games, winning 137 gold medals in Hiroshima in 1994 – a number that was later modified downwards because of positive drug tests.

During the author's period as a coach with the national track and field team in Beijing in the mid-1980s, there was considerable reluctance on the part of provincial teams to release top athletes for national teams. Coaches and provincial organizations were very protective. Through the performance of an athlete, a coach in China gains status, financial reward and, perhaps, 'promotion' to an administrative position. The situation has since changed. To encourage provincial teams to release their top athletes for the 1996 Olympic Games, medals and points won in the Olympic Games counted towards the final standings at the 1997 National Games.

If the results of the Chinese team at the 1988 Olympic Games were relatively disappointing – five gold, eleven silver and twelve bronze medals – the results in the Barcelona Olympic Games in 1992, reflected the continued progress of sport at elite level. The medal haul was sixteen gold, twenty-two silver and sixteen bronze. However, China has yet to emulate such feats at the Winter Olympic Games. Indeed, China only won its first medals in the Winter Olympics – three silver medals – at the 1992 Games, held in Albertville, France. Two years later, in Lillehammer, Chinese athletes won a silver and a bronze medal in speed skating and a bronze medal in figure skating to take nineteenth place in the medal table.

China's international sporting image has undoubtedly been tarnished since 1994 by drug scandals. Doubts were first raised when Chinese female swimmers won twelve of sixteen titles in the 1994 World Championships, setting five world records in the process. The positive tests at the 1994 Asian Games – when eleven athletes, including seven swimmers, tested positive for performance-enhancing drugs – threw the sport of swimming into turmoil. Ironically, an Anti-Doping Congress had been organized in Beijing in April 1994, only six months before the Asian Games.

Numerous charges have been made that the country had adopted the former East Germany's systematic programme of doping. China's sports leaders have disputed the existence of such a programme, however, and claim that it is impossible to prevent individual athletes and coaches from taking performance-enhancing drugs. Whatever the truth, China was excluded from the Pan-Pacific Games swimming competition in August 1995.

A new 'get-tough' campaign on banned substances was launched during the 3rd National Urban Games in October 1995, with more than 300 random tests being carried out; until then, tests had previously only been carried out on race winners. All members of a team were to be banned for a year if two individual team members tested positive. The ban would be extended to two years if four athletes from the same team were caught using banned substances. Subsequently, the bans were extended to include coaches. Swimming and athletics were the major targets of the new policies.

Also in October 1995, the National People's Congress in Beijing unanimously adopted a law introducing additional drug testing during, and outside, competition and stipulating tougher punishments for failed drugs tests. The following month, another Anti-Doping Congress was held.

Clearly, China hoped that these measures would help erase the memory of the positive dope tests of 1994. China's athletes are now subject to a strict programme of testing. The International Amateur Athletic Federation, for example, employed two full-time foreign experts in 1995 to travel throughout China conducting random tests. The Chinese Olympic Committee has a similar group working full time. Indeed, just two days before the Chinese track and field team were due to fly to the Hong Kong Sports Institute in January 1996 for a three-week training camp, a number of the athletes were tested in Beijing.

ATHLETE DEVELOPMENT

In parallel with the competitive sports system is a system designed to facilitate the progress of young athletes through various levels of development until they reach national level. The journey starts at the spare-time sports school and, for the best, ends with the national team. Most of China's top athletes have, at some time, passed through the sports school system during their progress to national level.

As a technical consultant with the national track and field team from 1984 until 1986, the author was able to observe the system and a number of schools and provincial teams in operation. Comments that were recorded during this period are shown in the extracts.

The spare-time sports school

At the base of the pyramid is the spare-time sports school. There are more than 3,500 of these schools throughout the country, providing specialist coaching for more than 150,000 selected youngsters after school hours. In the mid-1980s, Shanghai alone had twenty-six spare-time sports schools.

The Tiyuguan Lu (Sports Hall Road) spare-time sports school operates in the National Training Centre where the author worked with the national track and field team every day. In the mid-1980s, the school offered coaching for children in seven sports – badminton, basketball, soccer, swimming, table tennis, tennis, and track and field. Track and field athletes started training at 5 p.m., when national team members had finished for the day.

> During discussions with two of the four track and field coaches at the school, it emerged that students in the 10–14 age-range, the 'first-class', are usually selected by the school's coaches. Some are recommended by their physical education teachers. There are no national standards for selection, even though such standards exist.
>
> In some cases, parents must be persuaded to allow their children to attend the school and may refuse permission, either because sport is not regarded by the family as a secure profession or because they would prefer their child to participate in another, currently more prestigious, sport such as gymnastics or volleyball. Some of the children receive a small amount of money each month – about 12 yuan (US$4) – to assist towards food expenses at home. All necessary clothing and equipment, however, are provided by the school.
>
> The coaches are employed full time. Those at the Tiyuguan Lu spare-time sports school hold the rank of 'top-class' coach, the middle point in track and field's five-level coaching structure, but such qualifications are not always necessary.
>
> Beijing is divided into thirteen or fourteen districts and each district holds annual competitions for the spare-time sports schools within its boundaries. District teams then compete in the city championships and the city team competes in a regional meet. In 1984, six athletes from the school had represented Beijing in the North–East meet in Shenyang

(Liaoning province), one of four regional meets in the country. From there, qualifiers had progressed to the national championships in Jinzhou, also in Liaoning.

Spare-time sports school students also compete in the national middle school championships which are held every four years. In 1986, the championships were held in Dalian in Liaoning province.

At the age of 13, athletes with little potential are dropped by the school while more promising athletes are either recommended by the respective head coach for admission to a central sports school or continue to train for another three years in the spare-time sports school's 'top class'.

The central sports school

Provincial central sports schools select the best athletes from spare-time sports schools and, in a few cases, the normal schools of the province or municipality. Students live and train together on one site and study either on-site or off-site at different schools. At the age of 16, athletes with little potential transfer to normal high schools while top athletes normally progress to the provincial team. Students usually study in the morning and train in the afternoon.

In May 1984, the author visited the Shanghai Sports School at the invitation of the Shanghai Physical Culture and Sports Commission:

> More than 500 youngsters in the 9–18 age-range live, study and train together from Sunday evening until Saturday morning each week. They are then free to go home for a few hours. The school has a faculty of fifty teachers and seventy coaches. Classes are held 8 a.m.–12 noon and 5 p.m.– 7 p.m. every day. The period from 2–5 p.m. is devoted to training every day. The school supports fourteen sports.
>
> Athletes are selected from residential sports schools which exist in each of the twelve districts of Shanghai. Competition for admission to the school is fierce. The entrance examination covers both general education and sport. Students with poor grades are not allowed to enter the next grade. Each student pays just six yuan (US$2) each month towards food expenses. All other expenses are met by the government.
>
> During my visit, I observed practices in softball, volleyball, gymnastics and track and field. The girls' softball team had six players in the national junior team. The boys' volleyball team – the national junior champions – was preparing for a trip to Japan. In the gymnastics hall, a group of twenty-five 9-to-11-year-old boys and girls were working either individually, in pairs or in larger groups, sometimes under the guidance of one of the many coaches but, more often, coaching each other. The standard of performance was high; I spotted a number of stunts that had been used by

members of the senior national team during a gymnastics competition in Beijing just two weeks before.

In June 1984, the author visited the Nanjing Institute of Physical Education (NIPE), a provincial level institute, which trains physical education teachers and coaches and serves as the training site for Jiangsu provincial teams and the province's central sports school. Two hundred students, selected from spare-time sports schools throughout the province, resided at the sports school, attending classes every morning and training every afternoon.

Twenty-five 11-to-14-year-old children were training in the modern six-lane 25-metre training pool under the direction of an Australian coach, currently completing her third three-month coaching contract in China. During her first two contractual periods, she had been in charge of the senior provincial team. Now, with increased emphasis upon age-group swimming in China, she was preparing the sports school swimmers for the 1st National Junior Games, to be held in October 1985. Her assistant and interpreter was the swimming coach at the institute. Visiting spare-time sports school coaches were observing her workouts as part of an ongoing seminar. In an adjacent gymnasium, I observed seven young divers performing exercises under the direction of two coaches, either on trampolines or from springboards on to thick mattresses.

In the badminton hall, I spoke with the provincial badminton coach; as we talked, the sports school's badminton players were practising under the direction of their own coach. There were twenty badminton players in the school. They had been selected from a large training camp organized earlier in the year and were preparing for the provincial junior and senior championships. The provincial team coach himself worked mainly with his own players and only supervised the sports school players. He had just returned from Malaysia where the men's national team had won the Thomas Cup, but the women's team had lost the Uber Cup. Four of his players – two men and two women – had been in the team. He also worked occasionally with the institute's physical education students.

Two separate groups were working in the gymnastics hall. At one end, a group of fifteen 9- and 10-year-old boys were practising. At the other end, twenty 8-to-16-year-old acrobats were working individually or in groups under the direction of a number of young coaches and assistants. Some aspiring acrobats were lifting weights and performing bodyweight exercises. The girls, in particular, showed good development in the arms and shoulders.

As I watched, one youngster performed a press to handstand five times in succession without touching the floor with his feet. Two groups, each consisting of two girls and one boy, were working on balancing routines. The athlete at the top was attached to a safety harness. Each balance was held for a count of five seconds. Another stunt was then performed; after a five-minute rest, the routine was repeated.

Eleven years later, in October 1995, the author visited the NIPE for a second time. The sports school now had 320 students, aged from 7 to 16. This period represents the nine-year period of compulsory schooling in China. The goal of the school is to balance education with training. At the age of 16, students will either progress to the provincial team, enter the institute as a student – or find a job. During the visit, the author observed seven or eight divers undergoing dry-land training in a room adjacent to the pool. Five synchronized swimmers were working with their coach while seven or eight other girls were working unsupervised on the diving boards.

In May 1994, the author spent six days in Shenyang as a guest of the Liaoning Physical Culture and Sports Commission and observed the Liaoning sports system at work. The Shenyang Physical Culture and Sports School is one of fourteen city sports schools that feed top athletes to the Liaoning Sports Training Centre, the provincial team training centre. The school offers coaching in eight sports. Approximately 20 per cent of the students progress to the provincial team.

Besides preparing athletes for the provincial team, the school's major goals are to develop primary school physical education teachers and to participate in provincial and national inter-city competition; Shenyang had taken first place in the previous National Urban Games. The school's students, recruited from thirteen districts within the city, range from 6 (in gymnastics) to 21 years of age. One-hundred-and-twenty students attend elementary school. The majority (470) are middle-school students.

In June 1995, a delegation from the Hong Kong Sports Institute (HKSI) visited the Competitive Sports School at the Institute of Physical Education (a national level institute) in Wuhan, the capital of Hubei. The school was founded in 1980. In the mid-1980s, the school had drawn its talent from five southern provinces. Students are now recruited from spare-time sports schools throughout the country. The institute has an advantage over the Wuhan City and provincial teams in being able to offer students the opportunity to enrol as students when they reach the appropriate age.

The 250 students in the sports school live on campus, attending middle- or high-school classes in the morning and training in the afternoon; younger table tennis players and gymnasts attend primary school classes. Students follow a shortened curriculum but sit for regular school examinations. The school employs approximately thirty coaches, twenty teachers and thirteen administrators. The coaches work only with sports school athletes; a number are national or Olympic team coaches. Most athletes progress to municipal teams or to provincial or national teams. A number have won medals in the Asian and Olympic Games and World Championships; twenty-one athletes were currently training for the 1996 Olympic Games.

During our visit, we observed fourteen gymnasts training under the watchful eye of three coaches; the school has a total of twenty-four gymnasts and seven gymnastics coaches. The athletes perform early-morning exercises from 5 until 7.30 a.m., attend school in the morning and train from 2.45 until 6 p.m. One of the gymnasts that we watched was just 5 years old; she had trained at the sports school for one year. A second gymnast had joined the school when she was 7; she was now 11 years old.

The Beijing Sports Competitive school

At the top end of the pyramid of sports schools in China is the Beijing Sports Competitive School which operates at the Beijing University of Physical Education. In the mid-1980s; this was the only sports school that selected its students from the whole of the country. The author visited the school in March 1984 when the university was still known as the Beijing Institute of Physical Education.

> Instruction is provided in a number of sports, including basketball, gymnastics, rhythmic gymnastics, swimming, track and field, and volleyball. There are approximately 165 students, of whom approximately forty-five are training in track and field. The starting age of the students varies according to the sport. Gymnasts start as young as 5 or 6. Track and field athletes start at 13.
>
> Students attend classes every morning and evening. The sports school has its own teachers. The students train every afternoon. At 18, most progress to their provincial teams for further training. Those who do not make the grade enter college or university as undergraduates while others teach at middle schools or sports schools.
>
> Coaches at the school have various responsibilities. Some are involved solely with sports school students while others work with the institute's students or coach institute teams. A spare-time sports school is also attached to the institute.
>
> In the indoor hall, approximately 200 young athletes were working under the direction of twenty track and field coaches. These athletes were either students of the sports school or the institute or members of the institute's track and field team. Later in the day, students of the spare-time sports school began their training.
>
> Two 6-year-old girls were working on the asymmetrical bars in the gymnastics hall under the direction of a coach. The coach said little; the girls advised each other. Others were working on the beam and parallel bars. Again, little was said but there was much activity. In a second gymnastics hall, a group of 15- and 16-year-old boys and girls were working hard on various pieces of apparatus.

The provincial team

Provincial team coaches select their athletes from normal schools, spare-time sports schools and central sports schools within the boundaries of their respective provinces. At the provincial and national levels, Chinese sportsmen and women are professionals – and openly so. Free room and board, medical care, education and certain travelling expenses are provided; in addition, athletes are paid monthly according to their age, experience and performances. An athlete breaking a national record, winning a national title or winning a medal in a major competition will receive a monetary bonus from the provincial team, the national team, or both.

To prepare for their post-competitive careers, most athletes attend classes at local institutes of physical education or other institutions of higher education. Certain courses are mandatory. Each of the eighty athletes on the Liaoning track and field team, for example, must attend all classes. For those who wish to qualify as teachers or coaches, college classes are also provided. In Shanghai, the Shanghai Technical Sports Institute, using its own classes and teachers, prepares top athletes for careers in teaching and coaching. The course lasts for four years.

Only the best provincial athletes are retained as team coaches once their active competitive careers come to an end. The rest will either resume their education or join the general work force; many will finish up working in factories. At the end of their careers, Liaoning team athletes who cannot find jobs in sport can turn to the labour department for help in finding employment.

Provincial team coaches are employed on a part-time or full-time basis. If part time, they may also work at a local institution of tertiary education or in sports schools. During the author's period in China, coaches of the Zhejiang provincial track and field team were employed and paid by the Physical Education Department of Hangzhou's Teachers' College. To hold such positions, they had to be graduates of institutes of physical education. Liaoning provincial coaches are full time. They, too, must hold degrees. Most provincial coaches are former national-level athletes. In track and field, most have also qualified as top-class coaches under the coach education programme of the Track and Field Federation.

The training venues of provincial teams vary according to local conditions. As noted previously, many Jiangsu teams train at the Nanjing Institute of Physical Education. The Liaoning team trains in Shenyang during the winter but moves to Dalian, on the coast, to escape the summer heat. Shandong provincial teams train in Jinan during the winter but move to the coastal resort of Qingdao for the summer. The provincial (and national) sailing teams train in Qingdao all year round.

In October 1986, the author visited the Henan provincial team training centre in the provincial capital of Zhengzhou. In addition to the track and field, gymnastics and weightlifting teams, the centre catered for a number of team sports; target shooting and water sports teams trained elsewhere. The men's volleyball, wrestling, judo and track and field teams were amongst the province's strongest.

My visit took me first to the volleyball hall where the provincial men's team was performing a practice in threes; one man served, another set and a third spiked. The weightlifting team was training outside in the open-air.

From the volleyball hall, we walked to the general weight training hall; this is used by all teams. The equipment was very old and badly maintained. While we were inside the hall, the men's judo and wrestling teams arrived for group barbell work.

In the gymnastics hall, a group of seven 7-to-8-year-old girls were performing a group warm-up. Once they had finished, the girls divided into two groups; four girls each mounted a beam and, together, went through a series of posture exercises under the direction of a young coach; the other three girls worked on the asymmetrical bars. At the same time, five 9-to-10-year-old boys performed leg-circles using a buck; two older boys worked on the pommels.

Between the main hall and the entrance were two large pits full of foam rubber for practice on the horizontal bar and rings. The manager of the centre informed me that the gymnasts have classes every morning; the centre employs its own teachers. There is, as yet, no system by which older athletes, who also attend classes, can qualify as teachers or coaches, but a system is being devised.

Our next stop was the women's volleyball hall where the provincial team was training. We then walked to see the new indoor track and field hall being built. It will be an excellent facility when completed in 1987. The hall is adjacent to two football fields and the outdoor track. Both were deserted. The hall is also adjacent to the dormitory that is used by the track and field team; the team was competing in the national championships in the Henan provincial stadium at the time of my visit.

Our final stop was the basketball hall where the provincial junior men's team and women's senior and junior teams were training. The men were working on a fast break drill. The coaches stood and watched; there was little correction of faults. The men themselves, although tall, appeared to lack strength.

I left the training centre with a strong feeling of commitment on the part of the athletes. Within a twenty-five-minute period, I had observed nine provincial teams at practice. If every province in China has the same system in place, it will not be long before China catches up with the rest of the world.

In October 1992, the author visited the Guangdong Sports Technical Institute provincial team training centre, at Er Sha Tou in Guangzhou. At that time, approximately 500 athletes were training at the institute. Athletes are selected from thirteen sports schools in the province. Most athletes divide their time equally between training and studying. Approximately forty teachers are employed by the institute; classrooms are on-site. The institute accepts responsibility for placing retired athletes in appropriate positions of employment. Local employers co-operate in creating positions.

The institute employs either specialist sport coaches or sport science coaches who combine coaching with research. The institute does not employ specialist strength coaches but, at the time of the author's visit, was looking at the possibility of employing such coaches for groups of sports (e.g. agility sports).

The author visited a number of facilities, including the rehabilitation centre, with jacuzzi, flotation units, massage machines and hydrotherapy units; a 50-metre swimming pool and adjacent weight training facility with charts showing weekly training loads for each swimmer posted on the wall; weightlifting and table tennis halls; and an athlete recreational centre. New water polo and diving pools – the latter built as a result of successes at the Barcelona Olympic Games – were under construction. The institute was also developing a new rowing training centre and competition course.

A delegation from the HKSI visited the institute again in November 1995. During our tour of the facilities, it was obvious that most of the buildings had been renovated since the author's previous visit. The institute now caters for more than 700 athletes and employs approximately 500 staff members and 160 coaches. Foreign coaches are employed in gymnastics, pentathlon, rowing, shooting and track and field. The province has two other training centres. The institute's on-site school provides classes on Tuesday, Thursday and Saturday mornings at all levels up to university level; a number of athletes attend local universities. A few athletes have jobs.

Our first stop was the weightlifting hall. Three members of the provincial women's team were currently competing in the World Weightlifting Championships that were being held at the institute; the three athletes won a total of six gold medals. The provincial team coach informed us that the athletes normally train twice each day on Monday, Wednesday and Friday and once each day on Tuesday and Thursday.

From the weightlifting hall, we passed the table tennis training hall and athletes' living quarters, the building where chess and 'Go' players practise, two outdoor tracks, a large games hall, another building for rhythmic gymnastics, fencing and rehabilitation and the diving and swimming pools that had been under construction at the time of the author's previous visit. The water polo team was practising in the swimming pool.

Approximately thirty-six gymnasts were training in eight or nine small groups in the gymnastics hall. The institute employs ten coaches to train fifty gymnasts who train every morning and afternoon. We also observed thirteen young divers performing dry-land training under the supervision of four coaches and finished the tour at the badminton hall where approximately twenty players were training. The rowing training centre and competition course that had been planned in 1992 had still not been constructed.

Provincial team athletes are recruited to the Liaoning Sports Training Centre from more than fifty sports schools that operate in the province. The centre has five bases – three in Shenyang and two in Dalian. Provincial teams in selected sports undergo altitude training in Qinghai and Yunnan provinces.

In May 1994, the author visited the three training centre locations in Shenyang. Ten sports are based at the major campus. A number of provincial teams were training at the time of the visit, including the women's basketball and volleyball teams – both National Games champions. The second campus hosts eight sports including boxing, cycling, fencing and wrestling. Between them, Liaoning-based athletes in these sports won seven gold medals in the 1993 National Games. An on-site school, employing twenty-three teachers, provides education from elementary to high school standard. The third campus of the training centre caters for the shooting events. Athletes at the three centres train for approximately six hours each day.

Since Liaoning is the most successful provincial team in China, it seems appropriate to ask why is the Liaoning sports system so successful. First, the drive to sporting excellence is supported financially by the province and the central government. Few resources are directed towards public recreation. Second, key events in which Liaoning athletes can be expected to excel were identified in the mid-1980s, according to the physique of local athletes. Shooting, swimming and track and field were also identified as sports in which many medals could be won. Third, the physical attributes of Liaoning people give them an advantage. Liaoning athletes had recently been placed first in twenty-one of twenty-four indexes of physical performance adopted by the All-China Sports Federation. Fourth, the population of Liaoning is approximately 38 million. Liaoning emphasizes participation in competitive sport from an early age and has a systematic method of talent identification – perhaps the most systematic in China. There is a strong talent base which, through the network of county and city sports schools, is optimized. Fifth, a systematic coach education programme was initiated in 1988. Sixth, the system allows athletes to simultaneously prepare for competition and continue their education. Seventh, the adoption of scientific principles of training allows an individual approach to coaching and training. Coaches are encouraged to try new coaching methods. Finally, recent improvements in Liaoning's economy allow the province to send more than 100 coaches and 500 athletes overseas each year.

The development of sport to such a high level has taken ten years. Such has been the success of the Liaoning system that other provinces now come to Liaoning to 'rent an athlete'. Selected athletes sign contracts and either continue to train in Liaoning or move to their adopted provinces. Athletes can compete for their new provinces during the contractual period. In this way, more than 3,000 second- and third-tier Liaoning athletes have competed for other provinces. It does raise questions, however, concerning the relative inability of some other provinces to develop their own athletes.

A final word here about the People's Liberation Army team, or PLA. In theory, the army can recruit athletes from all provinces. However, this process often results in conflict with provincial teams which invariably block the registration of their capable athletes. In 1993, the Chinese Track and Field Federation and the army reached an agreement for the 1997 National Games: the army could recruit athletes in any province but any medal won by an athlete would be credited to both the provincial team and the army team.

National team

In May 1995, a delegation from the HKSI visited the National Training Bureau of the State Physical Culture and Sports Commission in Beijing. The bureau was established in 1951. The staff manage the National Training Centre and provide support for eleven national teams in nine targeted Olympic sports: badminton, basketball (men and women), diving, gymnastics, swimming, table tennis, track and field, volleyball (men and women) and weightlifting.

The objective of the bureau is clear: to produce Olympic champions. In the 1984 Olympic Games, athletes at the NTC won four of the fifteen gold medals gained by Chinese athletes. In the 1988 Olympic Games, all five Chinese gold medalists were based at the centre. In 1992, nine of the sixteen gold medals won by Chinese athletes were won by athletes training at the NTC.

Nearly all Chinese national teams in the major sports are sponsored by foreign sports footwear companies. The soccer team is now sponsored by Adidas, the swimming team by Mizuno and the track and field team, formerly with Nike and Mizuno, by Reebok. The gymnastics team is sponsored by Li Ning, a triple gold-medalist in Los Angeles, who is now a successful sportswear manufacturer in Beijing. Contracts between such companies and national federations vary in content but invariably provide for training camps overseas and visits by foreign coaches, as well as the provision of apparel, shoes and much-needed foreign currency.

From 1984 to 1986, the author spent two years coaching with the national track and field team at the NTC in Tiyuguan Lu, Beijing. The experience provided an opportunity to make a number of observations on elite sport in general and track and field in particular.

The author's role during the first six-month contract, from January to

June 1984, was to work with three Chinese sprint coaches and a group of eleven young sprinters – seven men and four women. The men had been selected to train for the 1986 Asian Games and 1988 Olympic Games and were expected to take over from the Guangdong provincial team as the top sprinters in the country.

The author's second contract started in February 1985. During this period – lasting five months – the author worked only with the women's group. This time, the objective was more focused. Because the group had shown no improvement since its formation four years earlier, the objective was to coach at least one member of the group on to the national team – to be selected at the national championships just four months later! If we failed, the group would be dispersed.

The two contractual periods followed similar patterns. The first few weeks were spent training and competing indoors at the NTC; it is too cold to train outdoors. Both training and competition moved outdoors at the end of March. In May, we attended a training camp in Wuhan, capital of Hubei province. Finally, after returning to Beijing for final preparations, the athletes competed in the National Championships in early June – in Nanjing in 1984 and Shanghai in 1985.

In October 1985, the author began his third, and final, contract in Beijing. This contractual period was to last thirteen months, a period which included the Asian Games, in September 1986, and concluded with the second annual national championships, in October 1986. The author was, once again, to work with the women's group but, this time, was allowed to invite additional athletes to join the group. With this in mind, the author attended the 1st National Junior Games in Zhengzhou in 1985 and then travelled to Nanjing to observe the second national championships of the year.

Contrary to what is told to foreign reporters, national team athletes in China do not compete 'for the motherland' or 'for the glory of socialism'. They compete for the same rewards that attract western athletes – status, the opportunity to travel overseas and, of course, financial reward. Overseas trips also mean pocket money in American dollars and, sometimes, the opportunity to shop in Hong Kong. Given the standard of living of the average Chinese citizen and the average annual salary – approximately Y1,000 (US$113) in urban areas – such benefits take on special meaning.

As noted previously, the best athletes usually become coaches when they retire, while the remainder return to their studies or to the workforce. The chance to study and to qualify as teachers or coaches is also provided during their competitive careers.

National team coaches are generally employed full time. In the past, the level of appointment of a coach reflected his/her competitive record as an athlete; the best athletes became coaches of the national team, the next best with the provincial team, and so on. Appointments were for life. The results of such policies were predictable. First, the coaches at the NTC were not necessarily the best coaches available; indeed, many had had no prior coaching experience. Second, successful coaches at lower levels had no chance of promotion.

Since the mid-1980s, increased accountability and mobility have been introduced into the system; coaches at the centre are now expected to 'produce' results or lose their jobs. A qualification in higher education is also required. Many of the younger coaches now hold bachelor's and master's degrees. Requirements for promotion from one level of accreditation to the next are clearly specified. Officials have also reviewed selection procedures to ensure that appropriate athletes are selected to represent China in international competition.

SOME OBSERVATIONS: 1986

After working for two years within the sports system in China, the author recorded the following comments:

> Many visitors from overseas have branded Chinese sport as propagandist and ideological on the basis of either only a few days in the country, preconceived ideas or simply the belief that sport in Communist countries is always used to promote political ideology. But China of the Cultural Revolution and of Mao Zedong is not China of the 1980s and it is my opinion that sport and politics are not as interdependent as they once were. China has a political system which its leaders consider appropriate to the needs of the people but they do not seek to impose that system on others; China has no intention of exporting its revolution. China, in fact, is adopting many western ideals – but at her own pace. Those who interfere with the country's internal affairs are told, politely but firmly, to attend to their own business.
>
> There is, of course, great national pride associated with sporting honours won by both individuals and national teams. When the women's volleyball team plays, it seems that the whole nation watches the game on television; there is pride in any victory. Successes at the 1986 Asian Games similarly stirred the nation. But these were sporting, not political, victories. Indeed, there is little difference between these displays of national pride and those observed in the United States during the 1984 Olympic Games in Los Angeles.
>
> It is also true that China is bent on sporting success, but so are other major nations throughout the world. The Chinese sports system is state-sponsored yet there is an ever-increasing demand for sport to be self-financing as in the West. China's athletes are professionals and openly so when compared with so many athletes in the West who earn lucrative rewards as so-called amateurs.

In general, China's sports administraters and leaders are working hard to close the gap on the rest of the world. Sport is progressing as fast as it can and on many fronts at the same time. No effort is spared. Facilities and competition are being upgraded and both athletes and coaches are being exposed to foreign influences at home and abroad, particularly in the country's weaker sports. There is tremendous enthusiasm among those involved in sport.

The problems that China faces in improving the standard of sport go far beyond the qualities of her athletes and coaches. Although living standards are improving rapidly, sport has little relevance to the lives of those in the rural areas of the country – approximately 90 per cent of the population; they have other priorities. As a result, most of the athletes within the system are based in cities, particularly those in the east.

Diet is another problem and the medical care of athletes, seemingly treading a line between traditional Chinese and western techniques, seems to be hopelessly inadequate at times, yet extremely effective at others. There is also little sign of any real contribution from the country's legion of sports scientists; the gap between theory and practice mirrors that found in the West.

Perhaps the greatest problem that China faces in attempting to close the gap in elite performance is the pressure from the country's leaders to do so as quickly as possible. As a result, changes may be occurring too quickly without time for consolidation at the various stages of development. Cutting corners will not ensure progress. The aim of China's administrators and coaches is to turn the country into a world sporting power by the end of the century. But the road from champion of Asia to world power is a long and difficult one. Only time will tell if the goal is realistic.

SOME OBSERVATIONS: 1996

Ten years on, much has changed. The objective of turning the country into a world sporting power by the end of the century has clearly been achieved in some sports. Talk to the top sports administrators and coaches in any province and the listener is left, above all, with an impression of teamwork, of a steady and relentless push towards excellence that involves everyone. The passion is obvious – but not over-excessive.

But, as some sports have risen to the top, others have languished in mediocrity. While China's gymnasts, female swimmers and table tennis players have achieved great successes in the Olympic Games and World Championships, the record in other sports, including the major team sports and track and field, is less impressive.

Indeed, it is tempting to suggest that, given the fact that twelve years have now passed since the 1984 Olympic Games, and given the vast resources that have been committed to the development of elite athletes by the central government and the massive population of more than 1 billion people, China's dominance of sport in the international arena is not what it should be. Perhaps the tendency for the less-successful provinces to 'rent' second-tier athletes from the more successful provinces is proof that the job is not getting done. The success of cities such as Shanghai (population 13.5 million) and Beijing (10.8 million) in the 7th National Games in 1993 suggests that having a large population is not enough.

It is doubtful, of course, if any country will ever replicate the efficiency of the sports system of the former German Democratic Republic. But why not? Nine provinces in China – Anhui, Guangdong, Hebei, Henan, Hubei, Hunan, Jiangsu, Shandong, Sichuan – have populations in excess of 50 million. They also have the political desire and the resources. An in-depth study attempting to identify the reasons why the Chinese sports system has not come close to emulating the results of a country with a population of only 16 million would make interesting reading.

One reason is undoubtedly the increasing affluence of the southern and coastal provinces of China. This provides potential provincial- and national-level athletes with alternative pathways to financial security; in these provinces, it is becoming increasingly difficult to retain top athletes. No longer does sport represent the only way out; there are easier ways of making money. Indeed, in time, the southern provinces may experience the same problem that Hong Kong now experiences in trying to retain top athletes in a society that values financial security above everything. This is particularly true of the male athlete who is usually perceived as the major bread-winner in the family. This will probably result in China's female athletes continuing to outdistance their male counterparts in terms of international success.

Another interesting trend is that the central government is now placing more responsibility on lower levels of the hierarchy for funding. This demand has passed all the way down to the districts and cities. As a result, sports marketing and sponsorship are beginning to play an important role and there is the realization that the influx of funds from the commercial world can have negative, as well as positive, consequences for the development of sport.

Indeed, there is now an increasing emphasis on cost-effectiveness throughout the whole system. This has resulted in a new interest in sports and facility management. Facilities are being upgraded and their use optimized. Facilities that were previously used only by elite athletes at various levels of the development hierarchy are now being viewed as potential money-makers.

It is clear that the challenges of the sports system in China of 1986 are not the challenges now. The momentum that was obvious in the mid-1980s appears to have been lost. After early gains, China now faces the same grind that other nations face in trying to reach the summit. The country's sports leaders must look at quality rather than numbers. Following the doping problems of 1994 and 1995, they also have to work to regain the trust of the international sporting community.

Chapter 7

Professional training

Dennis Whitby, Zhu Peilan and Zhang Baoluo

COACH EDUCATION

Following the 11th Chinese Communist Party Congress in 1987, the government stated that the country's future development depended on progress in science and elevation of the overall standard of education in the country. The government also stressed that a scientific approach to training was a prerequisite to raising the standard of competitive sport in China. Technology and human resources must be developed and deployed.

Coaches in China are recognized as a valuable human resource and the training of coaches is recognized as a prerequisite to raising sports standards. Considerable emphasis has been placed on the education of quality coaches ever since the Cultural Revolution (1966–76).

Until 1982, coach education in China was implemented through part-time, short-term courses organized by individual national sports associations (NSA), institutes of physical education, provincial sports technical colleges and universities. In 1982, a Coach Education Division (CED), previously known as the 'Education and Training Department for Elite Sports Teams', was established under the Department of Sports Science and Physical Education of the All-China Sports Federation. The major role of the division is to manage and co-ordinate the education of athletes and coaches throughout the country. The CED draws up broad principles and policies. With the exception of advanced-level refresher training courses, it is the responsibility of provincial organizations, working with provincial sports associations, to administer and implement programmes locally. Coach education is implemented through certification, refresher training courses, short-term training courses and the CED's information service. Coaches within the sports system are classified as national, advanced and level 1, 2 and 3 coaches. Unlike coaching classifications in the West, level 3 coaches are positioned at the bottom of the hierarchy. All coaches must satisfy basic requirements in academic certification, refresher training and coaching experience. The major emphasis within the Coach Education Programme is certificate education at the post-secondary or tertiary-education level. The purpose of certificate education is to improve the theoretical basis, common knowledge and basic techniques of coaches in the sports general theory component.

Most universities in China have separate sports and physical education departments; their role is to train coaches and PE teachers. Unfortunately, the number of graduates from sports departments who pursue careers in coaching is very few. However, coaches who do not satisfy requirements for admission to three-year full-time degree programmes may pursue a diploma course in sports training, either on a full-time (two-year) or part-time basis, or through distance learning.

The full-time diploma course is organized by the country's fifteen institutes of physical education and by sports technical institutes that have been established in ten cities and provinces – Beijing, Guangdong, Heilongjiang, Hunan, Liaoning, Shandong, Shanghai, Shanxi, Sichuan and Zhejiang. With the exception of the sports technical institutes in Beijing and Zhejiang, which have their own campuses, each institute also serves as the training venue for its respective provincial team and is managed by the provincial sports commission. The sports department at the Nanjing Institute of Physical Education also delivers the full-time diploma course.

Institutes of physical education and universities that administer certificate education follow a common syllabus set by the CED. The syllabus for correspondence and part-time diploma courses is identical to that for the full-time course for major (compulsory) topics, but differs for optional subjects. Since 1986, a national examination, set by the National Education Department and the Examination Management Centre, has been organized every November by the CED.

A survey conducted by the CED in 1982 revealed that only 17 per cent of all coaches held post-secondary education qualifications at diploma level or above. Most national coaches now hold such qualifications. In 1990, another survey showed that 56 per cent of the coaches held such qualifications. Few, however, hold university degrees.

Refresher courses

Coaches are expected to supplement certificate education with refresher courses, appropriate to their classification and particular sport. In contrast to certificate education, which provides a solid base of all-round education and theoretical understanding, refresher courses provide sport-specific training for coaches. Emphasis is placed on developing coaching and management skills, and coaching ethics.

Refresher courses were first initiated in 1987 in track and field for a trial period of eighteenth months. In 1989, a nation-wide pilot scheme was implemented for all sports when the Physical Culture and Sports Commission established a Leading Group for Coach Refresher Courses to establish relevant policies and guidelines. The CED implements these policies and administers the programme. The same year, each NSA was required to establish a Consultation Group for Coach Refresher Training to co-ordinate development of curricula and course content.

Course organization

Courses are organized at three levels: advanced (for national and advanced coaches), intermediate (for level 1 coaches) and elementary (for level 2 and 3 coaches). Elementary- and intermediate-level courses are organized by cities and provinces. The majority of courses are organized in sports departments of institutes of physical education and universities, and in provincial sports technical institutes. Organization of advanced-level courses is delegated by the CED to an institute of physical education which specializes in the sport. The institute then joins forces with the respective NSA to organize the course.

The Leading Group established a set of fifteen procedures to ensure the quality of courses organized by NSAs; these apply to areas such as course organization and management, selection of course tutors, teaching materials, course evaluation and the issuing of certificates. The procedures are distributed to all provincial organizations, NSAs and institutes of physical education. Course reports must be filed with the Leading Group.

There follows a list of institutes and their areas of speciality:

Beijing	Rhythmic gymnastics, soccer, swimming, track and field (field events), weightlifting and wrestling
Chengdu	Fencing and handball
Guangxi	Diving
Shanghai	Archery, badminton, cycling, table tennis, track and field (middle and long-distance running) and *wushu*
Shenyang	Winter sports
Tianjin	Softball, tennis and volleyball
Wuhan	Army sports and water sports
Xi'an	Judo

Advanced-level courses are also organized at the Beijing Shooting Centre and, in basketball, at the Beijing Teachers' College of Physical Education.

The CED has established broad principles and guidelines that must be followed by NSAs when developing course outlines for refresher courses. These emphasize integration of 'systematization' with sport-specialization, theory with practice and foundation with application. Course outlines must be approved by the CED before implementation. As soon as approval is given, NSAs may organize courses. Many professionals are involved in developing the outlines, including coaches, sports administrators, sports scientists and university teachers. The Division permits a high degree of flexibility in the course content of elementary and intermediate courses, but closely supervises advanced-level courses.

Local SAs and institutes of physical education are permitted to select their own course tutors for elementary and intermediate courses. However, the CED provides guidelines for NSAs to follow when selecting tutors for advanced-level courses and appointments must be approved. Teaching materials are expected to be systematically prepared, utilized, reviewed and refined.

Part- and full-time courses

Because of initial uncertainty concerning the suitability of material for full-time, part-time and correspondence courses, and because of a limited supply of course tutors and teaching materials, the emphasis was placed initially on organizing only full-time refresher training courses. To minimize disruption of training, most sports now organize full-time courses after a major competition at the end of the season. For this reason, most courses are organized between October and December. Although the normal course duration is two months, the CED allows individual NSAs to use a format which best suits the nature and competition schedule of the sport. Soccer, for example, organizes two one-month training courses during the first and second half of the year.

Pilot part-time courses started in 1995, however and, in the future, part-time courses are expected to replace full-time courses, providing the availability of a sufficient number of course tutors and appropriate teaching materials.

Funding

Government provides partial subsidies to provinces and cities to organize elementary and intermediate courses; provinces and cities normally have to provide some funding. Coaches' employers are responsible for paying some of the expenses. Government and NSAs provide all funding for advanced courses.

A new policy requiring participating coaches to contribute towards the production of course materials at all levels is currently under consideration.

Participants

Individual city and provincial sports commissions decide on the number of coaches who attend elementary and intermediate courses; coaches are released from their coaching duties. Coaches who successfully complete a course are awarded a Coaches' Refresher Course Diploma. This diploma is different from that received through the certificate education process.

Refresher courses will shortly become mandatory for coaches to retain their positions. Coaches will be expected to complete a minimum number of hours of training every four years. The first deadline will be 2000. Coaches who do not fulfil the specified requirements by that year may be released.

Coaches who are hoping for promotion will be expected to satisfy more stringent requirements. Promotion of coaches in a provincial training centre is determined jointly by the personnel department and the provincial sports commission. For this reason, provincial sports commissions are expected to maintain a record of all coaches and their training experience. Promotion in the National Training Centre in Beijing is determined jointly by the personnel department and the National Training Bureau of the State Physical Culture and Sports Commission.

National coaches

National team coaches are not all classified as national coaches; indeed, the majority of the country's national team coaches, and a number of provincial team coaches, are advanced coaches. Similarly, not all classified national coaches are national team coaches.

A systematic approach to refresher training for national coaches has yet to be established during the current transitional period; the development of such coaches is mainly achieved through self-study.

Seminars for national coaches are jointly organized by the CED, the NSAs and the National Training Bureau. These are based on the specific needs of a sport and problems encountered during training. By the end of 1995, two seminars had been organized – in gymnastics (on sports injuries) and track and field (strength training and recovery). National coaches are required to present a thesis following each seminar. The CED encourages NSAs to work with each other to jointly organize such seminars.

Currently, such development opportunities for national coaches are initiated and co-ordinated by the CED. In the near future, it is hoped that NSAs will recognize the importance and effectiveness of such courses and take over the work.

A meeting is organized annually to evaluate the refresher training programme. Participants include members of the Leading Group for Coach Refresher Courses, senior staff of the CED, institutes of physical education and NSA Consultation Groups for Coach Refresher Courses. The programme continues to develop. By January 1996, twenty-three of thirty-two NSAs had established consultation groups and, by the end of 1996, ten NSAs had finalised their course outlines. A survey has shown that coaches are generally content with the effects of the programme.

As expected, however, there have been some teething problems:

• By January 1996, only the Badminton Sports Association had completed all teaching materials. Another three or four NSAs, including winter sports and *wushu*, were due to have their teaching materials completed by the end of 1996. Teaching materials for all twenty-three sports are expected to be finalized by 2000.

- Course tutors are still refining their teaching methods and attempting to learn more about in-service training.
- By January 1996, only 2,500 coaches of more than 25,000 in China had participated in refresher courses. The number of qualified elementary and intermediate coaches is very few.
- Development of the programme lacks balance across different sports, levels and geographical areas.

Short-term courses are usually organized by individual NSAs after major competitions or during training camps. Courses last for only one or two days. Topics are very specific. The CED organizes similar short-term courses on sports-general topics.

Information service

The Information Service operates through publications such as *China Sports Coach*. The periodical contains updated information on coach education, training methodology and coaching.

General

The CED has encountered two major problems in implementing the Coach Education Programme. First, the majority of coaches do not understand the objectives and importance of the programme. Second, there is a discrepancy between academic qualifications and coaching standards. A number of coaches who are operating at the highest level lack requisite academic qualifications; conversely, many well-qualified coaches lack the ability to coach at a high level.

The CED used information from Canada, Germany, Japan and the United Kingdom as an early reference when establishing the coach education programme. Since then, however, the programme has developed on the basis of the characteristics and specific needs of the country's sports system. For this reason, a number of major differences exist between the programme and its counterparts around the world:

- In most countries, the central coach education agency is responsible only for the administration and implementation of the sport-general theory component. In China, the CED administers both sport-general theory and sport-specific components.
- China's Coach Education Programme services only those coaches who operate in the elite athlete development programme. Other coach education programmes do not normally have such a narrow focus.

- The programme integrates tertiary education with adult education, certificate education with refresher courses, and full- and part-time education with distance learning.

PHYSICAL EDUCATION

For historical reasons, education in China is less well-developed than in a number of other countries. In 1993, however, the government launched the Reformation of Education. In 1995 the Reformation of Education and Science Technology was launched. For the ninth 5-year plan (from 1996 to 2000), adult and in-service education are being especially emphasized.

The Education Department is responsible for determining physical education syllabuses for primary and secondary schools. Since 1986, universities have developed their own syllabus with advice provided by the Education Department.

The minimum numbers of hours of physical education required by students each week varies according to the level of education:

Level of education:	Hours weekly:
Primary	3 hours
Lower secondary	2 hours
Upper secondary	3 hours
University, 1st and 2nd year	2 hours
University, 3rd and final year	Optional

The Department of Science and Education of the All-China Sports Federation is responsible for training physical education teachers. Primary and secondary school teachers are trained in the country's sixteen institutes of physical education and 186 physical education faculties in teachers' colleges and universities. Subject areas and content are the same for all institutes for major subjects; optional subjects may vary.

The Chinese government has established a set of basic academic requirements for teachers at each level. Primary school PE teachers are expected to be graduates of sports technical colleges. There are, altogether, 300,000 primary school PE teachers; a number do not satisfy the basic requirement. Teachers in lower secondary schools are expected to hold diplomas. PE teachers in upper secondary schools are expected to hold bachelor's degrees. A master's degree is required of every university PE teacher.

In 1993, it was proposed that all PE teachers should satisfy these minimum requirements and thereby gain accreditation within ten years, either through normal education or continuing education. Provincial organizations organize courses for primary and secondary school teachers. The Department of Science and Education of the All-China Sports Federation organizes short-term courses in sports institutes every year for university PE teachers. Attendance, however, is not mandatory.

The Institute of Physical Education Section (IPES) of the Department of Sports Science and Physical Education of the All-China Sports Federation is responsible for all matters relating to the country's six major institutes of physical education, in Beijing, Chengdu, Shanghai, Shenyang, Wuhan and Xian, with the exception of personnel and finance matters which are administered directly by the personnel and finance departments of the Chinese government. The section is also responsible for the country's ten sports technical colleges which train respective provincial teams and, together with the institutes of physical education, play an important role in implementing the country's coach education programme. Matters relating to personnel and finance of these colleges are handled by the provincial governments.

The IPES has responsibility for administering the following specific areas: enrolment, course outlines, inter-institute competitions, library, teaching materials, information technology and research and teaching methodology.

The curriculum of the six institutes and ten sports technical colleges includes ten major subjects: Chinese medicine and orthopaedics, community sports, physical education, physical fitness and recovery, sports biology, sports journalism, sports management, sports psychology, sports training and *wushu*. The curriculum varies for different institutes and colleges; no single institute or college provides all ten subjects. The syllabus and content of major subjects are the same for each institute, but optional subjects vary according to the particular needs of each institute. The Beijing University of Physical Education provides most, but not all, of the topics.

If there is a need to add new subjects to the curriculum, the Section Chief of the IPES drafts a proposal for the Curriculum Committee; the Section Chief serves as general secretary of the Committee. Approval from the State Education Commission is required before any new subject is added.

For master's degree courses, the syllabus is the same for major (compulsory) subjects but, again, varies according to the institute for optional subjects. The IPES is also responsible for master's degree courses offered by the institutes.

The amount of funding allocated to institutes varies according to variations in the scale and profile of the institutes. The Beijing University of Physical Education, as the premier institute of physical education in China, receives more funding than its sister institutes.

In 1984 and 1985, while serving as technical consultant with the national track and field team in Beijing, the author (Whitby) had an opportunity to visit four institutes of physical education – in Beijing, Nanjing, Shanghai and Wuhan – and the Physical Education Department of the Beijing Normal University. Comments that were recorded following these visits are extracted below.

Since 1991, the author (Whitby) has revisited the institutes of physical education in Beijing, Nanjing and Wuhan. Additional visits have been made to the Guangzhou and Shenyang Institutes of Physical Education.

Beijing University of Physical Education

The Beijing University of Physical Education (BUPE), situated close to Beijing University and Qinghua University in the north-west corner of the city, is the country's major institution of physical education. Of the six institutes of physical education which operate under the jurisdiction of the Department of Sports Science and Physical Education of the All-China Sports Federation, only the BUPE recruits nationwide; the other five institutes recruit athletes and students on a regional basis.

The author (Whitby) visited the BUPE, then the Beijing Institute of Physical Education (BIPE), in March 1984 and, again, in 1993 and 1995. An informal meeting was also held with the new President of the BUPE, Professor Jin Ji Chuan, in Beijing in January 1996.

The BIPE was founded in 1953 and currently has a total of 2,000 students and 1,000 staff-members, including 400 faculty-members. The institute's main role is to train teachers, coaches and scientists.

There are five major departments in the institute: physical education, sports training, theory, graduate and *wushu*. The institute also has its own residential sports school and spare-time sports school.

The physical education department trains teachers of physical education for middle schools and universities. The sports training department trains coaches. The theory department is responsible for the development of scientists. The institute also provides two-year courses, various short courses and a correspondence course.

Students are admitted to the institute on the basis of examination marks and their scores on a battery of physical tests. Tuition, room and board and medical care are provided free of charge. A number of overseas students attend the institute but live in separate accommodation; they attend language classes every day.

Undergraduates undertake a four-year course of study, taking courses in anatomy, biomechanics, exercise physiology, foreign languages, the history of the Chinese Communist Party, Marxist political economy, pedagogy (teaching method), philosophy, sports medicine and sports theory.

Upon completing his/her course of study, each student is assigned a job within the government's centralized placement system. Since 1953, more than 10,000 graduates of the institute have accepted positions around the country.

The institute has awarded graduate degrees in physical education since 1954. Courses of study extend for three years. Research by graduate students and faculty members is published in the *Journal of the Beijing Institute of Physical Education.*

Facilities at the institute are extensive, covering 65 hectares and including eleven training halls and fifty outdoor sports grounds and courts. Buildings are more than thirty years old; the exteriors look dilapidated but the interiors are well-maintained. A new building programme is underway.

Our first stop was the indoor Olympic-size swimming pool where a small group of students was practising synchronized swimming. Our second stop was the indoor track and field hall where more than 200 students, track and field team members and sports school athletes were working under the supervision of more than twenty full-time specialist teachers and coaches.

The teachers apologized for the poor condition of the four-lane cinder track. The track is used by college students for competition during the winter. The institute also has two outdoor cinder tracks. Weight training equipment (and the techniques that were being used) were very poor.

In the games hall, classes in women's basketball and men's basketball and volleyball were in progress. In one building, a much-respected martial arts teacher was putting a group of six students through their paces for the benefit of a camera crew. There were also classes in rhythmic gymnastics, fencing, wrestling and weight training. These classes were held in smaller sports halls surrounding a courtyard; two *wushu* classes – one for men and one for women – were in progress in the courtyard. At the end of the class, the students lined up in front of the teacher to receive final instructions, bowed to the teacher and were dismissed.

I was particularly impressed by the amount of activity going on in each class. There was, on average, one foreign student in each class – three or four from African nations, two from Kuwait in the martial arts class and one European, looking totally exhausted, in the wrestling class!

Two or three teachers were working with each of the larger classes; specialist groups such as gymnastics and rhythmic gymnastics also had the services of pianists.

Guangzhou Institute of Physical Education

Founded in 1958, the Guangzhou Institute of Physical Education (GIPE) is located adjacent to the Tian He Sports Centre that was built for the 1987 National Games in the Tian He District of Guangzhou, capital of Guangdong Province. The institute is responsible for developing physical education teachers, coaches, sports managers and sports scientists. The institute currently has approximately 1,000 students and employs a total of 480 staff members; of these, approximately 50 per cent are teaching staff.

Two degree programmes are offered by the institute. The physical education personnel department offers a degree in physical education for prospective teachers. Graduates are appointed to teaching positions or coaching positions in schools or as physical education personnel in sports associations. The sport training department offers a degree in sport studies for prospective coaches. Graduates are employed as company, factory or school coaches or with Guangzhou City or Guangdong provincial teams. Master's degree programmes have been offered in sports administration, teaching or training since 1986. The institute also has research, adult education, ball games, multi-sport and track and field departments.

Indoor facilities include a teaching building, laboratory, library, indoor swimming pool and basketball, volleyball, *wushu*, table-tennis and badminton halls; outdoor facilities include a stadium for track and field, and a number of football and baseball pitches.

Currently, approximately sixty students from Hong Kong travel to Shenzhen every weekend to attend the institute's two-year part-time diploma in physical education; course graduates can teach at the middle and high school level in Guangdong. Another sixty students travel to Shenzhen every month to attend the institute's three-year part-time degree course in physical education. Approximately thirty Hong Kong students have completed these degree programmes.

Nanjing Institute of Physical Education

Founded in 1958, the NIPE is one of twenty institutions of higher education in the city. The institute was closed during the Cultural Revolution but re-opened in 1980. Many new facilities have since been built.

> The NIPE has approximately 500 students studying in either the physical education department or the sports training department to become teachers of physical education or coaches. Students receive bachelor's degrees.
>
> The institute also has a residential sports school and serves as the training site for members of the Jiangsu provincial team, the only institute of physical education which has this role. There are no graduate students at the institute.
>
> The institute has two tracks. A group of physical education students was practising on one track in the old stadium that was used for the 1938 Asian Games. The 400m cinder track in the stadium encircles a second, 300m track. On the inner track, a class of fifty students had been divided into groups; one group was practising the straddle. The institute also has a 200m indoor track that was built in the 1950s; this, also, was badly in need of repair.
>
> The swimming pool was occupied by athletes from the sports school during my visit and a group of physical education students were using

the diving pool. In an adjacent hall, provincial team members were refining their diving techniques using springboards, crash mats and trampolines.

In October 1995, the author (Whitby) again had the opportunity to visit the NIPE and was given a brief tour of some of the facilities by President Hua Xiong Xing. The institute now has 1,300 physical education students pursing two-year diploma, or four-year degree, courses. The institute has also acquired a number of new facilities, including a new swimming hall and a new track. The grandstand from the old track that was used for the 1938 Asian Games, however, is still standing.

Shanghai Institute of Physical Education

In 1984, the Shanghai Institute of Physical Education (SIPE) was ranked with the institutes in Wuhan and Shenyang as joint number two in the country, behind the BIPE. The author visited the institute in May 1984. The following notes were recorded at that time:

> The SIPE was established in 1952 by merging the physical education departments of Nanjing University, the East China Normal University and Jinling College. During the Cultural Revolution, the institute was integrated with other higher education institutes to become the Shanghai Normal University. The institute was re-opened in 1974. The institute currently employs forty professors and fifty-two assistant professors and has a total of 863 undergraduate and forty-three graduate students working on a full-time basis towards qualifications in teaching or coaching. Another 680 students are studying correspondence courses.
>
> Students normally attend classes in the morning and train in the afternoon. A number of the students train with the provincial team at the Sports Technical Institute but the institute has first claim upon their services.
>
> Master's degrees are offered in anatomy, biomechanics, exercise physiology, theory of teaching and *wushu*; doctoral programmes in anatomy and *wushu* may be introduced in the near future. Students who complete the three-year master's degree programme normally enter the coaching profession or accept research positions. The better students join the institute's faculty.
>
> I visited the volleyball hall (with its packed-earth floor) and a comparatively new sports hall, consisting of two connected double-storey buildings. In one building, the ground floor is used for table tennis; I counted twenty-five tables. The top floor is used for *wushu* and *taichi*. The ground floor of the second building is divided into two parts, one for basketball and one for gymnastics and judo. The top floor of the building is divided into two basketball halls.

Shenyang Institute of Physical Education

The author visited the Shenyang Institute of Physical Education in May 1994. The institute was established in 1954 and is one of the six institutes that operate under the jurisdiction of the All-China Sports Federation. The institute recruits athletes and students from Heilongjiang, Jilin, Liaoning and Mongolia.

The Shenyang Institute of Physical Education has a staff of 300, including twenty-two professors, sixty-eight associate professors and 100 lecturers, and 1,500 students. Students are admitted to study for a diploma in sports training (two years), a bachelor's degrees in physical education, sports training or *wushu* (four years), or a master's degree in health and fitness or training foundations and methods. The institute also provides distance learning courses for more than 600 students, leading to a three-year diploma or a bachelor's degree in sports training; students who are studying through distance learning must visit the institute twice each year.

Diploma-holders generally find jobs in the local community. Students who complete their degrees in sports training become coaches. Those with other degrees find employment in higher middle schools or universities. Graduate students normally find jobs at other institutes of physical education.

The author visited the biomechanics laboratory (housing a Cybex 6000), a cinder track (built in 1929), a ski jump and a brand new two-storey games hall for basketball and volleyball. This stands adjacent to the institute's indoor track and field hall, built in 1956.

Wuhan Institute of Physical Education

The author spent ten days at the Wuhan Institute of Physical Education (WIPE) in May 1984 and another twelve days in April 1985. On each occasion, the purpose of the visit was to attend a training camp organized jointly by the institute, the Hubei Provincial Physical Culture and Sports Commission and the Chinese Track and Field Association. The following comments were recorded following the second visit:

> Situated by the East Lake in Wuhan, the WIPE was founded in 1953 and serves the provinces of Hebei, Henan, Hunan, Guangdong and Guanxi. The institute has a total of 1,500 students.
>
> The institute's main priority is the preparation of teachers and coaches. Prospective teachers study in the physical education department; prospective coaches study in the sports training department. All students pursue a four-year course of study leading to the award of a bachelor's degree.
>
> The institute has its own residential sports school, graduate school and an adult education department for practising teachers; in-service

courses last for three months. Graduate students study for three years but receive no degree at the conclusion of their course.

The major areas of concentration of the sports training department are track and field, volleyball and *wushu*. Of the 150 students in the department, twenty-four are studying track and field. Students specialize in their chosen sport as soon as they enter the institute but do much of their work in the physical education department.

The institute is known nationally for its *wushu* programme. Students enter the programme two years before their fellow students and follow a six-year programme. Once qualified, *wushu* specialists are appointed as provincial team coaches or as coaches in institutes of physical education and universities.

Facilities at the institute include two cinder tracks, an indoor track, a gymnastics hall, basketball hall, volleyball hall and a number of general sports halls.

During my first visit in 1984, I observed two track and field classes for male physical education students in progress – for first and second-year students, respectively. While the second-year group practised putting the shot, the first-year group – one of fifteen in the year – practised hurdling. This group would participate in two two-hour sessions of track and field each week for three years. The instructor was the head of the track and field section.

At the beginning of the session, the class lined up in military fashion under the direction of one student. Standing to attention, the group was then handed over to the instructor. Instructions were issued and the warm-up began. This consisted of running round the track in two lines and performing group exercises. The instructional part of the session consisted of progressive hurdles drills followed by block starts and three-stride hurdling over five or six hurdles.

My host apologized for the level of skill displayed by the students but the level was higher than I had previously experienced in either England or the United States. What was lacking was conditioning. I was informed that the students would have two months of teaching practice during their last year at the institute. When they graduated, they would be appointed top teaching positions in their home provinces.

In June 1995, a delegation from the Hong Kong Sports Institute (HKSI) visited the WIPE. The visit took place exactly ten years after the author's previous visit to the institute. As noted previously, the WIPE is now one of the country's six major institutes of physical education which operates under the jurisdiction of the All-China Sports Federation.

In 1995, the WIPE had approximately 2,000 full-time students, 800 correspondence-course students and 800 members of staff. The institute continues to service a number of students from other provinces. The major role of the institute continues to be the preparation of teachers of physical education and coaches. Emphasis is also being placed on the development of sports administrators and sports psychologists. The institute is organized into five departments: physical education, sports training, sports management, sports psychology and *wushu*. The graduate school, adult education school and residential sports school continue to operate.

The institute established the country's third department of *wushu* in 1984. The department has approximately 300 students and thirty-six staff-members and is well known for its expertise in free-fighting. Admission is very competitive. Students work for four years towards a bachelor's degree, attending classes in the morning and practising every afternoon. Following their studies, students progress to the provincial team, become teachers in institutes of physical education or universities, or join the police or public security. The department also offers a three-year master's degree programme.

Besides *wushu*, the institute excels in sports such as boxing, gymnastics and water sports and takes a leading role in coach education. Facilities at the institute include ten dedicated facilities, including halls for artistic gymnastics, basketball, boxing, rhythmic gymnastics, table tennis, track and field, volleyball and *wushu*. In the *wushu* hall, the delegation observed different groups of first-, second- and third-year students performing free-fighting and routine exercises in preparation for a competition in the afternoon. Professor Jiang Bai-long, Dean of the Department, was planning to start a self-funded residential high school in September 1995. He hoped to have approximately 100 fee-paying students enter the school each year.

Our delegation also observed WIPE students training in three sports – canoeing, rowing and wrestling:

- The institute employs six coaches to work with a total of eighty canoeists. The delegation saw thirty canoeists training on the East Lake; all are students at the institute. Four students were training elsewhere with the national team.
- Rowing is one of the institute's strongest sports and attracts athletes from other provinces. The institute has approximately 100 rowers. The delegation saw sixteen members of the women's team performing weight training; all were students of the institute or of the residential sports school. Four rowers were currently training with the national team in Guizhou.
- The institute employs six coaches to work with seventy wrestlers. The delegation observed demonstration competition-bouts in three styles of wrestling – freestyle, traditional Chinese and Greco-Roman.

Beijing Normal University

As noted previously, primary and secondary school teachers are also trained in physical education faculties in various teachers' colleges and universities.

The author visited the physical education department of the Beijing Normal University (BNU) in April 1985.

The university, founded in 1902, has more than 5,000 students. The majority study for four years towards bachelor's degrees in education and subsequently enter the teaching profession; language students study for five years. All students study English or Japanese for two-and-a-half years.

The BNU offers doctoral degree programmes in more than twenty disciplines.

Each student is required to perform early morning exercises at 6.30 a.m. and, during the first two years' study, to participate in a physical education class each week, lasting for 1 hour 40 minutes. During my visit, I observed seven or eight of these classes in progress in basketball, volleyball and *wushu* in a large outdoor area consisting of twelve basketball courts. Courses in gymnastics, skating, soccer, swimming and track and field are also offered. These classes are similar to the in-service classes that are required in many American universities and are considered to be part of the student's personal education. Discipline was good and the students worked hard.

The physical education department has approximately 300 undergraduate students. There are eight groups of students in each year, four for men, four for women. Each group stays together for the full four-year period. Entry into the department depends upon academic performance – slightly lower than in other departments – and students' performance on field tests such as a 100m sprint, chins (push-ups for women), sit-ups, etc. The department employs 115 staff members who also teach the non-specialist classes.

The university and the Beijing Institute of Physical Education are the only institutions which are allowed to send their physical education graduates anywhere in the country; the graduates of other institutions, including the Beijing Normal College, must work locally. Twenty per cent of the BNU's graduates are assigned positions; the remaining 80 per cent obtain positions through direct contact with prospective employers. From 1986, all students will be free to obtain jobs by applying directly.

Although the Department's students are qualified to teach in lower- or upper-middle schools or high schools, 80 per cent had obtained employment in universities, factories or research institutes in 1984, thanks to the rapid increase in the number of research institutes in China. The best students are sometimes retained by the university.

From 1986, the department plans to offer graduate courses leading to the award of a master's degree. Possible areas of study include biomechanics, exercise physiology, history, theory of physical education and track and field.

I was accompanied during my visit to the BNU by Mr Tian Jizong, Head of the Physical Education Department. Mr Tian had studied in Moscow for four years in the 1950s and at the University of Massachusetts in the United States for eighteen months.

My visit took me to a track and to the sports and gymnastics halls. I also observed an outdoor class in *wushu*. The track that we visited is used exclusively by physical education students; another track is used by students from other departments. Three groups, each consisting of approximately twenty male students, were practising various events. The department has nine staff members who specialize in track and field.

The sports hall has four courts – two for basketball and two for volleyball. While a first-year class of male students practised their volleyball skills, a class of second-year male students was receiving instruction in the basics of zone defence; a *wushu* group worked outside.

The gymnastics hall was small and old but the gymnastics equipment, permanently in place, was quite adequate. Second-year students were undergoing a practical assessment in the vault under competition rules. The technical level appeared to be quite good.

SUMMARY

A unified classification system for sports officials has been established at six levels – international, national and advanced levels, and levels 1, 2 and 3. Institutes of physical education are responsible for training and accrediting level 1, 2 and 3 officials. Students can sit the level 1 examination at the end of their final year of study. National sports associations are responsible for training and accrediting advanced- and national-level officials.

In general, the current group of top sports administrators in China gained their management experience in education, the army and youth societies. Few have undergone formal training; formal training started in 1985. Short-term in-service training courses are now organized by the Department of Sports Science and Physical Education of the All-China Sports Federation.

ACKNOWLEDGEMENTS

The authors would like to thank Alison Wong, Assistant Manager, Coach Education Department, Hong Kong Sports Institute, and Yin Fei-fei, Coach Education Division, Department of Sports Science and Physical Education, All-China Sports Federation, for their assistance in developing this chapter.

Chapter 8

Chinese women and sport

James Riordan and Dong Jinxia

INTRODUCTION

The performance of top Chinese women athletes in the 1990s has been
unprecedented in the history of sport. Not only have they made remarkable
progress from virtual obscurity to world champions and record breakers,
they have far surpassed the performance of their male compatriots in international sport. This unique phenomenon extends from middle- and long-
distance running to swimming and diving, from weightlifting and chess to
volleyball and basketball, from shooting and archery to wrestling and rowing, from badminton and gymnastics to softball and soccer – and table tennis
dating back to the early 1970s.

In running alone, within the space of one year, 1993, Chinese women won
three world titles, set three junior records and three world records, ran the
four fastest marathons of the year and filled the first four places in the World
Cup Marathon. At the World Championships in Stuttgart, Chinese women
won four gold medals (Chinese men won none), putting China second in the
medal table behind the USA, but ahead of Russia, Germany and Britain.
They made a clean sweep of the 1500m, 3,000m and 10,000m. Until then,
Chinese women and men had won just *seven* medals in world track and field
championships, including two golds, in the three previous meetings put
together. Chinese women had taken no more than two of those medals.
Further, at the 7th National Games held jointly in Beijing and Chengdu,
Sichuan in September 1993, Chinese women athletes broke six world records
– the 10,000m by as much as 42 seconds.

An even more remarkable success occurred at the 7th World Swimming
Championships held in Rome in September 1994; Chinese women won twelve
of the sixteen swimming and diving world titles (and five silver medals),
setting five world records. Chinese men won no swimming medals at all.
While the men had also won no medals at the inaugural World Short-Course
Swimming Championships in December 1993, Chinese women won ten world
titles, setting ten new world records; they also won five world diving titles at
the 8th World Cup Diving Championships the same year.

In terms of swimming progress, suffice it to say that Chinese women had won no gold medals at the 1988 Olympics, took four gold medals at both the 1991 World Championships and the 1992 Olympics; in 1994, they had trebled that total. An idea of the rapid progress may be gained from Chinese women's place in world rankings:

Chinese women ranked in the world top twenty swimmers in all swimming events

1991   10
1992   28
1993   96

By contrast, only three Chinese men made the top thirty in all swimming events in 1993.

Source: Craig Lord, 'China's women shake the world', *Sunday Times*, 11 September 1994, Sport Section, p. 10; *The Times*, 13 September 1994, p. 42.

These noteworthy achievements established China in 1993 and 1994 for the first time as a major world power in sport. The attainment was gained thanks almost entirely to Chinese women's success, what is referred to in China as the blossoming of the Yin (female) and the withering of the Yang (male).

THE DRUG ISSUE

A number of commentators on Chinese sport, citing drug scandals, have cast doubt on the sporting achievements and called into question the very validity of the record and China's status as a world sports nation. While the drug issue is dealt with in more detail later, it needs to be raised here inasmuch as it casts a long shadow over all that follows.

The basic facts are that since 1988 as many as forty-seven Chinese athletes have tested positive for anabolic steroids; they include thirty-eight in 1994 alone, including eleven swimmers. During the Asian Games of October 1994, eleven Chinese athletes, including seven swimmers, tested positive; and two female weightlifters tested positive a month later at the World Championships in Istanbul. All but one of those positives were for a potent anabolic steroid called dihydrotestosterone (DHT); a significant number of other Chinese athletes had elevated levels of DHT in their urine at the Asian Games, but not enough to be declared positive. The eleven swimmers who tested positive have to be set beside the ten from other nations who tested positive in the twenty-two years since testing began. What is in the minds of many critics of China's sport and drugs record is the revelations following the demise of Communist countries in Eastern Europe. It is now known that there was long term *state* production, testing, monitoring and administering of performance-enhancing drugs in regard to athletes as young as 7–8. It was this mendacity of the old regime – loudly condemning drug abuse in the West as a typical excess of capitalism, while concealing its own involvement in a far more extensive programme of state manufacture and distribution of drugs, from growth stimulants to growth retardants, anabolic steroids to blood doping and hypnosis – that so tarnished the image of sport among many people. In late 1991, the year that the Soviet Union disintegrated, four one-time leading East German swimming coaches issued a statement confessing to widespread use of anabolic steroids among their swimmers in the 1970s and 1980s. And a long stream of evidence has been emerging, particularly from the ex-USSR and GDR, of state-controlled administration of drugs (Berendonk 1991; Mader 1983; Kuhnst 1982; Heinrich-Vogel 1981; Riordan 1993, 1994). We now know that, following the unification of Germany, a number of East German sports doctors and coaches went to work in China.

While it is true that drugs were used in Eastern Europe and are now being used in China, the same is also true of the West. Whatever the political ideology, the stakes in international competition are high. Victory brings increased status for the individual and his/her family, it results in financial and career rewards and boosts the image of the nation. Defeat can result in personal humiliation, loss of career and it does nothing for the image of the athlete's nation.

Today, in international sport, there are relentless pressures on athletes from coaches, sponsors, the public and even governments. Certain countries with few social, economic or scientific achievements, or countries who wish to demonstrate the superiority of their socio-political system, use sport to enhance their prestige. The promotion of sport has become a major political concern and, if success is believed to be possible through the use of drugs, then drugs are used. It is possible that in some countries, athletes, coaches or doctors, although not believing in the ethics or benefits of doping procedures, may be forced to use them.

For a genuine understanding of drug-taking in Chinese sport, it is important not to make sweeping generalizations, nor to take a holier than thou view of China, performance enhancing drugs or the old Communist system in Eastern Europe. What follows is an attempt to provide a broad understanding of Chinese women and sport putting the drug issue into perspective.

CHINESE WOMEN'S CONTRIBUTION TO THE OLYMPICS AND WORLD CHAMPIONSHIPS

An examination of Chinese women's contribution to China's Olympic record between 1988 and 1992 reinforces the Chinese women's achievements; it is a phenomenon unique in Olympic history (see Table 8.1). While men won eight

Table 8.1 Chinese women's and men's contribution to China's results in the summer Olympics, 1984–92

| Summer Olympics | Medals won | | | Place | Men (gold) | Women (gold) |
	G	S	B			
1984	15	8	9	4th	8	7
1988	5	1	12	11th	2	3
1992	16	22	16	4th	5	11

Sources: Stan Greenberg, *The Guiness Olympics Fact Book* (The Guiness Publishing Company, 1991); *Whitaker's Almanack*, 125th edition (London, 1993), pp. 1222–3; Howard G. Knuttgen, Ma Qiwei, Wu Zhongyuan (eds), *Sport in China* (Human Kinetics Books, Champaign, 1990).

Note
In 1984, men won gold in weightlifting (four medals), shooting (two) and gymnastics (three), archery, fencing, shooting and volleyball. In 1988, men won gold in gymnastics and table tennis; women won gold in diving (two) and table tennis. In 1992, men won gold in shooting (two), table tennis, gymnastics and diving; women won gold in swimming (four), diving (two), table tennis (two), judo, gymnastics and track (10km walk).

gold to women's seven gold medals in 1984, they won fewer gold medals than Chinese women in 1988 and 1992 (two to three, and five to eleven respectively). What is more, while the men's gold medals were confined to five sports (weightlifting, shooting, gymnastics, table tennis and diving), women's gold medals were spread over twice as many sports (gymnastics, archery, fencing, shooting, volleyball, diving, table tennis, swimming, judo and track and field).

In the winter Olympics, China has competed since 1980, though initially merely as a symbolic gesture: in the three Games up to 1988 the best result was sixteenth place in the women's 5,000m speed skating at Calgary in 1988. It was, nonetheless, women who provided the breakthrough. While men won no medals, women took three silver at Albertville in 1992 and a silver and two bronze at Lillehammer in 1994 (see Table 8.2).

An idea of the emphasis placed by the Chinese authorities on women as the vanguard of the Chinese international sporting thrust may be gained from the male–female composition of China's and other teams in the 1988 summer Olympic Games (see Table 8.3). Although they had more men in their squad than women, the Chinese easily had the highest percentage of women.

Table 8.2 China's performance at the winter Olympics, 1984–92

| Olympics | Medals won | | | Men | Women |
	G	S	B		
1984	0	0	0	0	0
1988	0	3	0	0	3
1992	0	1	2	0	3

Source: *China Sports*, June 1994, p. 13.

Table 8.3 Numbers of male and female competitors in Olympic teams, 1988: countries with established sports traditions

	Males	*Females*	*% females in team*
China	158	135	46
GDR	173	115	40
Belgium	39	26	40
Bulgaria	122	74	38
USA	388	224	37
GB	238	132	36
USSR	351	173	33
Denmark	62	26	30
Canada	265	117	31
FRG	288	119	29
Australia	216	79	27
France	225	82	27
Finland	76	27	26
Japan	213	75	26
Brazil	138	35	20
Italy	243	53	18
Spain	231	42	15

Note

It is important to bear in mind that at the 1988 Olympics there were twenty-six sports and 165 events for men compared with twenty-two sports and eighty-three events for women; overall, women constituted 25.84 per cent of all competitors.

An illustration of Chinese women's comparative contribution to China's overall performance at the 1988 and 1992 summer Olympics is given in Table 8.4.

Apart from confirming the Chinese improvement from five to sixteen gold medals on aggregate, including three to twelve to women, Table 8.4 shows that Chinese women had caught up with the world's top women by 1992 and made a substantial contribution to China's rise to become a leading sports nation.

But China's success is by no means confined to a handful of sports. As the following list indicates, the spectrum of Chinese women's success extends to twenty-one sports.

Table 8.4 Chinese women's comparative contribution, 1988 and 1992 summer Olympics

	1988 summer Olympics				*1992 summer Olympics*			
	China	*USA*	*USSR*	*Japan*	*China*	*USA*	*USSR*	*Japan*
Total gold medals	5	36	55	4	16	37	45	3
Women's gold medals	3	12	13	0	12	14	12	1
Women's %	60	33	24	0	75	38	27	33

Sports in which Chinese women have achieved world success in the 1990s:

Archery	Wang Xiaozhu	OGM and WRH	1993/94
Badminton	Ye Zhaoying	WC (singles)	1994
Basketball	Team	2nd in W Cup	1994
Chess	Xie Jun	WC	1991/95
Disabled*	Zheng Peifeng	POC	1992
Diving	All 3 golds	WCC	1994
Fencing	Foil	OGM	1992
Gymnastics		OGM/WC (2 medals)	1992/94
Judo		OGM	1992
Rowing		2nd in 'fours' in WC	1994
Shooting**	Li Duihong	OGM (air pistol)	1992
Shot putt	Huang Zhihong	WC	1994
Soccer	Five times Asian Games champs and World University Games champs		
Softball	2nd in WC		1994
Speed skating	Ye Qiaobo	WC (500m)	1993
Swimming	12 WC, 5 WRH		1994
Table tennis***	Women's team champs		1992
Track athletics	Won 1500m, 3000m and 10,000m at WT&FC		1993
Volleyball****	Team	OGM	1992
Weightlifting	19 WRH and 10 WC		1993
Wrestling	3 WC		1993

Notes

* Unlike other state socialist countries, China set up national sports associations for the disabled from the early 1980s, held three national paraplegic games and hosted the 6th Far East and South Pacific Games for the Disabled in September 1994, at which it completely dominated the other forty-one states, with a total of 298 medals (Australia in second place won fifty).

** Chinese women won the air pistol title at the 1987 WC.

*** The first Chinese player to win the WC (singles) was Qiu Zhanghui as far back as 1961.

**** The Chinese women's team first won the WC in 1981, retaining it five consecutive times, creating what many Chinese describe as the 'breakthrough' for China into world sport and provoking the outrush of mass feeling that may well have caused the Chinese leadership to try to link patriotic feelings with world sports success.

Legend

OGM = Olympic Gold Medal; WRH = World Record Holder; WC = World Champion; W Cup = World Cup; POC = Paraplegic Olympic

Champion; WCC = World Cup Champion; WT&FC = World Track and Field Championships.

As evidence of the sexual imbalance in Chinese world performance, it is noteworthy that Chinese women in 1992 and 1993 contributed seventy-one and seventy-seven world titles won by China out of eighty-nine and 103 respectively. Outside competitive sport, Chinese women are demonstrating considerable endurance and skill by, for example, climbing Mount Everest and crossing one of the world's most extensive (and dangerous) deserts – Xinjiang's Taklamakan – a first for women explorers. This swift emergence of Chinese women as a dominant force in such a wide range of sports, cerebral as well as muscular, raises a number of questions. What are the reasons for these achievements? How have Chinese women evidently evaded many of the obstacles confronting western women in sport (such as societal prejudice against 'muscular' women)? What is the government motivation in apparently prioritizing women's sport? How has the success been attained and at what cost?

ROLE OF SPORT IN CHINESE SOCIETY

As we know, for newly-independent nations trying to establish themselves in the world as world powers to be respected, even recognized, sport may uniquely offer an opportunity to 'win' against the best in the full glare of world publicity, for example at the Olympic Games. This is particularly apposite to those nations faced by boycott and/or subversion from big powers. Where other channels have been closed, success in sport would seem to have aided such countries as Cuba, the USSR and East Germany – as well as other modernizing states – to attain a measure of recognition and prestige internationally. Sport here is unique in that for such nations it may be the *only* medium in which they are able to take on and beat the economically-advanced nations. For some politicians, sports success can mean more than medals. As Jiang Yun has put it:

> Victory in the Olympics or World Cup can bring instant acclaim, international respectability and status. Sport, therefore, is no longer used merely to judge the competitive level of a country's athletes, but it is also an instrument to demonstrate the physical, economic, military and cultural superiority of a political system.
>
> (Jiang 1994: 34)

This puts particular responsibility on athletes from developing countries insofar as they are viewed by politicians as imbuing a sense of pride in their team, nationality or country, even political system.

For China, as with other state socialist countries, sport has traditionally been controlled by the state. Material and human resources may therefore be concentrated on prioritized goals, like 'sporting diplomacy' or Olympic performance far more easily than in a market economy. Sport in China, furthermore, has since 1949 reflected foreign policy and, on occasion, been blatantly utilized to effect foreign policy changes – as with the so-called ping-pong diplomacy in the 1970s. 'This was a shortcut that China took to restore diplomatic relations with the USA' (Jiang 1992: 7). As Dong Jinxia writes:

> sport is used to serve international diplomatic ends and to demonstrate superiority over capitalist systems. Sport is directed by state policies, decrees and plans. The policy of developing competitive sport was established in 1956 when the first Chinese athlete broke the world record in weightlifting. But until 1979 competitive sport was restricted to the domestic arena or international friendship tournaments because China was isolated from international sport for two decades. Moreover, during the ten years of Cultural Revolution from 1966 to 1976, the competitive spirit was discouraged, even criticized; Chinese competitive sport was seriously hindered. However, with economic reform in the 1980s a great change took place in every aspect of society . . . National sports policy was revised from 'Friendship First, Competition Second', advocated by Mao Tse-tung, to an all-out quest for global recognition and status.
>
> (Dong 1995: 11)

The primary target in China's sports policy since the early 1980s, therefore, has been to produce a winning formula in Olympic and world arenas – as other state socialist nations (notably the Soviet Union, Cuba and East Germany) had done from the 1960s. Chinese sports officials made no bones about the fact that 'The highest goal of Chinese sport is success in the Olympic Games' (Wu 1990), or that 'the all-important Olympic Games [is] the real yardstick for a nation's actual strength in sport' (Xu 1990).

But China was a 'late starter', making its Olympic appearance only in 1984, in Los Angeles (when most other Communist states boycotted the Games) after an absence of thirty-two years (since the 1952 Helsinki Olympics) during which time it had been prevented from taking part largely because of US opposition. Upon resuming its seat on the International Olympic Committee in 1979, its politicians sounded a clarion call of 'March out of Asia and into the world!' (Xu 1990). Although China made little impact at the 1984 and 1988 Games, by 1992 it was beginning to show signs that 'the tried and tested model of early selection and training, special sports schools and sports science was having an impact on results' (Jones 1993).

Sport then began to play a salient part in restoring pride and dignity to the world's largest nation. An American scholar has written that 'China's political and sports officials openly acknowledge that they view sport as one instrument for promoting national pride and identity, which is a primary motivation behind the expenditure of over 300 million yuan annually for [Olympic] sports' (Sage 1990). In other words, international sports success helps to bind the nation together as it goes through turbulent political and economic change. Such sentiments are explicit in statements by the Chinese themselves. Jiang Yun concedes that:

> In modern times, China has suffered from domestic unrest and foreign aggression, and has been in the position of a backward underdog. China has been described as 'the sick man of East Asia', 'a tragic race!' . . . Since it is unable to boast about its economic achievements, it is like the Soviet Union and war-devastated Japan in seeking a means to raise *political prestige* and show that it is *a large and powerful country.* It dreams, therefore, of becoming a strong sports nation.
>
> (Jiang 1992: 34; emphasis mine)

Li Hongbing, writing in the official sports monthly *China Sports*, talks of sports success helping to assuage the Chinese 'inferiority complex':

> Today the Chinese are not so impotent as they used to be in world sport. They can take *pride* in more than table tennis and women's volleyball; they have astonished the world by their *meteoric rise* in women's track and field where previously they had always hung their heads in *humiliation.* They have rid themselves of their *inferiority complex.*
>
> (Li 1994: 7)

As the most famous of all Chinese coaches, Mah Junren, has said of the spirit that motivates his team and himself:

> To win honour for our country – that is what motivates our team . . . The Chinese are not 'a nation of rice-eaters' or the 'sick man of Asia' – labels that westerners have stuck on our people. We can do what others can, perhaps even more. The worst thing is not that you are not able to to do something, it's that you dare not do it.
>
> (Song 1994: 11)

Having set a target of becoming 'a top world sports power by the end of the century' (Xu 1990: 466), Chinese officials set about prioritizing elite, especially Olympic, sport and working to fulfil this plan. It entailed massive financial investment: in the decade 1978–88, gross national income rose from 301 billion yuan to 1,177 billion, a 290 per cent increase. Government sports funding rose from 254m to 1 billion yuan, an over 200 per cent increase. Of that amount, two-thirds went into elite sport (Jiang 1992). To gain Olympic medals, moreover, the investment was relatively huge: it is estimated that

China spent US$52m on each gold medal won at the 1988 Seoul Olympics by contrast with the host country's US$9m. Altogether China invested US$260m in success at the Seoul Olympics (Jones 1993). Winning bonuses took a big part of that: rising from 8,000 yuan for gold medal winners in Los Angeles (1984) to 18,000 in 1988 and 80,000 in 1992 (with silver medallists receiving 50,000 and bronze medallists 30,000). The 13-year-old diving champion Fu Mingxia gained an additional 463,000 yuan from various sponsors (Jones 1993: 76). This may be a paltry sum when compared to the earnings of top US athletes, but it is a staggering fortune in a country where a school teacher, for example, earns some 150 yuan a month. In other words, the 13-year-old diver gained in winnings the astonishing amount of 3,620 times more than a teacher's monthly salary in 1990.

China had inherited the Soviet sports structure, with its professional coaches, sports medicine and science, major sports clubs sponsored and financed by the armed and security (*Dinamo* in Eastern Europe) forces, sports ranking system, residential boarding schools, etc. But China took the system further. Whereas the Soviet Union had forty-six sports boarding schools in 1990, and East Germany twenty, China had 150 (Riordan 1994: 74; Dong 1995: 62), whereas the USSR had 15,000 professional coaches, China had 18,173 in 1991 (Dong 1995: 63). It is revealed that full-time athletes in China spend an average seven to eight hours a day on sports training and they are distributed as follows: 15,602 in provincial team sports centres; 28,192 in sports boarding schools; and 47,315 in elite 'spare-time schools' (Dong 1995: 66). All training, board and lodging are free.

In order to improve the system and bring it into line with major reforms in the mid-1980s, the government moved to a multi-level, multi-channel system which, while still based on state overall control and planning, was made more flexible and polymorphous. Corporate sponsorship was introduced and the financial rewards were substantially increased. This, then, is the basic infrastructure of China's sports system and the springboard from which an assault was made on the world sporting citadels. In this context, the emphasis on elite women's sport may be seen, partly, as an attempt to win titles and recognition swiftly in events vulnerable to a concerted and well-planned assault – such as middle- and long-distance running, swimming, diving, weightlifting, soccer, wrestling, volleyball and table tennis – events that may be won more easily than others or those of men. As Thomas Lewis of *Transworld Sport* (which gave the long-distance runner Wang Junxia the 1993 Sportswoman of the Year award) has put it, 'women's long-distance running events are more than usually prone to a world record blitz' (Lewis 1994: 19). Lou Dapeng, Vice President of the Chinese Track and Field Federation, is reported as saying that 'it has been our policy to concentrate on women's sport' (Macleod 1993: 43). The swimming coach Chen Yongpeng has said that 'The outstanding achievements made by female athletes . . . have encouraged Chinese sports authorities to channel more funds and manpower to women's events than to men's, resulting in wider participation and higher technical standards among women' (Xie Yanmin 1994: 23).

Here, then, is one official reason for support for women's sport. But what of the women themselves? What has motivated them to undergo such rigorous training necessary to become world champions? After all, the path of world success and acceptance has been long and tortuous for western female athletes.

CHINESE WOMEN AND SPORT

In general, the greater the economic and social resources of a country, particularly in terms of education, health care and nutrition, the more likely it is that women will be part of a national sports scheme. But developing states (whose women make up two-thirds of women in the world) are relatively poor, with limited resources. In addition, other factors, such as tradition and religion, tend to militate against the promotion of women's sport. As a result, most developing countries have only a small number of female Olympic competitors, or none at all. Thus, between 1952 and 1972, the number of countries in the Olympics rose from sixty-nine to 121 – a 75 per cent increase. However, the number of countries that entered women (Asian states like Pakistan and Bangladesh had no women athletes at all in the 1988 Olympics) rose from forty-one to sixty-one – an increase of only 49 per cent (Hargreaves 1994).

China is highly eccentric in this general pattern. As we saw in Table 8.3, China headed all nations in 1988 in having 46 per cent of female athletes in its Olympics squad; the nearest Asian state was Japan in fourteenth place, with 26 per cent, while no other developing nation had over 10 per cent.

The answer to what factors, other than state encouragement, have facilitated women's progress in sport would seem to lie in a nexus of sources, several of which not only run counter to western experience, they actually challenge many dominant western theories of sporting activity.

I 'Chinese first, women second'

In connection with the official policy of giving priority to women's elite sport, the justification is frequently made by Chinese sources that their sportswomen are Chinese first and women second. In other words, in the overriding state priorities and among the public, in the patriotic zeal and social integration, produced by victories of Chinese women swimmers, runners, volleyball players, etc., their Chinese identity is seen as more important than their gender identity. Any polarization of males versus females is therefore overwhelmed by feelings of 'China vs the world'.

This is a phenomenon starkly at variance with the historical 'male vs female' dichotomy common in western sporting nations, but it is closer to the situation that existed in much of East European and Cuban sport. For example, at the 1976 Montreal Olympic Games, sportswomen from the Soviet Union made up over a third (35 per cent) of the Soviet team (all women comprising 20.58 per cent of competitors) and contributed thirty-six of the 125 Soviet medals (almost 30 per cent). The women of East Germany made up 40 per cent of the GDR team and won more than half the team's gold and silver medals. By contrast, US women comprised just over a quarter (26 per cent) or 112 out of 425, British and West German women slightly over a fifth (20.6 and 21 per cent respectively), and French women less than a fifth (18.3 per cent) of their teams. The teams from Latin America had virtually no women at all, with the notable exception of Cuba with fifty-five women out of its team of 200. Further, in the winter Olympics of 1976, Soviet and East German women contributed more than half their teams' medals – more than twice the number won by US, West German, French and British women put together (Riordan 1985). China therefore is following the path pioneered by other state socialist nations in seeking international sports success based on its women.

2 Traditional attitudes to women's sport

By contrast with western historical experience which, from at least Ancient Greece until recent times, has regarded most sports as male preserves, in China, martial arts (the principal form of indigenous sport to survive until today) have never been perceived as an area of life exclusive to virile young men. The figure of the female warrior (*wudan*) has existed down the centuries and is a stock character in martial arts novels (*wuxia xiaoshuo*) and other literary texts, and operas (*wuxi*) (Brownell 1995: 87).

There is evidence that in the Song dynasty (AD 960–1279) a form of football 'became more popular than ever for women, even with bound feet, spreading from court attendants to the general populace' (Brownell 1995: 88). Wrestling by both men and women was a popular court entertainment, and the top women's wrestlers became quite famous. In her seminal book on Chinese sport, *Training the Body for China*, Susan Brownell writes:

> For men, polo, kick-ball and wrestling were regarded as important methods of military training. Though there were certainly gender differences in the ways these sports were played and the meanings assigned to them . . . the fact that these were the same sports that women played seems to demonstrate that throughout Chinese history these sports were not regarded as an exclusive 'male preserve'.
>
> (Brownell 1995: 93)

This traditional involvement of women in combat sports helped to maintain women's active role in the face of the introduction of western sports with their male bias at the turn of the century – during the colonization of China and the Republican period (1912–49).

> Because Western sports were introduced into China through Western-run schools, and especially by the YMCA, the Western bias against women in sports was reflected in the limited participation of Chinese women from the turn of the century until the 1930s. Women were not included in the National Sports Games organised by Westerners in 1910 and 1914.
>
> (Brownell 1995: 96)

However, as the Chinese increasingly took over the organization of the Games, the situation changed. Thus the Third National Games, held in 1924 (i.e. in the Republican period), contained three exhibition sports for women, and the Fourth National Games in 1930 added four sports for women (track and field, volleyball, basketball and tennis). As Brownell (1995: 82) comments, 'Chinese women did not particularly lag behind men in sports that are strongly identified with masculine identity in the West'. Female athletes also participated in the Second Martial Arts Festival of 1932 and, in the Seventh National Games in 1948, women's wrestling was an exhibition event.

It is clear that not only have women had a long accepted involvement in sport in China, they have been able to practise 'muscular' combat sports like wrestling, boxing and *wushu* (various forms of hand-to-hand combat and weapon skills contests) with apparent official and male approbation and even encouragement. The same applies to Chinese women's involvement in body-building: the first Chinese Bodybuilding Championships for men *and* women took place in December 1994.

3 Sports as lower-class activities

From the Song dynasty onwards – i.e. after AD 960 – education for the elite in China increasingly emphasized the mind at the expense of the body. Henceforth sports tended to be marginalized in the education of the ruling class and its male offspring. By the Qing dynasty (1644–1911), scholars spent much of their lives memorising a vast amount of knowledge in order to pass the Imperial Examinations and therefore move up the social rankings scale. By the mid-nineteenth century, the Chinese situation differed singularly from that in western Europe, especially Britain, where 'character-building sports' were an integral part of the education of upper and middle-class boys. The influence of this historical denigration of engagement in sporting activity in China persists today in the popular consciousness:

> The influence of China's long history is evident in the fact that, despite the efforts of the state, sports still do not play an important role in the

educational system. Chinese parents do not like their children to devote too much time to sports because they perceive education as the way to a better life.

(Brownell 1995: 172)

A Chinese writer confirms that 'The Chinese put much store by intellectual education and display a negative attitude towards sport; some parents do not like their children to engage in sport' (Dong 1995: 83). As a result of this intellectual bias against sport, sport is still widely viewed as an activity engaged in only by 'lower-class, uneducated people' and, hence, an acceptable pursuit for women, thereby reinforcing the historical precedents described above. As we shall see below, a significant proportion of elite women athletes is from a rural, less educated background. By contrast with the United States and western Europe, and even Japan, therefore, 'Chinese athletes have a relatively lower standard of education' (Dong 1995: 84). For Chinese women athletes sport is an open channel to material and social advancement. Inasmuch as the state has substantially subsidized sport, this has enabled 'talented working-class and rural-based women' to enter sport and realize their potential (Dong 1995: 84).

It has to be remembered that China is a developing country. Only 1.8 per cent of the population had received a higher education in 1987, and only 33 per cent of those were women – the same figure as in 1976 and not even double the number of the 1950s (Dong 1995: 87; Rai 1992: 37). What is more, of the 230 million of the population that are illiterate, some 70 per cent are women. Women's education, therefore, is 'relatively restricted by comparison with advanced countries' (Rai 1992: 88). On the other hand, some dramatic changes have occurred in health: women's life expectancy rose from 35 in 1950 to 71 in 1991 (and to 76 in Beijing); the current women's life expectancy is therefore close to that in the world's richest countries (Liu 1995: 29).

Given the popular attitudes to sport and women's lower educational position, men (including those running a 'paternalistic' state) are unlikely to stand in the way of women who wish to engage in an activity that is relatively unimportant to men in the first place. This 'lower-class stigma' has implications for the way in which gender is linked with social class/status in contemporary sport.

4 Sport, the countryside and confucian philosophy

Of China's 1.2 billion people, 80 per cent live in the countryside. More than half of the rural population – some 550 million – is female. There are certain characteristics of rural women in China that predispose them towards sport. First, as noted above, sport traditionally has been regarded as a lower-class pursuit and therefore open to women as 'lower-class citizens', especially peasants, in the historically hierarchical, male-dominated society. Second, the very nature of peasant labour, requiring a strong physique and mental toughness, has some affinity with qualities required in sports training. Further, in a Communist country whose ideology has glorified manual labour and labourers, the notion of a strong, tough, muscular woman has been an officially-approved and propagated ideal stereotype that has re-inforced and authenticated the traditional stereotype described above.

It is therefore no surprise that the majority of Chinese women athletes come from an urban working-class or rural background, where the largest reservoir of sporting talent lies. Brownell attests,

> that a growing proportion of China's most outstanding athletes have come from the countryside. The low status of female peasants makes them superior for sports training because they are accustomed to physical hardship and are highly motivated to take advantage of sports opportunities in the face of limited options!
>
> (Brownell 1995: 74)

Xie Yanmin supports this view:

> Many girls in remote and poverty-stricken villages have become world-famous athletes . . . Although freed from the fetters of feudal custom . . . Chinese women, particularly in rural areas, have inherited the virtue of obedience to their elders, and to their coach in sports training. They can bear all hardships involved in training and obey their coaches.
>
> (Xie 1994: 23)

Brownell quotes a male sports official as an illustration of this point:

> Truly, women are more able 'to eat bitterness', endure hardship and labour. For thousands of years they did all the housework, they rose very early and toiled all day long, then went to bed and got up again. That ability, that tradition, persists. Women are therefore more disci-plined and obedient than men. If you are working with three women and three male athletes, you have to watch the men a lot closer; they're inclined to sneak off and cheat on workouts.
>
> (Brownell 1995: 76)

The official here unconsciously rejects the longstanding western notion of a polarization between biologically weak women and strong men.

It is perhaps significant that when the coach Ma Junren, under pressure to achieve with men what he had done with women, took on male athletes (in 1994), the experiment lasted no more than a couple of months before the men walked out, ostensibly 'because of a dispute over money' (Powell 1995a: 36). Ma Junren, incidentally, had deliberately taken on girls from villages:

'Most of them hail from the countryside and are therefore honest, obedient and hard-working' (Deng 1994: 12). His most outstanding protegée, Wang Junxia, the holder of world records from 1500m to 10,000m and recipient of the prestigious Jesse Owens Trophy in 1994, the world's highest athletic honour, grew up in a village, the daughter of poor peasants, and is said to have had to run 16km to and from school every day. During training with Ma, she and other female athletes had to run '220km a week or almost a marathon a day; sometimes she has to run as much as 170km in four days' (Yang 1994: 12).

Even some Chinese critics accused Ma of 'cruelty and inhumanity' in regard to his charges, intolerant of the slightest deviation from a strict regime which involved no boyfriends or make-up, and close-cropped hair (*China Sports* 1994: 24). On one occasion, he is said to have kept Wang's brother's death in a car crash and the subsequent funeral from her for several weeks until after the two championships in which she was competing; he did the same after the death of another runner's father. According to Ma, 'women are more susceptible to discipline and hard work than men' (Deng 1994: 12). Other Chinese experts, explaining Wang's remarkable achievements, have claimed that 'one reason she has been able to run so fast has to do with her rural background . . . the hard life in rural China is just what is needed to produce the kind of determination and endurance that Wang obviously has' (Yang 1994: 12).

A similar strict regime exists for female swimmers; they were reported in *Le Monde* as training and competing 364 days a year, with a daily two-hour gymnastics warm-up followed by six hours in the pool. No TV, no leisure time, no boyfriends, no right to visit their families during the training year, even on holidays. The 16-year-old world 400m freestyle champion, Yang Aihua, admits to swimming 120km a week in training (Georges 1994: 32). Some female divers are subjected to such training regimes even before their tenth birthday (Fu Mingxia and Sun Shuwei won world championships when they were 11 and 13 respectively).

This spirit of obedience and socially-conditioned aptitude for hard work and endurance have been reinforced by the philosophical traditions of Confucianism. In accordance with the 'three obediences' of Confucianism, women were expected to obey men (father, husband, sons) and to be humble, compliant, respectful. Despite attempts by the Communist authorities to root out such attitudes, as a Chinese scholar writes:

> Confucianism continues to have a substantial impact on Chinese female athletes to endure incredible training loads . . . that reinforces discipline in training and makes it easier to manage women than men . . . Women are socialised to be obedient, particularly to men from childhood; and since most head coaches are men, female athletes rarely violate regulations and schedules laid down by male coaches.
>
> (Dong 1995: 63)

To sum up, both a rural background and vestiges of Confucian philosophy stressing women's subordination to men have implications for women's greater involvement in and success at sport.

5 Sport and gender

In the West, sport with its heavy masculine image has complemented other socializing agencies – school, family, media, children's organizations and literature, religion and the state – in presenting stereotyped norms for girls and boys to develop their sexual identity. This growing-up process is based on a number of assumptions about behaviour being natural (or unnatural), universal and ageless, and being directly related to biological make-up. Boys and girls are 'born that way'. This rigid western conceptualization of gender has implications for those people who are perceived to cross the boundaries between 'female' and 'male' behaviour, nowhere more so than in the erstwhile 'male bastion' of sport where accusations of 'butch' and 'lesbian' have often been levelled at 'muscular' women. The Chinese attitudes have been quite different, as Brownell writes: 'in China, a woman who plays soccer might be considered "vulgar" (*cu*), but she is never considered "butch"; in other words, the primary axis for moral evaluations is based on class rather than "sexuality".' She sums up by maintaining that

> Although sports have played a role in changing perceptions of the body, they have not been used to separate females from males or to support claims to female biological inferiority as in the West . . . the successes of Chinese women athletes have now precluded this possibility.
>
> (Brownell 1995: 57–8)

All the same, times are changing, as anyone who has read *Wild Swans* will testify: it vividly shows how Chinese women have traversed three generations from feudalism to capitalism/Communism in a historical journey that took other nations six or seven centuries (Chang 1991). Today, the opening up of the country to the market, of television and other media to western 'culture', to women's fashions and other items of conspicuous consumption, are clearly contributing to a reformulation of gender and of women's role in society. Especially in urban centres, romantic love would appear to be rivalling social status in marital choice; men and women are becoming increasingly aware of their bodies (at an early age) as forms of sexual attraction, consumerism and hedonism are challenging for dominance in people's value systems, and increasing numbers of women are becoming economically independent of men. All this has led to a mounting debate on women's roles in society.

All these processes are bound to be reflected in sport. It is perhaps a sign of the times that in late 1994, sixteen of the nineteen female athletes walked out on coach Ma Junren. As Wang Junxia put it, 'We simply could not take it any longer. Ma made excessive demands, was over-critical and cruel . . . We had absolutely no freedom. The pressure was too great' (Powell 1995b: 46) Another bone of contention was money. Apparently, Ma had kept most of the athletes' winnings: of the 10 million yuan prize-money accumulated since 1993, he had given Wang 170,000 and his other star athlete, Qu Yunxia, 65,000 yuan, while spending 7 million on his own training centre (Powell 1995b: 46).

It appears that rapid social change is reinforcing the trend towards women's economic and social independence, and that is bound to have even greater repercussions for women's sport in the future.

6 Women, sport and socialism

The changes that have taken place in women's consciousness and economic position generally and in sport in particular are to a large extent the result of social transformations wrought by new attitudes to and of women and their roles in society, to which the Communist ideology has undoubtedly played a not inconsiderable part. As Shirin Rai has written:

> The Chinese communists regarded themselves as engaged not just in class war but also in social liberation: 'Women hold up half the heaven' was a favourite epigram of Mao. The post-revolutionary Chinese state was both socialist and developmentalist in nature. It was thus highly interventionist. This allowed it to affect the course of family life, the position of the woman within the family and within the public domain through policy-making and implementation. Under this paternalistic political system Chinese women did make significant gains in social status and economic position.
>
> (Rai 1992: 43)

Nevertheless, it has to be borne in mind that China, like almost all the erstwhile Communist states, emerged from a largely traditionalist, patriarchal, semi-feudal way of life only recently. Emancipation of women has been complex and uneven; there have been areas in which some western societies have progressed further in advancing women's rights. What is more, the point has to be made that the reasons for official encouragement of women to engage in sport have to be sought, too, in the state's political, military and material needs as well as its ideology.

In sport there is little doubt that the social policies pursued by the Communist government led to what a number of sources claim to have been 'fairly equal opportunities for men and women since the establishment of the sports schools in 1955' (Brownell 1995: 112). Brownell makes the telling point that

If one takes the passage of Title IX as the point when American sports-women began to achieve legal parity with men, then 1972 was the year when the American situation approached the Chinese. That means American women lagged 17 years behind the Chinese. If one considers the actual situation rather than the legal ideal, then American women have nowhere near the parity that Chinese women have.

(Brownell 1995: 143)

Such more-than-equal opportunities, however, by no means extend beyond sport. Even within sport, most of the major administrative and coaching positions are held by men, as Table 8.5 shows. Outside sport, the absence of women from political positions (discounting Mao's wife Jiang Qing) is glaringly apparent. In a continent not noted for women's leading roles in society, five other Asian states can boast women prime ministers past and present (Bangladesh, India, Pakistan, Sri Lanka and Turkey), while in 1990, as Shirin Rai reports, only 21 per cent of deputies to national and provincial people's congresses were women, and 29 per cent of political officials at all levels (Rai 1992: 74; Liu 1995: 23). The American authors Emily Honig and Gail Hershatter found in Shanghai (China's largest city) that only a quarter of the city's Communist Party members were women (Honig and Hershatter 1988: 17). We have already noted above the far-from-equal position of Chinese women in education.

At least the realities should warn against unreal assumption that if the social order is changed, women will be liberated almost overnight. As the two above-mentioned American authors write of China:

Perhaps the most serious flaw in Chinese discussions of gender was the assumption that since China had had a socialist revolution, time alone would solve all remaining problems. Yet until gender was put at the centre of an analytical model, it seemed likely not only that these problems would persist, but that their causes would remain opaque to those who raise criticism from within Chinese society about the situation of women.

(Honig and Hershatter 1988: 17–18)

Table 8.5 Respective numbers of male and female professional coaches, 1990

	Chief coach	Coach	Assistant coach	Total
Aggregate	1,669	8,448	8,056	18,173
Of whom:				
Female	220	1,601	1,706	3,527
%	13.2	19.0	21.2	19.4

Source: Dong Jinxia (1994) *Society, Women and Sport in Modern China*, unpublished PhD dissertation, Beijing University of Physical Culture, p. 39

Evidently, a socialist society may remove the class relationships between men and men, and women and women, but it does not necessarily promote emancipation of women at the same pace. Prejudice and traditional attitudes amongst both men and women, and a set of factors associated with economic backwardness and international tension, act as brakes on progress.

7 Other factors: physique, medicine and science

A consideration sometimes mentioned by Chinese sources in explaining the difference in international attainments of their men and women is that of height and weight. Thus, 'the sex difference in athletic achievements has something to do with the fact that Chinese women are by no means inferior (in physique) to their foreign counterparts in many sports, while Chinese men are often inferior in this regard (i.e. shorter and lighter)' (Xie Yanmin 1994: 23). While this may be true in some sports (in the 1992 Olympic swimming events, for example, the average body height difference between Chinese women and other finalists was insignificant, while there was a difference of 7–8cm in terms of the men) (Xie Yanmin 1994: 23), size has not prevented either Japanese or Korean (or, indeed, Chinese) men from performing well in a wide range of sports. It is also the case that in a nation of 1.2 billion people, it is surely possible to find the ideal anthropomorphic types for given sports. For example, the average height of the Chinese men's basketball team is 1.987m (the women's is 1.845m), with one member, Shan Tao, as tall as 2.15m. This, a Chinese source admits, 'is in no way inferior to European nations' (Xie Kainan 1994). Similarly, the Chinese men's volleyball team averages 1.95m in height (with four players over 2m) and the women's 1.85m (Huang 1994). It is hard to believe that such factors provide an insurmountable hurdle to Chinese men given the centralized sports system and the vast population.

A more complex and certainly controversial area is that of medical, including chemical, assistance to performance. Some claim that this assistance has a greater effect on women than it does on men. The Chinese swimming coach Chen Yongpeng has said somewhat nebulously that 'traditional Chinese regimens and medical theories have been widely applied to sports training for rapid recovery from fatigue. Perhaps some of these have produced more effects on women' (Xie Yanmin 1994: 23). What is unclear is whether traditional medicine and the state sports medical service give Chinese women the edge over opponents, whether fewer sportswomen in the world are on stimulants than men are, or whether they work better/faster on women (it certainly is true that women generally have lower testosterone and haemoglobin levels than men).

We know from evidence in other state socialist countries (e.g. the Soviet Union) that some women athletes have been encouraged to conceive and later abort, utilizing the body change benefits for sports training and competition.

Such evidence of cases of manipulation of female bodies has not emerged from China. What is abundantly clear, however, is that a significant number of top Chinese athletes (and very few men) have been identified in international drug tests as having taken performance-enhancing drugs (see earlier section on the drug issue).

The State Sports Commission started carrying out drug testing in some domestic competitions in 1988; the next year, it announced a three-pronged anti-drugs policy of 'strict prohibition, strict examination and strict punishment'. Three years later, in 1992, the Chinese Olympic Committee formed a special Anti-Doping Commission; at the end of 1993, this commission published the results of tests on 2,205 urine samples taken in random domestic tests during the year. It uncovered twenty-four cases of drug taking (mainly anabolic steroids) and meted out (undeclared) punishment to the guilty athletes (*China Sports* 1994: 58) The tests were conducted at the newly-established IOC-accredited Anti-Doping Centre in Beijing. It is an indication of the confusion prevailing over drugs that a month earlier, the same source had quoted 1,608 samples tested (1,032 in domestic events, 261 in international competitions held in China, and 315 in outside competitions) (*China Sports* 1994: 59). Both sources agree on the twenty-four positive tests.

However, it was the results of tests on Chinese athletes undertaken by non-Chinese bodies outside China that started in 1993 to record a high rate of positive drug tests. The first top woman athlete to fail a drug test was swimmer Zhou Xin in March 1993 (tested in January); she was banned for two years by FINA. Then came Zhong Weiyue, world record holder in the 50m and 100m back-stroke; she was suspended in February 1994 for two years by the Chinese Swimming Federation. These two swimmers were followed by Ren Xin and Bai Xiuyu in August 1994; they were also banned for two years. At the Rome World Swimming Championships in September 1994, Yang Aihua, 400m freestyle gold medallist, was caught and received a two-year ban.

The biggest haul of drug users came in early October, during the Asian Championships, when a further seventeen Chinese swimmers were tested, of whom as many as seven tested positive – an almost 50 per cent 'strike rate'. They included top swimmer Lu Bin who had won four gold and two silver medals in Rome. The same testing netted two canoeists, a cyclist and the women's 400m hurdles gold medalist Han Qing. Previously, in September, China's top discus thrower, Qiu Qiaoping, had been caught taking anabolic steroids.

Some idea of the scale of the positive tests in swimming may be gained from the fact that the number of apprehended Chinese swimmers exceeded the total number of failed tests recorded by all other swimmers in the previous twenty-two years (*Hong Kong Standard* 1994: 2). That is not to say that other nations' swimmers – or other athletes – take no performance-enhancing drugs or are less guilty than Chinese swimmers. It may be recalled that no East German woman swimmer tested positive, yet twenty East German swimming coaches admitted, after the fall of the Berlin Wall in 1989, that there had been systematic drug taking in East German swimming. As a punishment to Chinese swimmers and a warning for the future, the International Swimming Federation (FINA) is to conduct random tests in China and an on-site investigation there, while the four charter nations of the Pan-Pacific Swimming Association (Australia, USA, Japan and Canada) banned China from its championships in Atlanta in the summer of 1995.

What is not yet apparent is the extent to which the Chinese authorities (political as well as sports) are involved in the manufacture, testing, monitoring and administering of performance-enhancing drugs – as we now know the East German, Soviet, Romanian and Bulgarian authorities were. It is known that East German coaches and sports medical specialists have been working in Chinese sport since the mid-1980s; and one such swimming coach, Klaus Rudolph, has added his voice to those that believe that Chinese athletes are caught up in a state-run drugs programme: 'China, and particularly sport in China, is centrally controlled . . . a doctor is on constant call for national team members and permanent monitoring is provided by the Medical Research Institute in Beijing' (*Sunday Times* 1995: 17). As the *Sunday Times* commented, 'Rudolph casts doubt on the idea that those swimmers who have tested positive for steroids had acted unilaterally' (*Sunday Times* 1995: 17). Another source – a Chinese technician from the IOC-accredited Anti-Doping Centre in Beijing – claimed that China maintained a floating anti-drug laboratory off the shores of South Korea during the 1988 summer Olympics (the USSR did the same), and that the Chinese authorities had been involved in other cover-ups in Beijing (Almond 1995: 28).

As Wei Jiehong, Secretary of the Chinese Olympic Committee and head of the Anti-Doping Commission, admits, 'We recognize that doping ruins the image of Chinese sport'; he has threatened a lifetime ban for transgressors (Loh 1994: 41). The drug revelations have certainly caused considerable damage to China's chances of staging the Olympic Games in the near future and have caused embarrassment to IOC President Juan Antonio Samaranch (and others) who had declared several times, most recently during the 1994 Asian Games, that he was convinced that Chinese sport was 'drug-free' (Tait 1994: 41).

All that can be said for sure is that it is unlikely that a relatively poor country like China can match the huge amounts of money that prosperous countries like the USA can spend on drugs in sport, albeit on a private enterprise, not state-directed, basis. On the other hand, it may be tempting for a developing country that ardently desires international recognition and prestige through sports success to take short cuts. There are certainly fewer controls over the sale of drugs in China than in most western countries. However, the Chinese authorities are taking measures to combat drug taking in sport, including the threat of imprisonment, and are severely punishing drug cheats and those behind them (officials, coaches, medics). This is vital because, unless serious steps are taken to reassure the world public, much of the admiration for Chinese sports achievements generated by outstanding Chinese women athletes will turn to anger and contempt, and make China a pariah among sports nations.

CONCLUSIONS

Never in history has a nation's international sporting success owed so much to its women. Nor have women athletes made such rapid progress in a wide range of events in such a short time – some two or three years – or improved world records by such remarkable margins. The reasons for such progress have been located in the following factors.

1   There has been the absence in China of a number of deep-seated pre-judices in regard to sexuality that have been common in western his-torical development – prejudices centred on the notion that sport was a 'male preserve'. Chinese women are thereby challenging traditional cul-tural assumptions about behaviour being directly related to biological make-up, and demonstrating that many of the male and female charac-teristics for long taken for granted by the dominant ideology of western society are determined by social custom rather than by genetics.

2   That does not mean that the Chinese believe that the ability of male runners to run faster than female runners has no genetic component. Rather, there is a firm conviction that women's biological disadvantage in physical performance may be compensated for by socially-conditioned superior abilities of hard work, discipline and stamina.

3   The official prioritizing of elite women's sport as the principal thrust of China's international sports challenge has less to do with women's liberation than with national pride gained in the only clearly visible area where China can take on and beat the world's most economically advanced countries. That women's liberation is a secondary considera-tion is evident in the lack of effective government action to alter the relative subordinate position of women in sports administration and coaching, not to mention in politics, education and science.

4   The major factors that have facilitated Chinese women's progress in sport have to be sought in various elements intrinsic to Chinese society and shaped by historically-conditioned attitudes to sport and women which differ markedly from those that have formed the dominant values of sport in western society, at least since the time of Ancient Greece. Such factors include the long-standing involvement of women in martial arts, the general regard for sport as a low-class activity, the rural back-ground of many sportswomen, the influence of Confucian ideology in

inculcating such traits in women as obedience, sacrifice, discipline, humility and respect in regard to men. They also include the socialist ideology of equal opportunities for women in the period dominated by Mao.

5   The rapid economic and social transformation that has opened up China since the early 1980s to the all-pervasive influence of market values and western consumerism is undermining traditional attitudes, philosophies (Confucianism, Taoism, Bhuddism) and institutions. This trend is likely to grow stronger and, in sport, draw China's leading athletes into the mainstream of the transnational elite sports community dominated by western market values. This may provide more economic independence for Chinese women and erode patriotism and loyalty to Chinese society; it is also likely to make them less willing to undergo the sort of training regime associated with Ma Junren, though more susceptible to chemical manipulation of their bodies.

The next few years will give us a much better understanding of the progress, and reasons behind it, of Chinese women athletes and the implications that their progress will have for women and Chinese society generally. Certainly, the list of achievements by Chinese female athletes is long and imposing, particularly when set alongside those of women in the economically advanced nations of the West. Insofar as world-wide women's sporting attainments are reflecting, reinforcing and sometimes even precipitating processes of social change in the role and status of women, the Chinese women's example offers exciting prospects for the future of women in all societies, particularly the modernizing communities of Asia and Africa.

REFERENCES

Almond, Elliot and Tempest, Rone (1995) 'The Crooked Shadow', *Los Angeles Times*, 8 February: 28.

Berendonk, Brigitte (1991) *Doping-Dokumente: Von der Forschung zum Betrug*, Berlin: Springer Verlag.

Brownell, Susan (1995) *Training the Body for China: Sports in the Moral Order of the People's Republic* Chicago: University of Chicago Press.

Chang, Jung (1991) *Wild Swans, three Daughters of China* London: HarperCollins.

China Sports: 'Strict Anti-Doping Measures', June 1994; 'National Anti-Doping Conference' and 'Chinese Athletes Pass Tests', July 1994; see November 1994.

Deng Xuezheng (1994) 'Ma Junren: a thorny path to success', *China Sports*, October: 12.

Dong Jinxia (1995) 'Society, Women and Sport in Modern China', *Sports Science*, 1: 11.

Georges, Pierre (1994) 'Tais-toi et nage!', *Le Monde*, 16 September: 32.

Jiang Yun (1992) *China: a Developing Country, a Developing Role in International Sports*, unpublished Paper, Nanjing.

Hargreaves, Jennifer (1994) *Sporting Females* London: Routledge.

Heinrich-Vogel, Renate (1981) 'Mein Lebensweg vom sportbegeisterten Kind zur Hochleistungssportlerin der DDR', in Ehrich, Dieter, Heinrich-Vogel, Renate, Winkler, Gerhart (eds) *Die DDR Breiten- und Spitzensport* Munich: Kopernikus Verlag.

Hong Kong Standard (1994) 'China Drugs Shock', 29 November: 2.

Honig, Emily and Hershatter, Gail (1988) *Personal Voices: Chinese Women in the 1980s*, Stanford: Stanford University Press.

Huang Haiwen (1994) 'Will China Make it again?', *China Sports*, August–September: 43.

Jones, Robin (1993) 'Sport in China: a Current View', in De Lacey, Ann (ed.) *International Sports Systems: Past, Present and Future* Liverpool: Liverpool Institute of Higher Education.

Kuhnst, Peter (1982) *Das missbrauchte sport: die politische Instrumentalisierung des Sports in der SBZ und DDR, 1945–1957*, Cologne: Verlag Wissenschaft und Politik.

Lewis, Thomas (1994) 'World Beaters', *Britain–China*, 2: 19.

Li Hongbing (1994) 'Sports Make Our Life more delightful', *China Sports*, July: 7.

Liu Qian (1995) 'Respect and Protection', *Women of China*, 5: 23. The author reports that in 1993, 'women deputies accounted for 21.6 per cent of all deputies to provincial people's congresses'.

Loh, Matthew (1994) 'Chinese top brass meet over scandal', *Hong Kong Eastern Express*, 30, November: 41.

Macleod, Iain (1993) 'Life of extreme hardship lies behind China's revolution in athletics', *Telegraph Sport*, 18 October: 43.

Mader, Alois and Hollman, Wilmer (1983) 'Sportmedizin in der DDR', *Sportwissenschaft*, 2, June: 152–62.

Powell, David (1995a) 'Family regime at an end', *The Times*, 6 January: 36.

Powell, David (1995b) 'Divisions reported in athletics army', *The Times*, 5 January: 46.

Rai, Shirin (1992) 'Gender, employment and educational reforms', in Rai, Shirin, Pilkington, Hilary and Phizacklea, Annie (eds) *Women in the Face of Change*, London: Routledge.

Riordan, James (1985) 'Some comparisons of women's sport in East and West', *International Review for the Sociology of Sport*, 20(1–2): 117–28.

Riordan, James (1993) 'Rewriting Soviet Sports History', *Journal of Sports History*, 20(3), Winter: 247–59.

Riordan, James (1994) 'Russia and Eastern Europe in the Future of the Olympic Movement', in Barney, R.K. and Meier, K.V. (eds) *Critical Reflections on Olympic Ideology*, London: University of Western Ontario.

Sage, George H. (1990) *Power and Ideology in American Sport: A Critical Perspective*, Champaign, Illinois.

Song He (1994) 'He Means What He Says', *China Sports*, May: 11.

Sunday Times (1995) Sport Section, 1 January: 17.

Tait, Paul (1994) 'FINA "sting" Nailed Dopes', *Hong Kong Eastern Express*, 30 November: 41.

Women of China (1995) 4: 29.

Wu Shaozhu (1990) *Sports Science*, 4: 2, quoted in Jiang Yun.

Xie Kainan (1994a) 'Basketball: a look at China's Strength', *China Sports*, August–September: 43.

Xie Yanmin (1994b) 'Causes for female domination', *China Sports*, October: 23.

Xu Qi (1990) 'Sport awakening in China', *Olympic Review*, September–October: 466.

Yang Wanhua (1994) 'In a class by herself', *China Sports*, May: 12.

Chapter 9

The emergence of professional sport[1]

The case of soccer

Robin Jones

Within the space of just a few years, China has turned its sports system round from a centrally-planned structure to a more diverse, market-orientated system. This is in keeping with the government's general policy of reform. In sporting terms, the government has been determined to distance itself from its previous role of being 'sole provider' and today increasingly expects sport to adopt a 'pay as you play' approach. At the highest level, this has resulted in the development of professional sport on western lines – with Chinese characteristics. Of course, there has long been professional sport in China, as in other, former Communist countries, where 'state amateur' was a euphemism for 'professional', in that the athlete received money, housing, food, medicine, and sports clothing from the state, in return for a full-time commitment to sports training and performance. In China, provincial sports teams are the outcome of the special sports schools and are a regular form of paid employment for those who rise through the ranks of competitive sport. Beyond the provincial team is the national squad that, for the few, leads to Olympic and international glory. There is little doubt that such a system produces gold medals and it is a system that, under different guises, has been adopted in many countries, both East and West. But as the reforms in China, promoted by Deng Xiao Ping, have continued, a new focus has emerged in the last few years that is introducing professional sport. Commercial sponsorship and ticket sales now provide the financial underpinning to the system that was formerly provided by the government.

It was a government decision at the beginning of the 1990s to move certain sports in the direction of professionalism. The reform process – of which professionalism was part – introduced the idea and practice of accountability, at the same time separating the government to some extent from direct control of sport. Why did the government decide to promote professionalism in sport at all? There was the choice, after all, to simply pull out of sport, or just to reduce the funding. In choosing to retain some control, it has been able to retain the 'Chinese characteristics' of the system. For example, some of the key administrators of professional sports are from government offices such as the Sports Commission; and certain areas of professional sport receive provincial government support, such as accommodation for players. In addition, there is quasi-governmental involvement through the soccer team August First, which is linked to the People's Liberation Army and plays in the professional soccer league. It might therefore be reasonable to describe the present phase of development of Chinese soccer as transitional. Compared to South Korea, which developed its professional soccer league in 1983 (the first in Asia), China is still only in its third season and further change may be expected.

Soccer was 'chosen' by government sports leaders as the major sport to become professional because it has huge popular appeal worldwide, an established and prestigious World Cup, significant attractions for potential sponsors and a successful club system in Europe and elsewhere to copy. In China's case, however, their soccer system had not kept pace with developments in the structure of the game elsewhere, even though the Chinese Football Association was founded in 1924 and affiliated to the world governing body, FIFA, in 1931. The relative lack of international experience, though, showed in other Asian countries too, because whilst China has never reached the final stages of the World Cup, even the Asian Football Confederation (founded in 1954), has only ever provided eight countries for the final stages.[2]

Participation in the World Cup by Asian countries was extremely low until 1974. In the nine World Cups prior to 1974, only seventeen entries from ten national football associations had been received, and of these, seven were withdrawn, including the one from China in 1954. After its unsuccessful entry in the 1958 qualifying rounds, China then did not re-enter the competition for another twenty-four years, in 1982. It has since taken part in all the subsequent competitions. Figure 9.1 and Table 9.1 show the growth of Asia's involvement in the World Cup from 1930 to 1994.

The period 1958–82 spanned the austere years of China when the country withdrew from the IOC over the issue of the recognition of Taiwan, the years of the Cultural Revolution (1966–76) and the early years under Deng Xiao Ping, 1976–82, when he was establishing the approach that led to the 'open door' policies that have become a feature of Chinese government strategy.

From a modest starting point, international success was a distant objective in the early days and, in a sport as unpredictable as soccer, the route to this objective was far from clear. Again, as Cao Shi Yun[3] comments, simply copying from everyone without regard to China's own strengths meant that China 'actually learned very little from each of them and couldn't combine the skills together'. After many years of trying and failing to reach the World Cup finals, China has now set up a more coherent programme. By establishing a professional league system and building a supporting youth team programme, China hopes to bring about a change of fortune that could lead it forward internationally. Even if the World Cup finals remain elusive in the short term, however, China will have established a sustainable home-based market for soccer, with its own features, that may ensure the long-term

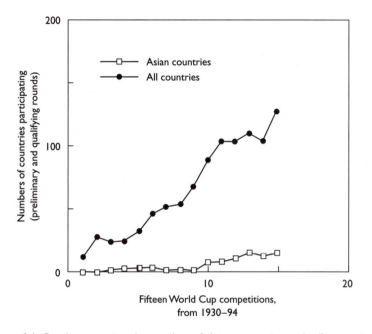

Figure 9.1 Graph comparing the number of Asian countries with all countries taking part in the preliminary and qualifying rounds of each World Cup, 1930–94

development of the game in China. The FIFA-Coca Cola World Ranking lists 1993–6 show that China has fluctuated by twenty-six places, but remains in the top third of the total number of 1996 listed teams (180). In the same period, Asia's rankings are shown in Table 9.2.

During the transitional phase of Chinese soccer, a fully independent, autonomous club system is not possible, principally because the clubs have to rely on their respective city or provincial government for the use of stadium and training facilities. In many cases, too, staff and players are housed in accommodation provided by the provincial sports commission. The stadiums are generally modern, large (40–60,000), with all-seating design, floodlighting and peripheral athletics track, together with electronic scoreboards and would certainly compare favourably with many British and continental clubs. The spectators are therefore used to good facilities at the grounds, for which they will pay between 10 and 20 yuan for a Group A match. Table 9.3 shows the structure of the league system.

Average attendance at Group A matches across all the twelve clubs in the league was 19,000 in the 1993–4 season, although the Sichuan Quan Xing club often gets a full house of around 40,000 for its home games. The training facilities and accommodation for the Sichuan club are provided by the Sichuan Sports Commission at their sports skills college campus in

Table 9.1 World Cup preliminary and qualifying rounds 1930 to 1994 – Asian countries taking part

1930	1934	1938	1950	1954	1958	1962	1966
None	None	Dutch Indies Japan (W)	Burma (W) India (W) Philippines (W)	**China (W)** Japan S. Korea	**China** Indonesia Taiwan (W)	Japan S. Korea	N. Korea S. Korea (W)
0	**0**	**2**	**3**	**3**	**3**	**2**	**2**
13	**29**	**25**	**25**	**34**	**47**	**53**	**54**
0	**0**	**8**	**12**	**8.8**	**6.3**	**3.7**	**3.7**

1970	1974	1978	1982	1986	1990	1994
Japan S. Korea	Hong Kong Indonesia Japan N. Korea S. Korea Singapore Thailand S. Vietnam	Hong Kong Indonesia Japan S. Korea Malaysia S. Korea Taiwan Thailand	**China** Hong Kong Indonesia Japan N. Korea Indonesia Macao Malaysia Singapore Taiwan Thailand	Bangladesh Brunei **China** Hong Kong India Japan N. Korea S. Korea Macao Malaysia Nepal Singapore Taiwan Thailand	Bangladesh **China** Hong Kong Indonesia Japan Malaysia S. Korea Malaysia Nepal Pakistan Singapore Taiwan Thailand	Bangladesh **China** Hong Kong India Indonesia Japan N. Korea S. Korea Macao Pakistan Singapore Sri Lanka Taiwan Thailand Vietnam
2	**8**	**8**	**11**	**15**	**13**	**15**
68	**90**	**104**	**104**	**110**	**104**	**128**
2.9	**8.8**	**7.6**	**10.5**	**13.6**	**12.5**	**11.7**

Key First number under each column = number of Asian countries taking part in preliminary/qualifying rounds. Second number under each column = total number of countries taking part in preliminary/qualifying rounds. Third number under each column = Asian countries as a percentage of total number. (W) = withdrawn after one or more matches.

Table 9.2 FIFA-Coca Cola world soccer rankings

Country	End of 1993 ranking	End of 1994 ranking	End of 1995 ranking	July 1996 ranking
Japan	43	36	31	25
South Korea	41	35	46	53
China	**53**	**40**	**66**	**54**
Thailand	69	85	76	61
Singapore	75	95	104	99
Malaysia	79	89	106	105
India	100	109	121	112
Hong Kong	112	98	111	116
Bangladesh	116	130	138	126
Indonesia	106	134	130	128
Sri Lanka	126	139	135	135
North Korea	62	84	117	138
Laos	146	160	152	155
Macao	166	175	180	166
Pakistan	142	158	160	167
Maldives	148	162	169	168
Philippines	163	171	166	169
Chinese Taipei	161	170	178	180
Cambodia	n/a	174	180	182

Source: *FIFA News*[4]

Table 9.3 Structure of the Chinese professional soccer league, 1996 National level

Group A – Premier league	Group B – Division I
Dalian Wanda	Qingdao Hai Niu
Shanghai Shen Hua	Guardians
August First	Foshan
Guangzhou Apollo	Shanghai Yuyuan
Sichuan Quan Xing	Liaoning Yuan Dong
Beijing Guo An	Hubei
Shandong Tai Shan	Shenyang
Guangdong Hong Yuan	Shanghai
Tianjin Samsung	He-nan
Guangzhou Panasonic	Locomotive
Shenzhen	Jiangsu
Jilin Hyundai	Dalian Shunfa
– two teams promoted/relegated at end of season	

Regional level

Four regional divisions. Thirty teams. Two teams promoted to the First Division on the basis of a regional play off

Chengdu, comprising a training pitch and access to other sports facilities. The team accommodation is conveniently located about 400 metres away from the training pitch. It is not uncommon in China for housing to be provided at the place of work, especially in state or state-related jobs. Since 1949, the government has gradually increased and improved the housing stock in the cities, but there is still a housing shortage (in the cities especially) and the pressure to find suitable accommodation is high. A consequence of the practice of tying housing to employment is that job mobility can be problematic. The stock of houses on the open market is both small and extremely expensive, further reducing the mobility of the labour force. Thus, behind the seemingly unusual decision to house all the soccer club players together lies an established practice of the Chinese Communist system. It is also the belief of the club officials that the players are less likely to stray from the straight and narrow path of clean living, regular habits, controlled diet and good training.

Overseas players in the Sichuan side also live in the same housing block but in better appointed flats. One Group A club did try allowing their players the freedom to live where they liked, but falling success rates were attributed to this and they reverted to the communal system. There is little evidence that the social psychology of small group cohesion is anything to do with the manner in which the team players are housed – which would seem to have the potential to create as many problems as it solves. Nonetheless, it would seem equally unlikely that the club will change this established pattern and it will remain part of the transitional phase of Chinese soccer for some time to come.

When the Chinese government, through the Chinese Football Association (CFA), took the decision to re-structure the game in the early 1990s, other Asian countries were in the process of setting up professional soccer leagues or had already done so (Japan and Korea, for example) and, of course, there was the much older European system. The Chinese Football Association then was not breaking new ground internationally, nor was it taking a unique course of action within the country. China was also re-structuring its industry on the free market model, with government quotas for production, differential pricing mechanisms, state subsidies and Communist Party intervention in company policy being phased out as the socialist market economy was phased in. A stock market was formed and private investment was allowed; overeas capital in joint venture schemes was actively sought and company decisions were taken on the basis of profit and loss. Much of this 'market driven' approach was adopted by the CFA; football had become an industry.

In the first instance, to be eligible for Group A or B, football clubs had to provide financial guarantees which, in the case of Group A, was, initially set at 1 million yuan per year. The source of funding for the clubs was, at the outset, to come from the commercial/industrial sector, and although there was some early reluctance for companies to commit funds, as clubs attracted sponsors, so others came forward as sponsors.

Sichuan Football Club now has an eight-year contract running from 1993 to 2000, with Quan Xing, a Sichuan-based but nationally known alcoholic drink company.[5] The 1 million yuan per year contract is no longer seen as a risky investment and clubs now raise far more than the minimum 1 million yuan. Some clubs have changed sponsors in the last two years in favour of better deals, even using a Beijing advertising agency, achieving an income of about 10 million yuan. It was further reported in *China News Digest*[6] that sports clubs have begun selling shares and that Liaoning (relegated from the Premier Division in 1995) had raised $3 million by this means. Not only have Chinese companies invested in soccer, three clubs have sponsors from outside China – Hyundai and Samsung from South Korea (Group A) and Panasonic from Japan (Group B). Thus, commercial investment in Chinese soccer is strong and lively. The money is used for the general administration of the clubs and the payment of players' salaries. In addition to its regular sponsorship, the Quan Xing company pays a match bonus to the club of 90,000 yuan for a win and 30,000 yuan for a draw, thus adding a potential 2 million yuan to their investment. The Sichuan club in the season 1994–5 spent a further 2 million yuan (US$200,000) on a four-month contract for three players from Brazil. This money was also provided by the Quan Xing company, bringing the season's total sponsorship to between 3 and 5 million yuan (US$350,000–600,000).

An unusual feature of the Chinese Soccer League is that ticket sales are not handled by the clubs themselves, but by the Chinese Football Association. With average attendances of 19,000 for a Group A match, and ticket prices of between 10 and 20 yuan, the income from ticket sales for the CFA is between 25 and 50 million yuan (£2–4 million; US$3.5–6 million) for the twenty-two match season. A small percentage of this is re-distributed to the clubs at the end of the season according to their final league position. Sichuan, in the season 1993–4, received 700,000 yuan for sixth place in the premier league. The CFA uses the surplus for the international programme – World Cup matches, FIFA fees, friendly internationals and the hosting of visits by foreign clubs – and is forging links with professional clubs in Europe, South America and Asia. In the twelve-month period 1994–5 there has been a succession of overseas clubs and countries playing against Chinese clubs or the national team, as shown in Table 9.4.

The Sichuan Quan Xing club retains a squad of about twenty senior players and a youth squad of the same number. The club also has links with a local middle school where it provides help with soccer coaching. Players in the senior squad receive a monthly salary of 2,500 yuan which, in 'new era' China, would put them in the wealthy, but not super-wealthy, class (a 40cc motorbike costs about 3,000 yuan, for example, and a small car around 100,000 yuan). Given that the players have their food and accommodation

Table 9.4 Soccer clubs and national teams playing in or
against China in recent years

Visiting club	From
Gremio; Palmeira	Brazil
Nacional; Penarol	Uraguay
Lazio, AC Milan, Sampdoria, Napoli	Italy
Anderlecht	Netherlands
Benefica	Spain
Waldhof Mannheim	Germany
KV Mechelen	Belgium
Sofia Locomotive	Bulgaria
Farmers Bank	Thailand
Arsenal	England
Visiting country	*Country visited*
England; New Zealand	Netherlands

Source: *China News Digest*[7]

Note
The table is not a complete list of all clubs and countries.

provided by the club, their salary is substantial, especially considering that they have a share in the 90,000 yuan win bonus, which almost triples their salary for that week. Certainly, for many Chinese people a salary of 7,000 yuan a month is a distant dream. A family of three (i.e. one child) could expect to cover their basic needs (in 1995) with an income of 800 yuan a month. Many couples have joint incomes that take them up to this figure and beyond. Extrapolating from these figures, the Sichuan club faces a basic monthly salary bill of 50,000 yuan for players in the senior squad, or 600,000 yuan per year (about £50,000 per year; US$75,000 per year).

As yet, the promotion of soccer is under the control of the CFA and the clubs. Television, although paying 1 million yuan to the CFA in 1995 for the right to televise live matches, exerts less overt influence over such things as timing of matches. A proportion of the TV fee is, like the ticket sales, paid to the clubs, but the signs are there that the influence will grow. Advertising boards along touchlines, shirt logos and the like give important TV prominence to company products and the symbiotic relationship between soccer and the media is firmly in place.

There has been an influx of soccer icons, symbols and images. Soccer has adopted many of the trappings of the world game – the sports hero, the partisan fan support, the soccer transfer market, elements of crowd behaviour such as throwing of paper streamers onto the pitch (which, interestingly, are sold to the fans around the ground), chanting and singing in the street outside the ground. These elements have not escalated to – or are not seen as likely to lead to – violence and problems of crowd control, but there is still the presence of police around the perimeter of the pitch during the match.

The buying and selling of players on the transfer market is now well established. Sichuan Quan Xing at the end of the 1994 season sold a player to Guangdong Hong Yuan for 420,000 yuan (US$49,000). The total value of transfers for the Chinese Premier League in the period prior to the opening of the 1995 season was 3,700,000 yuan[8] (US$447,000) for fifteen transactions, with the highest single transfer fee being 660,000 yuan (US$78,000). The home transfer market operates in *renminbi* (Chinese currency) but transactions for overseas players are usually in US dollars.

During the seasons 1994 and 1995, at least five of the Group A clubs in China contracted overseas players from a total of six countries, Russia, Georgia, South Korea, North Korea, Brazil and France. The principal motive behind such deals was the perceived weakness(es) in the teams that could not easily be met by local players and the expectation that bringing in foreign players with experience in professional soccer would 'rub off' on local players and strengthen the club. By mid-season 1996, there were still relatively few overseas players on contract to Chinese clubs. It is not easy to be precise about the figure because some players only come for a short contract of less than a season whilst others spend a longer period than this. Shanghai Shen Hua, for example, in April 1996, brought in three experienced French players from Nîmes, Gueugnon and Lille.[9] Liaoning, relegated to Division 1 in 1996, have four players from North Korea.[10] At any one time, the figure is about ten overseas players in the Premier League. Few Chinese players have any experience playing for clubs outside China (the exception being one or two players in Japan and Germany), yet this is likely to change as Chinese soccer progresses.

Some of the experiments with overseas players have been unsuccessful and shrouded in controversy over contract details, with the result that the number of overseas players in China has remained fairly static, even falling at one point in 1996. It is too early to say whether this decline will continue, but clubs are now exercising more caution in drawing up contracts because of earlier problems, when some players were demanding better terms after arrival than were originally agreed. In a few cases, contracts were cancelled and players sent home.

Depending on the country of origin, the cost of bringing in overseas players may be relatively high. Because the Chinese currency (*renminbi*) is not at present a convertible currency on the international money market, making high salary payments in foreign currency to overseas players can be problematic and certainly is a consideration in selecting a particular country as a source of players or coaches. From the former Soviet Union, where a consequence of the collapse of the political system in the late 1980s was large-scale unemployment or redeployment amongst sports personnel, a number of players and coaches (of various sports) found employment in China. A Russian canoeing coach explained that he received US$350 per month coaching in China compared to US$10–20 (equivalent) he would expect to receive in Russia.[11]

For the second half of the 1995 season, which runs in two halves with a break of one month in the middle, Sichuan Quan Xing contracted three Brazilian players aged 22 and 23 years. The players, a central defender and two forwards, came from the second rank of clubs in Brazil and were expected to play in the remaining eleven matches to help the Sichuan club ensure that they stayed in Group A. The assistant coach at the club described the situation in the following way:

> Japan and South Korea have both improved their soccer by employing overseas players and the Sichuan club decided that seeing what others do and learning from them would be beneficial. We thought that the Brazilian style of football and the sort of players they had matched the style of Quan Xing, which is based on fast, attacking, skilful players showing awareness and determination. Matches are played according to pre-match plans that take account of the opposition's style. Players train six days a week for three to four hours a day.
>
> I don't think the Brazilian players are so much different from our own. We are the first club in China to employ players from Brazil. Our sponsors were fully supportive of our decision to seek overseas help and willingly agreed to provide the money for the deal.

The club's general administrator explained further:

> The contracts were drawn up very carefully, involving the embassies of both countries. We sent four club officials to Brazil, who visited eleven clubs before choosing these players. A Chinese staff member at our Embassy had a personal contact at the club.[12]

The contracts covered accommodation, special food in case they did not like the local Chinese dishes, and the transfer fee. The whole deal, including the costs of the delegation to Brazil, amounted to 2 million yuan (about US$200,000). US$20,000 went to the Brazilian club with the rest going to the three players at the end of their four-month contract. They did not receive a transfer fee, but they shared a match win bonus of US$300–500, separate from the *renminbi* bonus paid to their Chinese teammates. Although the players live in the same housing complex, the Brazilians have better rooms, which might be expected to cause some discontent with the Chinese players, but it seems generally the case in China that foreign 'specialists' should be given good treatment and the situation is accepted. At the end of the 1995 season, Sichuan Quan Xing just managed to avoid relegation to Group 2 (i.e. Division 1), coming third from the bottom of the Premier League.

China's progress in international soccer is a demonstration of:

1 *The commitment to the government's 'open door' policy.* Membership of FIFA carries an obligation to accept the international consequences of being in World Cup competitions. The issue of separatism, typical of the earlier years of the People's Republic, when China was absent, by choice, from most (but not all) international competitions and of the still present issue of Taiwan,[13] over which China has maintained a clear and unequivocal stance, have been superseded, as far as sport is concerned, by the new policy.

2 *The growing potential of sport for the public.* As a mass sport, soccer has no equal, and the modelling of the game on western lines is likely to lead to increased pressure for more and better facilities in schools, colleges, universities and new clubs. The Chinese Football Association and the newly created Football Management Office will have an important role in this, following the closure of the Sports Commission in 1998, although continued government support would be needed in planning new facilities, if not financial assistance as well. The rapid growth of soccer can be explained by two factors. First, there is the inherent popularity of soccer as a global game. It is covered extensively by the media in China, with weekly soccer newspapers, monthly magazines, and local and national network television coverage. And second, there is the Chinese government decision to make soccer stand on its own feet in the reform of the sport system, without the guarantees that the government hitherto provided via the financial support of the national Sports Commission. The Chinese Football Association had to take the plunge – and it went for the big splash! However, the growth of soccer seems to be somewhat limited to the development of a regional and national league system involving around fifty or sixty teams. Two newspaper surveys, in the *Guangzhou Daily*[14] and Beijing *Xin Min Evening News*,[15] asked readers to nominate their top ten sports persons. The Guangzhou survey (250,000 responses) ranked a soccer player in fifth position, after table tennis (two players chosen), gymnastics, badminton and *go* (a Chinese board game), whilst in the Beijing survey (560,000 responses), no soccer player was ranked in the top ten (gymnastics, table tennis, track and field were the top three) – a reminder that soccer may not yet have reached the levels of popularity to match the passion of Britain, Germany or Italy.

At junior level fewer opportunities exist for playing because of the lack of facilities and the fact that in schools, soccer does not have the prominence in the physical education curriculum that it has in England, for example. Soccer has yet to become a major game of Chinese schools – it is still not part of their school culture. School playing fields are limited in their provision of soccer pitches, and public parks are even more limited. However, soccer is a growing attraction for school age youngsters in China and they may be able to attend junior soccer clubs operating after school or in the evenings (for which a charge may be made), or even aspire to the youth teams run by the professional clubs. Part of the CFA development plan has been to send a squad of juniors to live, train and play in Brazil for a period of up to five years, depending on their progress and sponsorship.

3   *The possible demotion of Chinese indigenous sport.* There is no reason to suppose that soccer will not sweep across China and in so doing will challenge the position of indigenous sports. The Chinese National Games (held every four years) have already suffered in this way from Olympic sports.

4   *The arrival of commercialism in Chinese sport.* With the encouragement of the government, Chinese sport is seeking sponsorship, with soccer leading the way and with basketball also developing its share. Although the government has been in the past the major provider of finance for sport, and even though it will provide substantial monetary rewards for Olympic medals (80,000, 50,000 and 30,000 yuan for gold, silver and bronze respectively),[16] the advent of commercial backing for sport from both Chinese and non-Chinese companies represents a major departure from former policies.

5   *The growing divide between rich(er) and poor.* Average salaries in Shanghai are now 9,000 yuan per year compared to the neighbouring provinces' average of 3,000 yuan, whilst the average yearly income for the poor in China is still only 300 yuan.[17] Thus, attendance at soccer matches, including travelling to away matches, is part of the growing affluence that some are experiencing and of disposable incomes hitherto unheard of.

6   *Inter-provincial/inter-city rivalry.* All the Group 1 teams (except August First) are from major cities – some cities also have more than one team – and this has added to the attractiveness of the big cities, underlining their 'glitz' and success and, potentially at least, increasing rural–urban drift that in China overburdens city services and facilities.

7   *Reform of the sports system.* 'Socialism with Chinese characteristics' has been the government description of the reform process and there is no doubt that the Chinese Football Association mirrors this in several ways. On the other hand, it must be cause for some speculation as to how this reform process will develop in sport. Will there, for example, come a time when a Chinese Professional Football Players' Association is formed; or will players begin to negotiate their contracts through agents; will ultra high salaries enter the game; will clubs be bought and sold as commodities; will the hiring and firing of managers become a regular issue; will television contracts become the dominant influence in scheduling fixtures?

As a model for other parts of the Chinese sports system to follow, it is important that soccer is successful in its transition to professionalism.

Basketball and volleyball have also moved in the same direction and, as the reforms continue, the planned introduction of sports management offices will take over the running of sport. The impact of the new policy on sports may see a division of sports into those that 'need' government support and those that don't. Those sports that would be less likely to attract commercial backing will still have to rely on government support.

Women's soccer – perhaps somewhat paradoxically – achieved international success in the Olympic Games at Atlanta, where the Chinese national women's team gained a silver medal, losing 2–1 to America in the final. Although the pattern of national strength in women's world soccer is not as clear as for the men's game, China's success in reaching the women's final at Atlanta underlines their determination to raise the profile of the game at home. Given the relative newness of women's international soccer, China has, arguably, been able to make greater international progress than in the men's game.

Comparisons between the Chinese, British and other soccer systems are instructive:

1   *Clubs.* Profits from matches are channelled back to the clubs by the CFA on the basis of their league position. This applies both to television fees and to ticket sales. Salaries have not reached European proportions, but they nevertheless represent considerable wealth in China. Clubs do not own their own grounds so matches tend to take place in multi-purpose stadiums.
2   *League.* There are fewer teams in the leagues and thus fewer games per season. The league has a mid-season break of about one month, during which the cup competition is held.
3   *Players.* No players' professional football association exists in China nor any football agent acting for individual players. Players have to meet a minimum level of fitness, as laid down by the CFA, which at the start of the 1995 season meant running 3,100 metres in 12 minutes and a 5×25 metre shuttle run in 34 seconds.[18] All players in the league have to attend the central testing camp and failure to reach the standard results in cancellation of the player's registration (in 1995, 86 per cent passed the test first time and three or four players failed the second test). Such control over player fitness is not exercised by the Football Association in England, and much more loosely by the trainer/manager at club level.
4   China has few overseas players and, conversely, few Chinese players play outside China. The Japanese J-League, which started at almost the same time as the Chinese league in 1993, comprises sixteen clubs with fifty-nine players from overseas, with every club employing from three to five overseas players.[19] The source of the overseas players in Japan is predominantly South America (see Table 9.5).

Table 9.5 Country of origin of overseas players in Japanese J-League, August 1996

Continent and number		Country of origin and number
South America	41	Brazil 32, Argentina 8, Paraguay 1
Europe	15	Netherlands 3, Italy, Germany, France Croatia, Yugoslavia, each 2, Ukraine, Czech Republic, each 1
Asia	3	Korea, Africa, New Zealand, each 1
		None listed from China
Total	59	

Source: *Official J-League Information* (Homepage, internet)[19]

Europe, perhaps, is able to keep its players home based because of the high salaries available and because of the standard of competition. China, by comparison, in its Premier League has far fewer overseas players (average about one per club, but not all twelve clubs in the Premier League employ overseas players).

5   *Level of financing.* The transfer in August 1996 of Alan Shearer from Blackburn Rovers to Newcastle United in the English Premier League for £15 million (US$22 million) gives some idea of the scale of financing that is now engulfing the English Premier League. In the season 1995–6, total revenue for the seventy-two English league clubs was £468 million (US$700 million),[20] of which the Premier League took £323 million (US$480 million). This gave profits of about £49 million (US$75 million) to the twenty-two clubs in the Premier League – but somewhat masked a loss of about £28 million (US$44 million) for the remainder, showing that there are financial 'flaws' in the professional game for the lower clubs, but that Premier League membership carries substantial rewards. Shearer is expected to earn £35,000 per game (US$52,000).

In the season 1995–96, the English Premier League clubs spent £97.67 million (US$150 million) on player transfers (an increase of about 10 per cent on the previous season), at the same time receiving £43.425 million (US$65 million) from player sales. Between the end of that season and the start of the 1996–97 season alone, English Premier League clubs spent £45.4 million (US$67 million) on the import of new overseas players. Helping the funding of such deals has been the advance payment of £50 million (US$75 million) from the new Sky Sports television deal, due to start in 1997.[21]

This puts into perspective the earlier figures quoted for the Chinese Premier League and Sichuan Quan Xing club. Whilst it would be foolish to suggest that the financing of soccer in one country is necessarily going to be repeated in another country, escalation has already occurred in the financing of Chinese clubs. That suggests that the effects of professionalisation may not be dissimilar, in kind at least, from country to country. Comparing the total level of transfers in the premier leagues of

China and England, the English Premier League is operating at 330 times the level of China, whilst at club level, the annual salary bill for all the senior players in the Sichuan Quan Xing club would barely cover two weeks wages for Alan Shearer at Newcastle. Such stark comparisons though, should also be a warning that it is soccer in the social setting of China or England that must be considered, if we are to fully understand their meaning and significance.

CONCLUSIONS

- *The transitional nature of sport in China.* Amongst the teams in the top soccer and basketball leagues are six from the armed forces, demonstrating that professionalisation of sport has not exactly followed the western pattern.
- *The rapid pace of change.* Sport is part of the surge in the Chinese economy, which in turn, is part of the economic situation of the 'Pacific rim' countries.
- *The arrival of commercialization.* Companies from within China and beyond are contributing in a major way to the financing of professional sport in the People's Republic, although the government is still a key part of the process. The presence of overseas sponsors in the soccer league is clearly related not only to the huge potential for generating profits directly from sports but to the broader commercial market of China.
- *The adoption of western soccer symbols.* Once wary of influence from outside the country, China now embraces influence from outside its borders (not simply western) but is aware that 'cultural imperialism' can be a double-edged sword. Hence the government's policy phrase, 'socialism with Chinese characteristics'. As professional sport in China grows, its own cultural identity will reflect this, even though western symbols can be seen.
- *Where does Chinese soccer go from here*? This chapter has suggested that sport in China is in a transitional phase. The obvious and immediate objective of the professional soccer league is consolidation – continued investment from sponsors coupled with continued public interest, i.e. media and live support. The future success of the league system may be indicated by the degree to which it attracts outside attention. During spring 1996, Transworld Sport on Channel 4 television in Britain featured Chinese Premier League matches, which is a sign of growing recognition. A further indicator is the inflow of high quality players from other countries, and here, although the numbers are still small, the transfer has begun. The three French players brought into Shanghai Shen Hua in August 1996 have a strong pedigree in the French premier

league over the last five seasons and one of the players, Christian Perez, has at least twenty-two appearances in the French national team, and it would seem only a matter of time before there is an equivalent movement of high quality Chinese players to clubs in the stronger soccer nations around the world.

The Chinese Football Association is aiming for international success, and here, several developments show the way to qualifying for the World Cup finals:

Asian and regional championships
Asian Games
Olympic Games
Invitation international tournaments in China and abroad, at club and national level

The CFA have, in the past, employed coaches from overseas for the national team, but currently the coach is Chinese, as indeed are the coaches in the Premier League. If this continues, there is the possibility of a distinctive Chinese style of soccer emerging, although the globalization of soccer and the exchange of players and coaches internationally may be an inhibiting factor in this respect.

Finally, the future lies with youth. In the long term, the success of Chinese soccer is likely to depend on the development of the junior and youth game, which points to schools, children's and young people's clubs. Here, China is in a strong position to develop the game because of the way in which their sports system is organized, allowing for curriculum development in schools to be planned centrally and for talented youngsters to feed into the existing system of spare time and full-time sports schools. It is notoriously difficult to 'programme success' in soccer, but as one Chinese writer said, 'Surely, out of twelve hundred million people, we can find eleven who can play soccer.'

NOTES

1 The background data for this chapter have been gathered over several field visits to China, spanning nine years. The assistance of Mr Ye Guo Zhi, formerly of the Sichuan Sports Science Institute, in arranging interviews and discussions with key soccer personnel in August 1995, and his contribution to my understanding, have been invaluable in preparing this chapter.
2 Cao Shiyun, 'Looking Back and Pondering on the Rise of Asian Football. Proceedings of the Asian Conference on Comparative Physical Education and Sport', *Journal of Tianjin Institute of Physical Education*, 1995, pp. 178–80.
3 Cao Shiyun, *ibid.*

4 G. Tognoni and A. Herren (eds), World Rankings in *FIFA News*. Monthly publication by FIFA, Hitzigweg 11, 8030 Zurich, Switzerland, December 1994, pp. 5–6 and K. Cooper and A. Herren (eds), News, *FIFA News*, June–July 1996.

5 The general name of the Chinese white spirit made from several grasses is 'bai jiu' but there are many brand names, the most famous being Mao Tai. Quan Xing is the company/brand name of the Sichuan soccer sponsor.

6 Reported in *China News Digest*, 10 March 1996, p. 3.

7 Table compiled from reports in *China News Digest*, over the period 1995–6.

8 Reported in *China News Digest*, 27–8 March 1995, p. 4.

9 Reported in *China News Digest*, 29 April 1996, p. 3.

10 Reported in *China News Digest*, 29 May 1996, p. 2.

11 Author's conversation with Russian canoeing coach, Sichuan, August 1995.

12 Author's discussions with Sichuan Soccer Club officials, August 1995.

13 Under the present situation, China maintains that Taiwan is still a sovereign part of China. In Olympic and World Cup soccer competitions, Taiwan appears as Chinese Taipei, whilst the mainland appears as the People's Republic of China.

14 Reported in *China News Digest*, 13 March 1996, p. 3.

15 Reported in *China News Digest*, 29 March 1995, p. 4.

16 Reported in *China News Digest*, 21 July 1996, p. 1. The money provided by the Chinese government for Olympic success goes directly to the athlete. Other money from sponsors, for example, goes to the particular sports association for distribution to the coach(es) and other key personnel. The *China News Digest* report lists sixteen countries that offer cash rewards to successful Olympic sports people, showing that China offers the third lowest amount. Singapore was top of the list at US$700,000, although it was not clear if this was government money.

17 Reported in *China News Digest*, 1 May 1996, p. 3.

18 Reported in *China News Digest*, 24–5 March 1995, p. 4.

19 Players from outside Japan (1996), Official J-League home page http://www.dentsu.co.jp:80/J-LEAGUE/index.html

20 Deloitte and Touche, *Annual Review of Football Finance*, Deloitte and Touche, Accountants, London, August 1996.

21 Reported in the *Daily Telegraph*, 16 August 1996, p. 34 and p. 40.

Chapter 10

China and the Olympic movement

Hai Ren

INTRODUCTION

There is, perhaps, no other term related to sport with greater popularity in China than 'Olympic'; no other cultural term is better known. The Olympic Games are watched by a vast television audience; Olympic champions are treated as national heroes, entertained with luxurious banquets, hosted by the State Council and attended by state leaders. IOC members, especially its president, are welcomed like royalty and the Olympic Games are extensively covered on television, in newspapers and magazines. Olympic Day (23 June) is celebrated by a large group of runners wearing T-shirts with the Olympic rings on them, and a mass bicycle rally, organized under the name of the IOC president, attracts a million cyclists annually. The Olympic Games are a frequent topic of conversation, and it is no exaggeration to say that the word 'Olympic' has penetrated every corner of society. It seems strange that an oriental country with a long Confucian heritage should demonstrate such an enthusiastic affection for a sport phenomenon originating in the West which has much closer historical links with the Olympic movement.

Historical background of Olympic diffusion in China

China's attitude towards the Olympics is rooted in events from the middle of the nineteenth century.

Social dimension

Prior to the Opium War (1840–2), the social pattern in China was mainly feudal. Ruled by the Qin royal court, the last feudal dynasty followed precedents whose origins date back to the third century BC. Feudal society was highly centralized politically, with all power concentrated in one person, the emperor. In contrast, the country's economy tended to be decentralized, with thousands of small farmsteads locked in a cycle of 'husband tilling and wife weaving'.

The Opium War interrupted the static social position of the feudal dynasty and was followed by a series of unprecedented events that resulted in such 'unequal' treaties as the Sino-British Treaty of Nanjing (1842), the Sino-American Treaty of Wangxia (1844), the Sino-French Treaty of Huangpu and Sino-French War (1884–5), the Sino-Japanese War (1894–5) and Treaty of Shimonoseki. Relying on powerful gunboats and privileges enshrined in the treaties, the western powers gradually established their dominance over China and turned the once independent country into a country with semi-colonial status.

So the most urgent task for China since that time has been national salvation, that is, to free the country from the danger of partition by foreign powers and to save it from any exploitative government. A strong national patriotism was invoked by events of the nineteenth century. There was disappointment with the conservative and corrupt Qing court and fear of collapse of the once mighty nation, so patriotism became the underlying theme of the dynamic process of the next 150 years.

Sport dimension

Before the Opium War, the dominant forms of sporting activities in rural agrarian China were traditional, mainly *wushu* (martial arts), *Qigong* (a popular form of breathing exercises) and a variety of other folk activities. These traditional physical activities focused more on enjoyment than competition, more on moral cultivation than physical development, more on the consumption of scarce leisure time rather than material gain. The absence of competition in traditional Chinese activities resulted in few standardized rules and great diversity of form and pattern.

After the war, China recognized its military weakness and updated physical training in order to strengthen the military forces. Thus, under the guidance of foreign instructors, military gymnastics was introduced to the army and navy in the period 1869–90, which marked the first stage in the modernization of China's sport. This 'westernization' movement also launched education reforms, setting up schools with a western curriculum, employing foreigners as instructors for military and normal gymnastics, vaulting, exercises on parallel and horizontal bars, fencing, boxing, weight-lifting, football, hurdling, race walking carrying a weighted load, long jump and high jump, stick climbing, swimming, and skating. In the period after 1872, students were also sent abroad to study in England, France, Germany, the United States and Japan, and their experiences of physical education and sport enabled them to play a considerable role in spreading western sports in China when they returned home.

Almost at the same time, schools established by missionaries, especially those from the YMCA, were introducing sport activities as part of their educational programmes. A competition, mainly for athletics, was held in 1890 at St John School, sponsored by the Christian Church. This was the first competitive sports event. Athletics accompanied the spread of church schools during the early twentieth century. In 1910, the first National Games, with athletics as the core of the programme, were held. However, until 1919, sport was principally confined to schools, and sports competitions were mainly organized between schools and monopolized by male students.

Review of the development of the Olympic movement in China

Inititial involvement (1920s–49)

China's involvement in the Olympic movement can be traced back as early as 1922, when Mr Wang Zhenting, a high ranking diplomat and sports leader, was selected as the first Chinese member of the IOC. But the Olympic Games attracted little serious attention from China, mainly because the nation was engaged in other, more urgent tasks to survive the threat from foreign powers. However, although the formal organizational link between China and the IOC was established, recognition of the key Chinese sport organization, the Chinese Society for Sport Promotion, as the national Olympic body, came much later, in 1931. In 1928, when the Ninth Summer Olympic Games were held at Amsterdam, China sent only an observer to the Games, Sun Ruhai.

In 1932, China initially did not intend sending competitors to the Games in Los Angeles, instead planning to send an observer, Sheng Sitong, as before. However, as rumour spread that the puppet state installed by Japan after their occuption of north-east China (renamed Manchuguo) was trying to send a sport delegation to the Olympics, which would have been a great embarrassment to China, a small Chinese sport delegation was hurriedly made up, comprising five members. The group had only one athlete, the sprinter Liu Changchun, and he was disqualified in the preliminary heats. All the same, this was the debut of Chinese athletes in the Olympic arena.

Four years later, in 1936, the Eleventh Olympic Games were staged in Berlin under the Nazi regime. China sent a sports delegation numbering sixty-nine athletes in the following events: football, basketball, boxing, weightlifting, athletics, swimming, cycling and *wushu* (the traditional martial arts), and an additional observer group comprising thirty-four members. The poor performances of the Chinese athletes at the Games revealed that a big gap existed, not only between China and western nations, but also between China and Japan. However, the *wushu* demonstration drew extensive attention and was warmly welcomed.

In London, when the Olympic Games of 1948 were restored after the

Second World War, thirty-three Chinese athletes – in basketball, football, track and field, swimming and cycling – participated in the Games, but they did no better than the team twelve years previously and won no medals. What made things worse was that when the Games ended, the delegation found themselves unable to pay for their return journey, so they had to send a telegram back to the government for assistance, only to be told that they would have to solve the problem themselves. The delegation was thus obliged to raise the money to return home.

Controversy (1949–79)

With the establishment of the People's Republic of China in 1949, a new era began in Chinese history and with it started a controversial period in the relationship between the IOC and China over the issue of China's seat on the International Olympic Committee. The IOC, led by its president at the time, Avery Brundage, decided to recognize the National Olympic Committees of both China and Taiwan, thus violating the Olympic Charter, which allowed for only one NOC per country. Thus, the serious issue of 'two Chinas' was created. In protest, the Chinese Olympic Committee suspended its membership of the IOC in 1958, which was unfortunate both for sport in China and the Olympic movement.

After twenty years of controversy and negotiation, the IOC, under Lord Killanin's leadership, finally recognized the legitimate seat of the Chinese Olympic Committee at the IOC session in Nagoya, Japan, in November 1979, with sixty votes for, seventeen against and two abstentions. The resulting resolution stipulated that the name of the Olympic Committee of the People's Republic of China would be the 'Chinese Olympic Committee' and that the national flag and anthem of the People's Republic of China would be used in all ceremonies. Further, the name of the Olympic Committee in Taiwan would be the 'Chinese Taipei Olympic Committee' and the flag, anthem and emblem formerly used by them would not be used in the future. Referred to as the 'Olympic Model' in China, the resolution provided athletes in Taiwan and mainland China with opportunities for competition in the same Olympic arena, symbolically, as brothers and sisters of one motherland. It was also, in a sense, an early sign of the 'One country, two systems' policy, proposed by Deng Xiaoping, and quickly opened the doors of other international sports for Chinese athletes. Now, with a broad programme of international sport, China is faced with the challenge of rapidly improving performances to catch up with other world sport powers. International competitive sports are cultural symbols closely related to the image of a nation. Although the IOC insists that the Olympic Games are competitions among individual athletes rather than countries, all the rituals of the Games, especially the medal awarding ceremonies, obviously intensify national awareness and highlight national image. Major international sport events, in a sense, may thus logically be viewed as competitions among nations. Taking into account the humiliating experiences at the hands of foreign powers in its modern history, China has been eager for success in international sport, and in particular its Olympic effort has had a significant impact on its sport policies and management.

Before 1979, hardly any serious study related to the Olympics had been carried out in China, and during this period of nearly thirty years, only thirty-three articles were published on the Olympics, with two-thirds of them being translations. The fact that the Olympics were so little studied may be attributed to the abnormal relations between China and the IOC, and later the Cultural Revolution, which was a social disaster that isolated China from the outside world and impeded international exchanges involving Chinese sport.

New era (1979–88)

A significant turning point was reached with China's return to the international Olympic family in 1979. During the 1980s, a developmental strategy for sport was proposed by the National Sport Commission; it attempted to balance the requirements of high level sport with sport for all. Notwithstanding, competitive sports in China have been orientated towards Olympic glory, and steps were taken to revamp the sports programme of the National Games in line with Olympic events, with the exception of *wushu*, one of the traditional sports. The National Games are the most important domestic sports meet, organized in a four-year cycle, and bring together athletes from all provinces, autonomous regions and trade unions. In this way the National Games actually serve as preparation for the Olympics. This policy did produce positive results in terms of China's performances at the Olympic Games, as Table 10.1 shows, but it also brought a degree of negative influence on those non-Olympic events and team sports, such as football, basketball and volleyball, which may be deemed to be less medal-intensive.

Because of a lack of knowledge of the Olympic movement amongst both the general public and sport specialists, most newspapers and articles focused on a historical description of the Olympics, with the exception of a few studies concerning professionalization and women's participation in the Olympics Games.

The success achieved by the Chinese team in the 23rd Summer Olympics in Los Angeles in 1984 stimulated a great deal of Olympic enthusiasm in China.

Further development (1989 onwards)

After the 24th Olympic Games, the development of the Olympic movement in China entered a new stage, mainly for the following reasons. First, the disappointing performance of the Chinese team at the Seoul Olympics,

Table 10.1 Summary of China's participation in the 23rd, 24th, 25th and 26th Olympic Games

Year	No.	Venue	Participants	Events competed	Medals won
1984 28 July to 12 August	23rd	Los Angeles (United States)	304 (224 athletes)	Basketball, volleyball, handball, athletics, gymnastics, swimming, weightlifting, shooting, archery, fencing, wrestling, judo, cycling, rowing, canoeing, yachting, tennis	15 gold 8 silver 9 bronze
1988 17 September to 2 October	24th	Seoul (South Korea)	445 (298 athletes)	Athletics, swimming, gymnastics, basketball, volleyball, soccer, table tennis, tennis, handball, shooting, archery, weightlifting, wrestling, judo, boxing, fencing, modern pentathlon, cycling, rowing, canoeing, yachting, badminton (demonstration), women's judo (demonstration)	5 gold 11 silver 12 bronze
1992 25 July to 9 August	25th	Barcelona (Spain)	380 (250 athletes)	Athletics, cycling, swimming, judo, wrestling, badminton, archery, basketball, boxing, canoeing, gymnastics, tennis, table tennis, rowing, fencing, shooting, volleyball, yachting, weightlifting, modern pentathlon	16 gold 22 silver 16 bronze
1996 August	26th	Atlanta (US)	495 (310 athletes)	Athletics, cycling, swimming, judo, wrestling, badminton, archery, basketball, boxing, canoeing, gymnastics, tennis, table tennis, rowing, fencing, shooting, volleyball, yachting, weightlifting, softball, handball, football	16 gold 22 silver 12 bronze

compared to the excellent results they had achieved four years earlier in Los Angeles, stimulated much debate on the value of Olympic gold metals. Second, the hosting of the 11th Asian Games in 1990 was the first time China had organized such a large international competition, and no efforts were spared to ensure its success. The Asian Games sparked great public interest in international sporting issues, including the Olympics. Nevertheless, no matter how important was the influence of these two events on Olympic studies in China, they could not match the impact generated by Beijing's bid for the 2000 Olympic Games.

Bidding for the 2000 Olympic Games

At midnight on 23 September 1993, millions of Chinese were waiting in front of their televisions for the result of the voting by the IOC 101st session on the host city for the 2000 Olympic Games. When IOC president Samaranch announced that it was Sydney instead of Beijing, many Chinese were upset. It was understandable, since they had enthusiastically hoped for positive news. A survey carried out by the Beijing Statistical Bureau of 10,000 city residents showed 98.7 per cent support for the city's bid. The Beijing 2000 Olympic Games Bid Committee, set up on 1 April 1991, comprised staff mainly from the National Sport Commission and the Beijing municipal government, and for two years they had held a series of campaigns, including popularization of Olympic history. Although the bid itself was unsuccessful, it did educate the public in the Olympic movement, Olympism and, of course, the Olympic Games.

Beijing's bid was the largest campaign to spread Olympic information in China's history. As a result, academic study of the Olympic movement attracted increasing attention as an emerging field of sport science. Olympic studies are now offered as a subject in some physical educational institutions; a university-based Olympic studies centre has been formed; various reading materials have been written, such as *Olympic Encyclopedia* and *Olympic Mass Readings* for the general public, *Olympic Stories* for elementary school students, *Olympic Knowledge* for secondary students, and *Olympic Movement* as a textbook for university students. It is no exaggeration to say that Olympic study has become one of the focal points of sport in China. Figure 10.1 shows the ratio between research papers and the introductory articles relating to Olympic topics in three periods, indicating that research papers have increased rapidly.

With more attention now being given to Olympic study, the scope of the academic area has also expanded, and certain issues, such as Olympic philosophies, organizational structures, operational mechanisms and Olympic problems, have been researched. Table 10.2 compares the content of Olympic studies in China in three time periods.

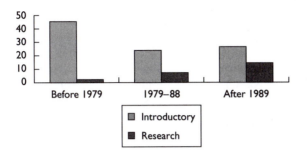

Figure 10.1 Comparison of research papers and introductory articles

Table 10.2 Content change of Olympic studies in China in different periods

Time	Content
1984	Professionalization, Women and sport
1989	Olympic ideals, Olympic studies, the Olympic Movement and economics, Olympics and education, Women and sport, Professionalization
1992	Olympic philosophy, Olympics and society, Olympics and culture, Olympic issues (commercialization, professionalization and political interference, etc.)

Future trends

Structural reorganization of sport

China's participation in the Olympics has been based on a strong, multi-level sport training system directly supported and organized by the government, mainly through the Sport Commission at local, provincial and national levels. The system has concentrated the country's relatively scarce sports resources on international competition. However, the shift from a planned economy to a market economy has seen corresponding changes to sports organizations. All formal administrative agencies for sports events have now been separated from the Sports Commission (which itself has been restructured as a Sport Bureau) and twenty sport event administrative centres have been formed to run affairs relating to their particular sports, including top-level training, competitions and mass sport participation. At this stage, strong government support is still available, but the centres are being encouraged to develop their own programmes and financial resources, assuming the roles of decision maker and co-ordinator, as the government reduces its direct involvement. This change of organizational structure will in the long run strengthen the basis of China's Olympic participation.

Linking high performance sport to mass sport

Although China has tried to harmonize its high performance sport and mass sport participation, in reality in the quest for Olympic glory, more emphasis has been put on Olympic effort, whilst mass sport has lagged behind. Since the mid-1990s, a new attempt has been made to bridge the gap, the most striking measure being the National Fitness Promotion Programme, launched on 20 June 1995 by the State Council. It has now been adopted by all provinces in China and is expected to redress the previous over-emphasis on competitive sport.

Integrating Chinese culture and the Olympic movement

The Olympic movement is not merely a set of highly standardized sport competitions, it is also a synthesis of complex cultural patterns and forms – in education, philosophy, morality and behaviour, which may or may not differ from Chinese culture. By trying to combine Olympic ideals with traditional ethics in moral education in universities, some Chinese scholars have attempted to find connecting points between the Olympic movement and Chinese sport culture.

China's potential contribution to the Olympic movement

The over-emphasis on winning, drug abuse, lack of democracy in sport management, commercialization, professionalization, Olympic gigantism, political interference and so on, are all problems that might suggest that the Olympics are seeking extrinsic ends instead of the intrinsic value of harmonious human development, as Olympism declares. This has concerned many scholars around the world, and it is clear that the Olympic movement is entering a crucial period towards the end of the twentieth century, and as the twenty-first century begins.

Of all the problems faced by the Olympics, two in particular stand out, namely, western ethnocentrism and the conflict between sport commercialization and the Olympic ideal. These two issues hold profound consequences for the Olympic movement.

Western ethnocentrism

The Olympic movement originated in the West, but today it has developed into a worldwide movement. However, the movement remains dominated by western culture, as shown by the lack of non-western sport in the Olympic programme, of non-western cities as Olympic hosts, and of non-western sports leaders in the international sports organizations.

Historically, western culture is rooted in Ancient Greek civilization, but the values of today's industrial society are associated with fair play, striving to be best, pursuance of truth, individual liberty and so on. It is exactly these qualities in western culture, with the powerful support of the material base accumulated in the Industrial Revolution, that have spread all over the world and become the dominant form of contemporary society. However, western culture has its own inherent shortcomings for the Olympic movement.

Materialism-oriented values

Industrial society tends to give prominence to the pursuit of material goods. The widespread materialism in western culture has placed material wealth above spiritual well-being, external rewards over internal ones, and physical gains over human values.

Emphasis on 'outcome' and neglect of 'process'

Being part of western culture, modern sports readily adopted the dominant material values and, in the sports arena, tremendous emphasis has been put on the outcome of sport competitions, namely, win or lose, whilst the process of competitions or games themselves is neglected. It indicates alienation of sport from its intrinsic values because the educational and cultural values of sport mainly lie in the process of competitions or games, not their outcomes. This value judgement of sport has inevitably diminished the educational and cultural worth of athletes.

Athletes as 'means' instead of 'ends'

Following the above, neither industrial society nor modern sport would regard the sound development of athletes as the ultimate end of sport. Instead, athletes are treated merely as a means for economic or political and other external ends.

Because athletes' sporting skills and physical prowess are the most useful parts of these external objectives, industrial society attempts to focus only on these aspects, which would inevitably lead to unbalanced development between the physical and mental aspects of athletes, as Baron de Coubertin realized 100 years ago.

Conflict between sport commercialization and Olympic ideals

Commercialization has become a powerful trend in contemporary society, and is inherently apt to stress tangible values, material gains, and monetary benefits, whilst denying intangible values such as morality, ethics and those upheld by Olympism. Obviously a serious conflict between the tangible and the intangible may occur, and evidence indicates that commercialization has had some negative impact on athletes, coaches and referees. Linked with commercialization, directly or indirectly, are the serious problems in today's sports world of corruption, bribery, cheating, drug abuse and so on.

However, it would be too simple and naive to keep the Olympics separate from commercialization, in order simply to maintain their 'pure and noble' goals. As a worldwide social and cultural phenomenon, it seems inevitable that the Olympic movement should attract commercialization; the two may even be mutually beneficial, posing the question not whether commercialization should be involved in sport, but how to use it. Unfortunately, a proper way for handling these two does not seem to have been worked out yet, though various attempts have been made.

According to the Olympic Charter, 'the goal of Olympism is to place sport at the service of the harmonious development of man', but the concept of harmonious development is itself complex, involving development of the individual, the individual and society, and the individual in the natural environment. Obviously, Olympism sets itself very difficult goals, and raising interest in sport is one means by which Olympism may reach them. Having noted the shortcomings of modern sport, it is perhaps doubtful whether we can reach such high and noble goals through current sport practices. Considering that the problems of high performance sports are mainly rooted in western culture, the Olympic movement could enrich itself with new blood from other cultures and in this respect Chinese culture may deserve attention.

The potential contribution of Chinese culture to the Olympic movement

A striking feature of Chinese culture that is particularly useful to the Olympics is its stress on harmony. According to Chinese philosophies, harmony is a basic feature of the formation of the perfect world, as the master of Taoist teaching, Lao Zi, states: 'Both Yin and Yang are unified through harmony in the invisible breath.'[1] A Confucian classical work, *Doctrine of the Mean*, also called harmony of 'the universal path'.[2] Moreover, Confucius claimed that 'In practising the rule of propriety, harmony is more important'[3] and Confucian scholars regarded harmony as 'the highest virtue'.[4]

Based on such philosophies, Chinese culture stresses the following:

1   With regard to the relationship between an individual and society, it emphasizes the collective spirit rather than individualism.
2   In terms of the relationship between society and the natural environment, it emphasizes following the natural way to integrate human beings into the natural world.

These characteristics may possibly help to compensate for the excesses of western culture and some shortcomings of the Olympic movement. For example:

- emphasis on the mental and moral aspects in comparison with the physical may strengthen the Olympic ideal which is so essential to the Olympics;
- emphasis on internal body training may counterbalance the external body training stressed in western sport;
- emphasis on the 'process' of sport may help to set up a healthy relationship with the 'outcome' of sport and make people take a more reasonable attitude towards winning and losing;
- emphasis on a harmonious relationship with the natural world may help the Olympic host cities take more care over ecological problems when planning and building sports facilities.

A new trend may gradually be taking shape, as human society enters a new century, suggesting that China will contribute more to the Olympics in the next century. This is not only because Chinese culture may compensate the Olympics, not only because China is the world's largest country, but also because the social conditions for China contributing more to the Olympic movement are improving, following reforms over the last twenty years. A long history of 5,000 years has endowed China with a unique cultural heritage, interwoven with Confucianism, Taoism, Buddhism and traditional medical theories. It will be interesting to see how the practice and theories of Chinese sport will contribute to the Olympic movement in the future.

NOTES

1 *The Book of Lao Zi*, Beijing, Foreign Language Press, 1993.
2 *The Document of the Mean*, Changsha, Hunan Press, 1992.
3 *The Confucian Analects*, Changsha, Hunan Press, 1992.
4 Dong Zhongshu, Chun Qiu Fan Luo, in *Selections from Chinese Philosophy*, Beijing, Chinese Press, 1984.

Chapter 11

Sports science

Dennis Whitby

As a technical consultant with China's national track and field team from 1984 until 1986, the author was able to visit a number of research institutes of sports science. Extracts contain comments that were recorded during this period. First of all, a description is given of the sports science system. At the apex of the pyramid of research institutes are the National Research Institute of Sports Science and the National Research Institute of Sports Medicine, both based in Beijing.

NATIONAL RESEARCH INSTITUTE OF SPORTS SCIENCE

The National Research Institute of Sports Science (NRISS) is situated in Tiyuguan Lu (Sports Hall Road). The major role of the institute, founded in 1958, is to provide sports science support for the eleven national teams that train in the National Training Centre (NTC) across the road. Services also include medical supervision of national team members, treatment of injuries and the provision of postgraduate education.

The author has visited the NRISS on two occasions. Observations that were recorded following a guided tour of the institute in 1984 with then-director Wang Ruying follow. Most of the information included in this section, however, has been updated as a result of a second visit to the institute in May 1995 when a delegation from the Hong Kong Sports Institute (HKSI) visited Beijing. On that occasion, a meeting was held with Director Zhao Bingpu, Vice-Directors Gao Da'An and Cao Wenyuan, and a number of departmental heads.

The NRISS currently employs more than 250 people, including research professors, associate research professors, and scientific and technological researchers, in ten departments. The athletic training department works with coaches in gymnastics, swimming and track and field. At the time of my first visit to the NRISS in 1984, and according to the official guidebook, the department – then the training science department – had taken part in studies of 'the morphological features and physical qualities of Chinese elite athletes, the results of which have provided a scientific basis for the training and identification and training of potential athletes'.

Of the eighteen staff members, four had qualified in the Soviet Union and a fifth was currently studying at the German Sports Institute in Cologne. Eight departmental members work in track and field; two, including the departmental head, work with my own group of athletes at the NTC. The area appears to have great potential in its attempts to link theory with practice. Studies in the field of gymnastics, in particular, have clearly contributed to improved performances at the highest level.

Today, the twelve members of the department work with coaches on a two-year cycle of development, aiming at either the Asian Games or the Olympic Games. The department's major tasks are to study athletic training theory, develop scientific training methodology for elite athletes, improve sport techniques and methods of technique development and selection. Coaches propose different areas for research each year. Individual athletes are often targeted for analysis. Certain areas for study require co-operation between different functional units. Data are provided for the coach and, later, summarized in the form of a thesis.

The ball games training department provides assistance to three sports – soccer, table tennis and volleyball. Basketball was also supported at the time of the author's visit in 1984 but has since been dropped. Nine training scientists and one technician, all holding master's degrees, currently work with the sports – three with table tennis, four with soccer (two with the men's team and two with the women's team) and two with volleyball.

Valuable insight into the work of the department was provided during our visit in 1995 by Associate Professor Qin Zhifeng, a training scientist who had worked with the national table tennis team for ten years. His role is to assist with preparations for either the Asian or Olympic Games. The coach first highlights areas that require investigation. A discussion paper is then considered by the institute's scientific research management department and the president of the institute decides whether to submit the paper to the State Physical Culture and Sports Commission. The Commission makes the final decision on which research should proceed. The training scientist's work in table tennis covers four areas: the technical evaluation of opposing players; the provision of tactical information; basic research in areas such as spin, speed and service; and research into different styles of play.

Information concerning opponents is summarized and given to the head coach. A written paper on each opponent is prepared and updated every two years. Players attend lectures during which individual opponents are discussed and observed on video. Based on the information provided, training programmes can be developed or modified. Assimilated training is often used with a fellow team player in the role of opponent. The department first conducted an analysis of Hong Kong's players in 1992. This detailed attention goes a long way towards explaining Chinese table tennis success. The team won all seven gold medals at the World Championships, held in Tianjin in May 1995.

In 1984, the sports biomechanics department, established two years before, had undertaken an analysis of various techniques used in gymnastics, skating, track and field and weightlifting. Anthropometrical data had also been collected from 5,000 elite athletes in the four sports and from youths and children of different ages. In a laboratory, a technician was analysing a weightlifter's movements using a film motion analyser and mini-computer. Apparently, this equipment, imported from Japan, was the latest available. The department now has a total of seventeen staff-members and reacts to enquiries from individual coaches, providing them with data to assist them with technical analysis, evaluation and problem-solving. Data are released immediately to coaches.

The sports medicine department was visited in 1984 and recorded in the following way:

> Fifteen members of the department hold medical degrees. Another six staff members hold graduate degrees in various areas of physical education; four of the six studied in the Soviet Union. Another seven staff members have other postgraduate study experience.
>
> There are laboratories for animal experiments, biochemistry, cardiac function evaluation, ECGs, EEGs, histology and pathology, physiotherapy, ultrasonic cardiograms and X-rays. A sports medicine clinic is attached to the department.
>
> Areas of research include overtraining and the evaluation of physiological function in athletes subjected to heavy load training and intense competitions. Members of the medical supervision group are assigned to work with national teams. Two medical doctors from the department, Dr Wu Zhennie and Dr Wang Yigin, worked with my own group of athletes.
>
> My guided tour took me to eight laboratories in the department. In one, members of the sports injuries group were tending a number of outpatients. In another laboratory, a cyclist on the national team was receiving treatment for injuries suffered during a fall. In a third laboratory, a swimmer, sitting in an adjacent darkened room with her head covered with electrodes, was undergoing an EEG examination; a technician and graduate student were collecting and analysing the data using a computer. At one point, the swimmer was asked to hyperventilate. The doctor in charge informed me that EEGs are used to monitor overtraining, the effects of high-altitude exercise and the extent of head injuries.

In another laboratory, I watched a technician preserve and mount slivers of heart muscle taken from a mouse for microscopic analysis.

In April 1996, Dr Guoping Li, Chairman of the Sports Medicine Department at the NRISS, provided the following information concerning the work of the department today:

The department is the largest in the institute with a total of thirty-three staff members, including seven research professors, ten associate professors and ten lecturers. The majority are qualified medical doctors. The department operates in three areas:

- Medical supervision

  - diagnosis and exclusion of pathological conditions in sports participants such as congenital heart diseases, heart murmurs, etc.;
  - medical consultation for elite athletes in a variety of physical activities;
  - functional evaluation of physical work capacity of elite athletes, including cardiovascular and nervous functions;
  - determination of aerobic and anaerobic metabolic capacity;
  - prevention and treatment of overtraining and fatigue; and
  - facilitation of local and general recovery.

Many research projects regarding the medical aspects of training have been conducted in areas such as altitude training, overtraining syndrome, exercise related *arrhythmia*, etc.

- Sports injuries

  - an outpatient clinic is open to athletes and local residents suffering from sports injuries; these are treated mainly with Chinese traditional medicine, such as Tuina (manipulation), acupuncture, ear pressure and Chinese herbs.

Research in this area has mainly focused on the mechanism of some injuries to the knee, wrist, vertebrae and spinal cord, using animal models with biomechanical techniques.

- Histopathology, including

  - clinical and experimental pathology, sports injuries and diseases of skeletal muscle, tendons and insertions;

- studies of the athlete's heart;
- use of muscle biopsy for the analysis of muscle types for the purpose of talent identification.

The sports physiology department was visited in 1984, and the author's reservation were as follows:

> According to the official guidebook, the department is concerned with 'studies of aerobic and anaerobic metabolic capabilities, cardiovascular function, neuromuscular efficiency, and haematological and urinary systems in elite athletes.
>
> The department has four laboratories – biochemistry, neuromuscular function, gas exchange and metabolism, and respiration and circulation.
>
> In the biochemistry laboratory, a doctor explained that the work was primarily concerned with the effects of loading (intensity and duration) and the length of resting interval upon lactic acid concentration and pH levels. Research has been conducted on both distance runners and swimmers. The doctor showed me some of the equipment in the laboratory, including a Hitachi spectrophotometer, a radiometer from Denmark and two spectrophotometers made in China.
>
> In the neuromuscular function laboratory, another medical doctor was conducting research into muscle stiffness induced by exercise. Following the electrical stimulation of one of its hind legs, blood samples were drawn from the ear of an anaesthetized rabbit. The sample was then analysed for electromyoscopic changes and changes in the level of lactic acid.

Today, the department employs three exercise physiologists and five biochemists. Their work is separated into basic research and athletic science research. The latter involves research in areas such as biochemical changes during exercise, nutrition, the effects of Chinese herbs on recovery and training intensity and fatigue. Staff react to requests from individual coaches. Specific problems may be investigated through the use of animal research.

In 1984, according to the official guidebook of the NRISS, the main task of the mass sports department was 'to provide scientific bases for promoting sports on a massive scale so as to improve the people's fitness'. The guidebook indicated that the department had carried out research on spare-time training in factories, mines, enterprises, villages and schools. At the same time, Director Wang Ruying had identified physical culture in schools and physical fitness as the two major areas of concentration.

The department continues to engage in research in a number of areas, including sport in schools, workers' sports, farmers' sports, training and fitness of youth and children, broadcast exercises, National Physical Training

Standards, group calisthenics, rhythmic gymnastics and medical gymnastics. Award-winning studies have included 'A General Survey of the Anthropometrical, Physiological Characteristics and Physical Fitness of Chinese Children and Youth' and 'A Survey of the Physical Fitness and Health of Chinese Students in 1985'. The former involved testing 183,424 students and pupils, ranging from 7 to 25 years of age on twenty-three items of physical fitness in sixteen cities and provinces. Between 1985 and 1987, the department worked with Japanese sports scientists to produce a co-operative study on the physical fitness of children and youth.

Three new departments have been added to the institute since 1984.

- The sports theory department established in 1987, performs research on basic sports theories and conducts general surveys on competitive sports. A typical study was entitled 'Prediction of Chinese and World Track and Field Records by 2000 and China's Strategy for the Challenge'.
- The central laboratory also established in 1987, performs functional evaluations (cardio-pulmonary function, aerobic and anaerobic capability and muscular strength) of elite athletes.
- The sports psychology department was established in 1991. Until then, a sports psychology section had operated within the ball games training department. Today, the department has six staff, consisting of one associate professor, three assistant professors and two technicians. The department combines consultations and mental training for individual athletes with research. The department is currently planning to study aspects of teenagers' mental health and to use results from psychological tests to establish a data bank on China's top athletes.

The tenth and final department of the NRISS is the sports instrument department which designs, produces and maintains electronic sports instruments.

The NRISS also housed a sports information and documentation department. In 1987, however, the department was moved into an adjacent building to become the China Sports Information Institute.

Degree programmes

In 1980, the NRISS started three-year graduate programmes in biomechanics, exercise physiology, sports information, sports medicine and training science. By 1984, six students had already received master's degrees; another eleven students were registered. During the first eighteen months, the students attended classes at the Beijing Institute of Physical Education (BIPE), now the Beijing University of Physical Education. The students then transferred back to the NRISS to undertake research for an additional eighteen months.

The same degree programmes are offered by the institute today, with the exception of sports information. A doctoral programme in biomechanics is now jointly organized with the Shanghai Institute of Physical Education.

The coach–scientist link

During the visit of the HKSI delegation to the NRISS in 1995, Zhao Bingpu, Director of the Institute, explained that communication between sports scientists at the NRISS and coaches at the NTC was not particularly good. He expressed the belief that the sports scientists must educate the coaches concerning the potential uses of sports science research in performance enhancement. Some coaches do, however, provide ideas for research.

Working within the system

From 1984 to 1986, the author spent two years coaching with the national track and field team at the NTC in Tiyuguan Lu. During his first six-month contract – from January to June 1984 – he worked with a support group of sports scientists and medical doctors from the NRISS. The following observations were recorded:

> Six staff members of the NRISS – two biomechanists, two training-science specialists and two medical doctors – were assigned to work with the track and field group of four coaches and eleven athletes. One of the two biomechanists, Li Chengzhi, had already undertaken some research using the athletes. Mr Li studied biomechanics in the United States for two years and had previously conducted a comparative study of Chinese and American sprinters. The second biomechanist, Huang Zhongcheng, was head of the biomechanics department. He had received his degree in biomechanics in China while studying under a Russian advisor in the 1950s. At my request, Mr Huang undertook a comparison of the sprinting action in normal race conditions and in training with the stride length regulated.
>
> The two training scientists were Tang Li, head of the training science department, and Li Qing. Ms Tang had studied in the Soviet Union for four years in the 1950s. Li Qing was a graduate of the BIPE. He left Beijing with another training scientist from the NRISS in 1986 to study for eighteen months in Mainz, West Germany.
>
> The two medical doctors were members of the medical supervision group in the sports medicine department. Dr Wang Yiqing had received her medical degree from Shenyang, Liaoning province, and had previously studied medical aspects of mountaineering. Dr Wang was also working with the national swimming squad. Dr Wu Zhenmei had received her degree from Dalian Medical University, also in Liaoning

province, and had worked at the NRISS since the institute was established in 1958.

Each day, the two doctors measured the protein concentration of each athlete's urine; this was used as a stress indicator. Each athlete was also subjected to a series of tests every Saturday, including EEGs, ECGs (if necessary) and the measurement of blood pressure. Blood tests were taken immediately after each race during the indoor season.

During the author's second contractual period in Beijing, the amount of contact with the NRISS was reduced. At the end of February, however, the training scientists administered strength tests to the athletes at the author's request. In addition, the doctors continued to screen the athletes on a weekly basis and to take blood samples after competition. During this period, incidentally, the men's group was assisted by Gao Da'An, one of China's legion of West German-educated training scientists, who is now a Vice-Director at the NRISS.

NATIONAL RESEARCH INSTITUTE OF SPORTS MEDICINE

The National Research Institute of Sports Medicine (NRISM) was established in 1987. The Institute, located in the National Olympic Sports Centre, serves as the National Test and Research Centre for Doping and Sports Nutrition. The Doping Control Centre was established in 1989 as the third IOC-accredited laboratory in Asia (after Seoul and Tokyo). The centre has since successfully passed the annual reaccreditation test and had, in fact, passed the most recent test in the mid-1990s. Since the 1990 Asian Games, the centre has assisted a number of Asian countries in establishing testing programmes and has organized technical courses for doping personnel in North Korea, India, Indonesia and Taiwan. The centre employs twenty-six staff members. All are university graduates who are engaged in chemical or pharmaceutical analysis. The centre has three departments: diuretics, nitrogen containing substances (stimulants, narcotics and beta-blockers) and steroids. The instruments and equipment used in sample analysis are manufactured by China Hewlett-Packard Company which services the equipment at no charge.

The sports nutrition centre was also established in 1989 and now employs twenty-five staff members in four departments – nutrition and biochemistry, physiology, food production and animal experiment – and has laboratories for animal experiments, immunology, nutritional biochemistry, physiology and the manufacture of food products.

Following the doping scandal at the 1994 Asian Games, and in an attempt to counter the threat of drugs, more emphasis is to be put on sports nutrition because of the obvious beneficial effects for both health and performance.

Advice on nutrition is provided by the centre to national teams who train at the National Olympic Sports Centre; as noted previously, the NRISS provides nutritional advice to the national teams based at the NTC. Athletes also undergo physiological and biochemical testing and are counselled on specific problems such as anaemia, and training and competing in a hot climate.

The NRISM offers master's degree programmes in nutrition, exercise physiology and doping control. The institute hopes to introduce doctoral degree courses in doping control and sports nutrition in the near future.

PROVINCIAL RESEARCH INSTITUTES OF SPORTS SCIENCE

In terms of elite sports, the majority of the country's sports scientists are employed at research institutes of sports science that are administered by provincial physical culture and sports commissions. Every province, with the exception of Hainan and Tibet, has an institute. With the exception of Sichuan, each institute of sports science includes a department of sports medicine; only Sichuan has a separate institute of sports medicine – the National Research Institute of Sports Traumatology in Chengdu. Some provinces, including Guangdong (in Guangzhou), Liaoning (Shenyang) and Sichuan (Chengdu), also have institutes of sports science in their capital cities.

The Jiangsu Research Institute of Sports Science (JRISS) is situated on the campus of the Nanjing Institute of Physical Education (NIPE). The institute was established in 1978 but the institute's building was first occupied, and the staff appointed, in 1983.

In 1985, according to Chen Zhongyuan, the institute's director, while the NRISS and the Shanghai Research Institute of Sports Science are mainly involved in research which is not always transferable to the practical situation, the aim of most provincial research institutes is to perform applied research.

In general, the staff of the JRISS lack the higher academic qualifications and experience of researchers at the NRISS. Of thirty staff members, only five have master's degrees conferred by Chinese universities. The remainder hold bachelor's degrees, or the equivalent.

Director Chen, himself, is a former track and field coach. He started his career studying at the Nanjing Medical School before transferring to Beijing to train as a high jumper with the national team. On retirement, Director Chen coached with the Jiangsu team. His appointment as director, he thought, was indicative of the trend towards applied research: two former coaches had recently been appointed as directors of research institutes.

One of the obvious advantages of the JRISS is its location on the campus of the NIPE. Both work under the direction of the provincial physical culture and sports commission and a close relationship exists between the two institutes. Until recently, the vice-president of the NIPE had also held the position of vice-director of the research institute.

The location of the Jiangsu Central Sports School and of the majority of provincial teams at the NIPE provides the research institute with an ample supply of subjects and, in turn, enables the institute to play an important role in the development of the athletes. There is a continual interchange of information between coaches of the provincial teams and researchers. As is normal in research institutes in China, most staff members could speak some English.

The sports medicine department was originally concerned with the treatment of injuries. Although its title has remained unchanged, the department's major area of emphasis is now exercise physiology; it is also involved in selection procedures and problem diagnosis. The department has six staff members. One research assistant had graduated in sport physiology. The head of department holds a master's degree. The department has four small research laboratories that are used in the areas of blood chemistry and cardio-respiratory function. Most research is directed towards the determination of aerobic threshold. Two papers on the subject had recently been presented at an international sports medicine congress in Beijing.

Data concerning the athletes are passed directly to their coaches. Equipment included an oxygen/CO_2 analyser, the 'Eugo Screeb' and a 'Polygraph' system for monitoring ECG, blood pressure, etc. The equipment – manufactured in Britain, China, Japan, Sweden, the United States and West Germany – was well-maintained, modern and used very efficiently. All systems were computerized. The institute, however, finds it difficult to afford new equipment in the area of exercise physiology.

The biomechanics department also appeared to operate very efficiently. Using a basic but compact film analysis system, members of staff work closely with coaches who often assist with analyses. As was the case with the sports medicine department, the system was connected to an Apple II computer.

The sports training department was originally concerned only with training theory. Currently, however, members of the department work closely with provincial team coaches to improve sport techniques and methods of technique development, and selection.

The information department is concerned mainly with publishing a research journal every two months. Research from overseas is translated and, together with results of ongoing research at the institute and elsewhere in the province, published in the magazine.

The institute also has an efficient reading room for researchers. This contains numerous bookstacks and shelves carrying the latest periodicals in sports science from around the world. Every item is carefully catalogued.

The clinic is administered by the NIPE and is concerned with the diagnosis of injuries and treatment of students, provincial team members and athletes of the Central Sports School. Athletes receive treatment in three sparsely-equipped rooms. Staff-members hold the equivalent of degrees in sports medicine earned at various medical colleges.

The institute has been in existence for only two years yet is operating in a very efficient manner. Equipment, though not sophisticated, is obviously fully-utilized. In addition, research is being applied. The institute is clearly committed to the advancement of sport in the province of Jiangsu. For his part, Director Chen regarded the expense involved in research as an investment to be repaid, subsequently, in medals. Others, he hastened to stress, might not agree.

In December 1994, Yvonne Yuan, Sports Science Officer at the HKSI, visited the JRISS to study the provision of sports science support to the provincial swimming team and to compare this with the support system at the HKSI. Yvonne made the following comments on her return to Hong Kong:

> I worked with Sheng Lei who has been providing sports science support to the swimming team for more than eight years. The swimming team depends heavily on lactate monitoring during training. Lactate samples were taken almost every day, sometimes during both training sessions on the same day. Haemoglobin and body fat levels were also monitored on a regular basis. Other tests that are performed . . . can be of immediate benefit to our swimmers. For example, hormonal levels and the biological age of athletes can be important criteria in talent identification.
>
> I also visited the different departments of the institute to gain a better understanding of the province's overall support system for athletes. The biomechanics laboratory is the best-equipped laboratory in the institute. Equipment includes the latest Cybex (for isokinetic testing), a force platform and a system of high speed video cameras for filming various sporting activities.

In October 1992, the author visited the Guangdong provincial team training centre in Guangzhou and met with Mr Lin Zhenbin, deputy-director of the Guangdong Research Institute of Sports Science (GRISS), which is located on the premises.

The GRISS, established in 1982, has a staff of approximately fifty. The primary role of the institute is the provision of sport science support for provincial team coaches. Twenty-two provincial teams train at the training centre. At least one sport scientist – a biomechanist, physiologist or training scientist – is attached to each team on a full-time basis. The track and field team, for example, has four scientists attached to the team.

Sport scientists are expected to spend 50 per cent of their time with their teams. Both coaches and scientists identify areas for research; only applied research is permissible. Areas of concentration include optimum performance, recovery and nutrition. Scientists are permitted to publish their findings in professional journals.

Appointments at the institute are very competitive with only applicants holding master's degrees receiving consideration. Approximately twenty to thirty individuals apply for positions at the institute each year; only one or two are accepted.

Among the institute's centres and departments are:

- The biochemistry department in which six individuals – an exercise physiologist, a biochemist and four technicians – work. Most work is conducted to monitor training, recovery and athletes' general health. Up to 100 parameters can be analysed.
- The sports nutrition department had established guidelines for athletes and coaches prior to the 1992 Olympic Games and 1993 National Games.
- The testing centre, one of three in the country, is used for talent identification.
- The audio-visual research centre is connected to televisions in various training locations and allows videotaping, playback and conversion from tape to black and white photographs (fifty frames/second) for biomechanical analysis.
- The information centre contains information, often translated from English, Japanese, German and Russian, on training and skill development.
- The computer centre employs three staff-members to maintain a database on the top athletes at the training centre.
- The sport psychology department had only recently been established.
- The cardiac pulmonary function centre.

In October 1995, a delegation from the GRISS, led by Professor Lin Shenghao, the Director and Professor Lin Zhenbin visited the HKSI and provided additional information concerning the Guangdong Institute.

- The major roles of the GRISS are, first, to provide technical support for provincial teams as part of China's Olympic Achievement Programme, and second to provide support for the Sport for All Programme, also known as the All-China Achievement Programme. Although China has emphasized sport for all since 1949, the Sport for All Programme became law in October 1995 and is seen as providing a base for the Olympic Achievement Programme. The Olympic Achievement Programme is the responsibility of the central government. The Sport for All Programme is the responsibility of local government and communities. The premier of each province is nominally in charge of the programme within the province and funding is provided by provincial physical culture and sports commissions. All provincial research institutes of sports science are involved.

- The GRISS is conducting research into the effects of nutritional supplements and Chinese traditional medicine on performance. In doing so, the institute works closely with pharmaceutical companies and medical universities and follows the rules of the IOC. Some of the institute's products are considered to be better than those on the market. Products are sent to the NRISM in Beijing for further testing.

- The GRISS does not currently offer programmes of study. However, according to Professor Lin Zhenbin, the institute is considering whether to apply to the provincial Science and Technology and Education Commissions to organize its own courses or to place staff members under the supervision of another degree-awarding institute.

- Of the various disciplines within sports science, the institute has found that biomechanics has been the slowest to develop during the previous ten years. The interface between the coach and the scientists is clearly a problem with the information provided generally too advanced for the coaches to utilize. For technical reasons, the institute had also experienced problems in establishing performance norms. For now, coaches were provided with film prints to assist them with technique analysis. The institute is now attempting to address the problem.

- The institute operates under two provincial government departments. The Science and Technology Commission is responsible for providing funding for overheads, personnel and office administration. The Physical Culture and Sports Commission provides programme funds – currently Y1.5 million (US$210,000) per annum.

- Although the institute is based at, and works closely with, the provincial training centre, the two organizations operate independently.

In May 1995, the author visited the Liaoning Research Institute of Sports Science in Shenyang. The institute was based at the provincial Sports Training Centre until 1992 when it moved to its present five-storey building. The institute, headed by Professor Quan Zhifei, employs thirty-five members of staff, including three associate professors and fourteen research assistants. According to Professor Quan, the facility ranks among the top five in China – along with those of the NRISS and the Guangdong, Jiangsu and Shanghai provincial research institutes.

The importance of sports science in performance enhancement was first recognized in Liaoning in the early 1980s. The major priorities of the institute are the provision of sports science support for provincial teams and talent identification. Sport scientists are assigned to teams with good medal prospects. The type of support depends on the sport. If a scientist is assigned to a team on a full-time basis, the national sports organization foots the bill.

The institute works on a four-year cycle, based on the National Games. During the first two years, research assistants may work on research projects that are assigned to the institute by the State Sports Commission; they may also attend courses and undergo language training. For the last two years of the cycle, all activity is directed to enhancing the performance of the provincial teams.

The institute played a major role in the world-record performances of Mah Jun Ren's athletes in 1993. In 1988, Mah was transferred from the Shenyang city team to the provincial team. At that time, sports scientists in China knew little about training at high altitude. Mah was one of thirty coaches who attended a seminar on the subject. He then agreed to experiment with high-altitude training during preparations for the National Junior Games in 1989. In July 1988, the first group of coaches and athletes, including Mah and ten of his female athletes, travelled to Qinghai for high-altitude training. Following competition at sea-level and a second trip to Qinghai, Mah's athletes competed successfully at the National Youth Games. The rest is history.

Professor Quan, who supervised both training camps in Qinghai, claimed that high-altitude training is only one of the components that has contributed to Mah's success. Lessons learned working with his athletes are now being applied to other sports, particularly cycling and swimming. Professor Quan was, of course, aware of the charges of drug usage that had been laid against Mah, but emphasized that Mah's athletes have been tested many times.

To the question 'why had Liaoning's male athletes not shown similar levels of improvement?', Professor Quan replied that Mah worked only with female athletes. He would, however, be working with male athletes in the future. Professor Quan also emphasized the fine performances of Liaoning's male distance runners at the 1993 National Games. He confirmed that Mah's athletes were selected on the basis of their speed and agreed that the previous world records in the women's 1500m, 3000m and 10,000m had been weak.

During my first visit to the Guangdong provincial team training centre in 1992, I had been informed of a new breed of coach – the coach-scientist, or a coach who possesses a degree in sports science. I discussed the emergence of the coach-scientist with Professor Quan and Associate Professor Tang Ruan. Although one of the institute's medical doctors had actually crossed over to become a coach, Associate Professor Tang felt that it was more logical to keep the two roles separate.

We also discussed how provincial coaches in Liaoning had come to accept the importance of sports science. Originally, the sports scientist had to lead the coach. Now, as coaches have become more familiar with sports science, it is they who ask the questions.

We visited three biochemistry laboratories, which include state-of-the-art equipment imported from Japan and the United States, and a cardio-respiratory function laboratory. Other equipment included a Cybex 6000, soon to be linked to EMG and video equipment, and manual digitizing equipment. Interestingly, the institute employs no sports psychologists. Psychologists are employed from the Shenyang Institute of Physical Education to service the psychological needs of the province's athletes.

It was clear that Liaoning is a leader in China in the provision of sports science support to athletes and coaches. Such support is undoubtedly a major reason for the success of Liaoning teams since the 1987 National Games.

INSTITUTES OF PHYSICAL EDUCATION

China's institutes of physical education also provide a valuable source of sports science and sports medicine support for provincial- and national-level athletes and coaches. The Wuhan Institute of Physical Education, for example, has both a sports science department and a separate department of sports psychology.

The sports science department was established in early 1995 to provide support for the institute's athletes and coaches, the institute's competitive sports school and selected Hubei provincial and national teams that train at the institute. The department now employs a total of twenty staff members in five units – biomechanics, exercise physiology and biochemistry, sports psychology, sports information and equipment research. The various units often combine to provide support for a particular athlete or team.

The State Physical Culture and Sports Commission is planning to target ten institutes and sports science departments nationwide to provide sports science support for national teams; the department at the WIPE will probably concentrate on water sports. The department is also involved with the Sport for All Programme.

The institute's separate sports psychology department – one of five departments in the institute – is one of the best in the country. The department, which employs twenty staff-members, has three roles:

- Services Hubei provincial teams and four national teams – archery, canoeing, fencing and windsurfing.
- Offers bachelor's and master's degrees in sports psychology – the only department in China to do so. The department also plans to offer a PhD programme in the near future.

- Uses data that are collected fulfilling its service role for research purposes.

The Wuhan Institute of Physical Education runs a separate sports medicine department, which is involved in teaching and research, and a sports injuries clinic.

SOME FINAL COMMENTS

Research is certainly very active, but how much it is contributing to performance enhancement in elite sport in China may be open to question. Certainly, the structure is in place. As noted previously, almost every province has an institute of sports science and the major role of each provincial institute is to assist the provincial team in its preparations for the quadrennial National Games. Everything else is of secondary importance.

The number of sports scientists employed at each institute also appears to be more than adequate; but, given the number of provincial-team athletes that need to be serviced, this observation may be a little unfair. The athlete: sports scientist ratio of 14: 1 at the Guangdong provincial training centre, for example, is identical to that at the HKSI which is considered to be a lean and efficient sports science support service.

Another positive characteristic of the system is that, while the institutes work in isolation in their attempts to develop their provincial teams, research throughout the system is co-ordinated, and research projects assigned by the State Physical Culture and Sports Commission, through the Department of Science and Physical Education of the All-China Sports Federation. Research is also co-ordinated on an informal basis through frequent meetings of specialist associations such as the China Sports Science Society and China Sports Medicine Association.

Surprisingly, however, the NRISS and NRISM have no formal leadership role in sports science and sports medicine. Links are established either through business or, unofficially, through exchanges, seminars and staff exchanges. There are few official links between the two national institutes and the provincial institutes.

In Chapter 6, it is suggested that, given the vast resources that have been committed to performance enhancement and the country's population of more than 1 billion, China's dominance of sport in the international arena is not what it should be. Even in sports that are producing world-leading performances, the question must be asked: how much progress is due to quality coaching and sports science support and how much can be explained by pure numbers? In the author's view, the major reason for progress has been the number of athletes within the system. Until now, the coaches and sports scientists have had what is, essentially, a free ride. The majority of coaches continue to use coaching techniques that worked for them as athletes; accountability was introduced only in the late 1980s. The lack of interaction between coaches and sports scientists that exists in many provinces has also minimized the effects that sports science could have on performance. This must now change. With further gains in performance levels becoming increasingly difficult to achieve, China will undoubtedly have to turn to its research institutes of sports science for the answers. The future of sport in China, as in any society, depends upon the technical people. In time, you have to know what you are doing, and why. For this reason, sports scientists in China now occupy a position of considerable responsibility. For China to close the gap on countries such as the United States, Russia and Germany, and to become increasingly dominant in international sport, the country's legion of sports scientists must move towards the level of efficiency of their former East European counterparts. They must also convince their coaches that sports science has an important role to play in performance enhancement. If they fail to do so, China will probably remain an also-ran in the international arena of sport.

ACKNOWLEDGEMENTS

The author wishes to thank Li Guoping, MD, Head, Sports Medicine Department, and Ding Xueqin, Head, Sports Psychology Department, National Research Institute of Sports Science, for reviewing the content of this chapter.

Chapter 12

Sports medicine

Frank H. Fu

INTRODUCTION

The development of sports medicine in China is divided into two parts: pre-1949 and post-1949. For the period before 1949, the focus is on the historical development of acupuncture and Meridian network, massage and physical therapy, *QiGong* and *wushu*. The post-1949 period addresses the development of sports medicine under the present government in the People's Republic of China (PRC).

PRE-1949 PERIOD

Acupuncture is presently accepted by the medical profession for treating specific illnesses, for example, arthritis, paralysis, digestive system disorder, high blood pressure, and muscle atrophy (China Medical Rehabilitation Research Society 1984). As early as 2,300 BC, sharp stones were used to relieve pain and illness, an early form of acupuncture (Chin 1985). Without any sophisticated equipment, networks of nerves were identified and documented by 200 BC. These networks are still used by acupuncture doctors in giving treatment. At about the same time the subcutaneous network was discovered. This network of nerve neurones or concentration of nerve sensors/receptors is somewhat similar to that used for acupuncture, and is known as the Meridian network. Its significance and acceptance are still being debated and investigated by Chinese doctors.

There has been speculation that massage was used in China some 3,000 years ago. Certainly, the use of massage for treatment was documented during the Chou dynasty (1112–770 BC). By the time of the Western Han dynasty (200 BC–AD 25), it was widely used for treating a variety of diseases. Its uses include improving blood circulation, joint function and mobility, concentration and overall health. Massage is presently classified into five types: pushing, friction, kneading, cupping, and hacking. It is commonly accepted that massage also aids the recovery of fatigued muscles and is used during warm-up and cool-down routines as well.

The use of *Qi* (air) in treating illness was documented over 2,000 years ago (China Medical Rehabilitation Research Association 1984). It was believed that Qi was vital as the material that made up the human body, being responsible for all physical functions and connecting the body to its external environment. Thus, breathing came to hold a key position in exercise. Qi's indications include treating such diseases as high blood pressure, coronary heart disease, digestive disorder, nervous breakdown, respiratory malfunction and even cancer. In its early stages, Qi involved postural meditation, such as 'Anqiao' and postural/breathing exercises, such as 'Daoyin'. Both exercises were recorded in the *Huan Di Nai Jing*, the first publication in traditional Chinese medicine (the Warring period, 475–221 BC) (see Figure 12.1). Postural exercises were further developed in subsequent years. Wu Quin Xi was most popular during the Three Kingdoms (AD 220–80), with exercise postures imitating the tiger, bear, deer, monkey and bird (see Figure 12.2). Each posture would contribute to the development of Qi and benefit the lungs, liver, stomach, kidney and heart respectively. Ban Duan Jin was another popular exercise practised by people during the Sun dynasty (AD 960–1271) (Qu and Ya 1988). This series of postural exercises would contribute to better concentration and relaxation, and to cardio-respiratory functions (see Figure 12.3).

The addition of the element of movement to postural exercise led to the development of Tai Chi Quan, which emphasized body relaxation, breathing, concentration, and smoothness of muscle movement. There are twenty-four fundamental movements, but these can increase to forty-eight or more (see Figure 12.4) (China Medical Rehabilitation Research Association 1984). The exercise could contribute to the development of Qi, physical stamina and concentration/will power through a combination of postural and movement exercises. Development of other forms of Quans followed, such as Yi Jin Jing during the Ming dynasty (AD 1368–1644) and many became components of modern *wushu*.

Before the fall of the Ching dynasty in 1911, China's closed door policy had limited the influence of western ideology and technology, and during the period 1911–49 China was in turmoil – with the two world wars, the Civil War lasting from the 1920s to the 1940s, and the Japanese invasion. Thus, despite its long history of adopting 'therapeutic exercise' and 'development and application of Qi' as a form of sports medicine, and since modern competitive sport was only a western import during the last 100 years, sports medicine in its modern form did not really exist in China before 1949.

POST-1949 PERIOD

With the founding of the People's Republic of China in 1949, and the emphasis on enhancing national prestige through sport and the productivity

Figure 12.1 Silk painting of 'Daoyin' found at the grave of Emperor Ma (475–221 BC). Each postural/breathing exercise is for treating a specific illness

五　禽　戏

Tiger

Bear

Deer

Monkey

Bird

Figure 12.2 Wu Quan Xi – postural exercises imitating animals – popular during the Three Kingdoms (AD 220–280)

of the workforce, the political climate was conducive to the introduction and development of sports medicine. In the early 1950s, graduates from medical colleges were assigned to various national teams. The first breakthrough in importing overseas expertise was the visit of a delegation of Soviet sports medicine experts to the Beijing Institute of Physical Culture in 1956, which led to the introduction of graduate programmes in sports medicine and sports physiology. In the following year, China sent a group of medical doctors to study in the Soviet Union and Hungary. Among them were

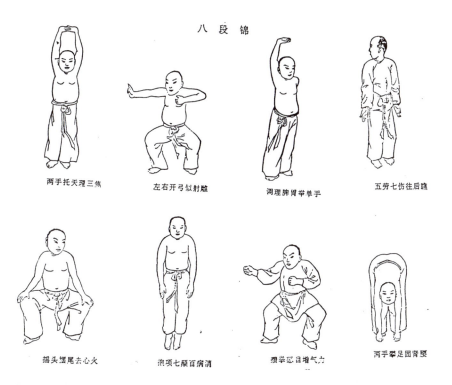

八 段 锦

两手托天理三焦   左右开弓似射雕   调理脾胃举单手   五劳七伤往后瞧

摇头摆尾去心火   背项七颠百病消   攒拳怒目增气力   两手攀足固肾腰

Figure 12.3 Ban Duan Jin – postural exercises popular during the Sun dynasty
(AD 960–1271)

Professor Qu Mianyu, Professor Yang Tienle, Professor Yang Xirang, Professor Cen Haowang and Professor Lu Shaozhung, who have provided leadership in this field over the last forty years. This trend in exchange programmes with the Soviet Union and Eastern Europe (e.g. Hungary) continued until the Cultural Revolution (1966–76). With the 'ping pong' diplomacy in the 1970s, China resumed its interaction with the rest of the world. The first delegation to the USA in 1978 comprised three coaches to Springfield College for three months. In the following year, sports medicine experts were allowed to spend up to two years at US universities for academic exchange programmes. In 1989, the Tiananmen Square incident again put a temporary hold on all exchange programmes as well as the overall development of sports medicine in China. However, with the support of the government and a strong desire among Chinese sports medicine professionals to interact within the country and with foreign institutions, sports medicine in China continued to develop. The following section briefly describes the development of various aspects of sports medicine in China.

太极拳动作

Start →

Figure 12.4 (i) Tai Chi Quan
Source: China Medical Rehabilitation Research Association 1984

Figure 12.4 (ii) Tai Chi Quan

PROFESSIONAL PREPARATION

Throughout Chinese history, *wushu* has been an important part of overall culture. As injuries would occur during practice and competition, many *wushu* 'masters' were also competent 'doctors' in sports medicine, and some are still referred to as 'bone-setters' today. The learning of the art of treating injuries usually took the form of passing on family 'secrets' or an apprenticeship. It was only recently that emphasis has been put on training

Figure 12.4 (iii) Tai Chi Quan – fundamental movements
Source: China Medical Rehabilitation Research Association 1984

for, and the practice of, Chinese medicine. There is still, however, no formal legal structure or institution offering a formal education programme in 'bone-setting' per se.

In the early 1950s, medical school graduates with no specialized training in sports medicine were posted to work with national sports squads. They were the pioneers of sports medicine in modern China. The influence of the Soviet Union resulted in an awareness of the need to develop formal institutions to train sports medicine personnel. In 1958, the State Research Institute of Sports Science was established in Beijing with specialization in sports medicine, sports biomechanics, sports physiology and sports biochemistry. In 1959, the Beijing Medical College became the first institution in the country to establish research departments in sports traumatology, sports nutrition, sports biochemistry, medical supervision and rehabilitation. At the same time, graduates from medical schools were sent overseas to study in the Soviet Union and in Hungary in specialized areas of sports science and sports medicine (as mentioned above). As more and more trained personnel became available, research centres in sports science were established in different provinces, with funding from the central government. By 1966, there were eighteen research centres in twenty-nine provinces. At the same time, sports science personnel (non-medical) were trained by various institutes of physical culture in the provinces. There are presently seventeen such major institutions funded by the central government, while the remaining ones (over 100) are funded by provincial governments.

The training of sports medicine personnel in China is well established. Undergraduate programmes of four to five years are offered by medical colleges and institutes of physical education. Graduate degree programmes with various specializations follow, with emphasis on research, clinical and sport-related areas. Some of these programmes are offered by universities or research institutes of sports science and/or sports medicine. As Chinese athletes are winning more medals in international competitions, exchanges with overseas institutions continue to be important in the professional preparation of sports medicine personnel, especially in the area of surgery and pharmacology. Some traditional medical practice, for example acupuncture, Qi and Meridian network, and use of herbal medicine, are likely to become the focus of further research in the next century.

PROFESSIONAL INSTITUTIONS

As sport was regarded as a means of nation-building after 1949, institutes responsible for the training of sport-related experts were founded in the early 1950s. Key institutes, such as the Beijing Institute of Physical Culture, were funded by the central government with an emphasis on training athletes, coaches, physical education teachers and sports scientists (who included sports medicine in their qualifications). During the same period, ten medical colleges offered specialized programmes in sports medicine with a focus on care and prevention of sports injuries. The first graduating class of 1956 provided today's leaders in sports science and sports medicine.

Apart from the institutes of physical culture, many medical colleges with sports medicine departments were formed after 1958, providing training programmes in care and prevention of sports injuries and related research opportunities, for example the Institute of Sports Medicine at Beijing Medical University. Others, funded by the central government through the All-China Sports Federation, include the National Research Institute of Sports Science and the National Research Institute of Sports Medicine. There are also numerous research institutes of sports science/sports medicine funded by provincial governments, for example the Guangzhou Institute of Sports Science at Er-Sa-Tow.

In China, sports science commonly includes sports medicine, with the exception of the courses at medical colleges. The founding of the National Research Institute of Sports Medicine in 1992, an independent body separate from the National Research Institute of Sports Science, is a good example. At present, six major specializations within sports medicine are recognized, with degree programmes offered at various institutions:

1   Medical supervision
2   Preventive medicine
3   Sports physiology
4   Sports injuries
5   Sports biochemistry
6   Sports nutrition

Despite the desire to establish sports medicine as an entity separate from sports science, areas of common interest exist, especially when they involve the training and preparation of national team athletes. It is envisaged that this symbiotic relationship will continue in view of the need to integrate traditional Chinese medicine with western technology. A Doping Control Centre was also set up in Beijing in 1990, but it failed to prevent the incidence of drug violations by Chinese athletes at the 1994 Asian Games in Hiroshima. Much more effort will be needed by sport administrators to ensure full compliance with drug regulations by coaches and athletes in the future.

PROFESSIONAL ORGANIZATIONS AND ACTIVITIES

The above-mentioned visit of Soviet medical experts in 1956 marked the beginning of a series of exchanges between China and the Soviet Union. This had a significant impact on the training of the pioneers in sports medicine and science. The first National Conference on Sports Science was held in 1964 but, because of the Cultural Revolution (1966–76), the next conference was not held until 1978. At present, the conference takes place biennially. The Chinese Association of Sports Medicine (CASM) was formed in the same year as the initial conference, and it became a member of the International Federation of Sports Medicine (FIMS) in 1980. Academic exchanges with the USA were renewed in 1979 (after a gap of some thirty years), and by 1980 China had established several exchange programmes with US universities and the American College of Sports Medicine (ACSM).

Sports Science, a periodical devoted to physical education and sport science, was first published in 1981. The first *Chinese Journal of Sports Medicine* was published by the China Sports Science Society in 1982 and now appears four times per year, with a circulation of over 4,000. In recent years, international conferences have been held by various institutions in different cities, while many scholars and students have also been sent overseas for further study. The 'brain drain' has been a major problem, especially with young graduates who left to study in overseas institutions. However, China's 'open door' policy has continued with the hope that many overseas-trained young professionals will eventually return home.

THE WAY AHEAD

In its short history since 1949, the development of sports medicine in China has been interrupted by the Cultural Revolution and the Tianmen Square incident (1989). Notwithstanding, it has managed to establish its own identity as a separate entity from sports science. As the emphasis on winning medals in sport continues to be a top priority in China, sports medicine has to continue to conduct applied research in sport performance-related areas in order to gain sufficient funding for its programmes – teaching, research and practice. Tian *et al.* (1993) have suggested that future research in sports science should focus on improving methodology, increasing the knowledge base and meeting the demands of society by conducting more applied research.

The future development of sports medicine in China will depend not only on government support, but also on the ingenuity used in securing funding from overseas or local companies anxious to take advantage of China's 'open door' policy. The continuing stability of the present government will have a direct impact on the growth of sports medicine in China in the years ahead.

REFERENCES

Chin, Hsiaoyi (1985) *Chronological Table of Chinese and World Culture*, Taipei: National Palace Museum.

China Medical Rehabilitation Research Association (1984) *Rehabilitation Medicine*, Beijing: People's Hygiene Printing Press.

Committee on Emperor Ma Grave (1977) *Medical Diagnosis and Prescription*, Beijing: People's Printing Press.

Knuttgen, H.G., Ma, Qiwei and Wu, Zhongyuan (eds) (1990) *Sport in China*, Champaign, Illinois: Human Kinetics.

Tian, Mai Jiu *et al.* (1993) 'Sports science research methodology – problems and issues in China', *Journal of China Sports Society* 13(3): 13–18.

Qu, Mianyu and Yu, Changlon (eds) (1988) *China's Sports Medicine*, New York: Karger.

Wang, B. (ed.) (1955) *Huang Di Nai Jing*, Beijing: Commercial Printing Press.

Zhu, Zongxiang (1993) *The Meridian Network and Longevity*, Beijing: Science Promotion Press.

Chapter 13

Mass fitness

Shirley Reekie[1]

FITNESS BEFORE 1949

Fitness activities have a long history in China. Some activities, such as archery, horseriding, spear throwing, tree climbing, shuttlecock kicking and Chinese martial arts, can be traced back several thousand years, and fitness for inner health has a similarly long history, especially *Qi gong* and *Tai ji quan.* These activities were very popular whenever the economy was in good condition, and various organizations were set up to deal with the activities, such as those for archery, ball kicking, and martial arts, in which ordinary citizens, as well as emperors and imperial officials, participated.

Modern sport was introduced into China at the end of the nineteenth century and began with military training and church-initiated physical education classes. Gradually, other sports, including basketball, gymnastics, volleyball, team handball, baseball, weightlifting, track and field and soccer, spread. Most of the participants, however, were school students or the rich, and these sports tended to be played only in the eastern regions and in large cities. The fitness pioneers worked very hard to promote sports in order to improve the fitness of ordinary people. They published articles in the newspapers, organized competitions, and taught school students, but their efforts were not particularly successful owing to the low level of the economy, the various wars, problems with drugs and natural disasters. By the 1940s, the average fitness level of ordinary Chinese was very low, and their average life span was only 40 years. China had few high level athletes; only one runner participated in the 1936 Olympics, and he was eliminated in the first round. Because of the low fitness levels, China at that time was sometimes referred to as the 'Sick Man of Asia'.

FITNESS BETWEEN 1949 AND 1979

After taking power in 1949, the new Chinese government decided to make fitness a priority. In the same year, the first national physical education convention was held in Beijing, and the State Physical Education and Sports Commission of China (SPESC, but also referred to at that time as the State Physical Culture and Sports Commission, SPCSC) was established as the executive body to promote fitness and health. In 1951, the SPESC created the first form of Chinese *ti cao* (callisthenics set to music), and promoted it through national administrative bodies. *Ti cao* was practised by school students and government employees during their recess time and the new form of exercise spread rapidly through the whole nation, attracting much attention. The SPESC further set a basic exercise standard for schools, factories, farms and the army and, by 1956, nearly a million people had reached the standards set.

The Chinese government also organized various sports competitions in order to promote exercise and sport. An impressive national folk exercise demonstration was held by fifty-six minority groups, but the largest event during this period was the national industrial workers' sports tournament in which 1,200,000 workers participated, during the preliminary stages, in various sports. This became the cornerstone of the worker fitness movement. In this period, more than twenty sports associations for state employees (such as those of mineworkers, and railway workers) were established, with 36,000 branches and more than 4 million members.

Ti cao was updated several times and, most importantly, the SPESC trained many *Tai ji quan* experts to develop a standard, simplified form of *Tai ji quan* – the 24 Form – to promote this Chinese traditional exercise (because there were several styles, it was difficult to make them all popular). It worked well and more people practised *Tai ji* afterwards. In 1959, the first national games of the People's Republic were organized, which reflected concerns about fitness and sport. However, this period was beset by natural disasters and severe political problems, and fitness and sport became neglected until 1965. As the economy recovered and the political situtation stabilized, China organized the second national games, which gradually restored people's interest in fitness and sport.

The Cultural Revolution in 1966 was a disaster for mass fitness. Virtually all sport and exercise ceased. This situation lasted for five years until, starting in 1971, sport and fitness returned in popularity, although the number of participants was far less than before the Cultural Revolution.

FITNESS IN THE 1980s AND 1990s

The 1980s was the boom time for the fitness movement and three factors facilitated this. First, the improved economy gave increased opportunity for fitness and exercise. Second, the publishing of a new style *Qi gong* – Crane style *Qi gong*, which spread to the whole country in just one year as an exercise and therapy for inner health – started a fitness fever. Third, the consecutive victories of the Chinese women's volleyball team in the world championships, and the achievements of Chinese athletes at the 1984 Olympic Games in Los Angeles, stimulated people's interest and attracted youth to sport training.

The reforms of the 1990s have had several repercussions. First is the change in people's attitude toward fitness, thanks to the influence of 'fitness fever' in developed countries. Before this time, the government used to assist people to participate in sports competitions or exercise. For example, when employees participated in competition and training, the government provided sportswear, transportation and meals. In the 1990s, however, higher salaries allowed more people to spend their own money to play or exercise, and such expenses have become a part of the everyday budget for many. Second is the changeover of the administration of fitness from government-based to society-based. This has led to greatly improved resources and opportunities. And third, in 1995, the SPESC started a national project, 'Fitness for All', which has attracted people all over China and has started an even bigger wave of fitness movements.

Fitness activities can be identified in four categories: government departments, national sports organizations, businesses, and spontaneous groups.

Government level

Restructuring of the government in March 1998 (see Chapter 1) is changing the former responsibilities of various departments. Although the closure of the SPESC reflects new government priorities concerning sport, it would be wrong to interpret the move as an abandonment of government interest, and much of the work and duties mentioned in this section will doubtless remain within government offices.

At the point of restructuring, several government departments were involved in the administration of mass fitness, but the SPESC had overall responsibility. Its duties included development of long-term, and annual, planning for mass fitness, development of budgets for mass fitness, management of mass fitness organizations, establishment of mass fitness policies and rules, supervision and evaluation of procedures, and organization of comprehensive fitness events.

Attached to the SPESC, the Mass Fitness Department, in 1997, was involved in research studies, drafting laws and regulations, organizing meetings, tournaments, national fitness events and international activities, and administrative work related to fund raising, publications, supervisor and instructor training, awards and fitness equipment testing. Assisting the SPESC, the Fitness Centre Society organized meetings, international fitness and recreation events, and directed activities such as youth fitness camps and youth weight control camps.

Other government departments included the Department of Health, Physical

Education and the Arts (attached to the State Education Commission, now Ministry of Education), dealing with schools; the Ministry of Health and its subordinates, for sport rehabilitation and therapy, health examinations, and fitness assessments; the National Minority Population Commission, organizing traditional minority population sport events; and the National Ministry for the Disabled, promoting and organizing sports and fitness for people with disabilities. Each of these ministries or commissions, funded by tax revenues, operates under the State Council, at national, provincial, city and lower levels.

Specific sports organizations

Beyond (and largely outside) the government ministries, there is an array of organizations that are involved with the organization of sport and fitness. They have in the past liaised with the SPESC and have received government financial support, but the latest reforms are likely to give them greater responsibility, or to lead to their closure, depending on their success in fundraising, recruitment of members, provision of facilities and equipment and consultation, and general organization. Some operate for specific groups of employees (e.g. the railway workers), or for specific groups of people (e.g. the elderly), or for specific sports (e.g. the Badminton Association).

Business-oriented clubs

With greater income and a shorter working day giving greater recreational opportunities, people are choosing to spend more time and money on fitness activities. In the new economic climate, many commercial sports clubs have opened, especially in the major cities, to meet the growing demand. Clubs for aerobics, martial arts, bowling alleys, *tai ji quan*, *qi gong*, golf and social dance may be found and, although expensive, they are becoming popular. The clubs attract the general public, but especially the self-employed. There are, however, many people who still do not have access to government-sponsored or ministry-run facilities, and who cannot afford the business-oriented clubs.

Spontaneous groups

These groups are both popular and active. The retired population, those who do not have access to other exercise facilities, do not have time to participate in other organized exercise, or do not have extra money for clubs, may form spontaneous groups. The groups are usually loosely organized, without formal organization or administration, and often grow from a small initial group interested in one type of exercise or activity. By starting and finishing before breakfast, participants are able to go to work. The scale of these spontaneous groups may be quite large, as the following example shows: at 5.30 a.m. in May 1996, at Beiling Park in Shenyang (capital city of Lioaning province in north east China), a group of about 100 swimmers was observed, along with a social dance group estimated at 700–800, a large Chinese folk dance group of at least 2,000 people, twenty-five *tai ji quan* and *qi gong* groups ranging from eighty to 200 participants, and several martial arts groups with thirty to forty participants. Besides these, other small groups and individuals were playing badminton and volleyball or jogging.

FITNESS TESTING PROCEDURES IN CHINA

Following the start of fitness testing in 1980, the SPESC established national standards of fitness in 1982, to be used for students and young people (other organizations, such as government institutions and community groups were also able to adopt part of the standards).

Students and young people

There are four age groups (9–12 years, 13–15 years, 16–18 years and 19 years or older) and three evaluation categories for each age group: outstanding (420–500 points), good (350–415 points) and pass (250–345 points). The government gives certificates to those who achieve the necessary standards, and recognition of these standards is given for admission to universities (see Chapter 5).

The national standards include five types of fitness test for each of the four age groups, but may overlap in some tests (50 and 100 metres, 1000 and 1500 metres for example) and lack other tests, such as those for flexibility (see Table 13.1).

Adults

Fitness standards for adults were designed for males, age 18 to 60, and females, age 18 to 55; 60 and 55 years are the standard ages of retirement for males and females respectively in China. This adult group is further divided into Group A, age 18 to 40, and Group B, age 41 to 60 (55 for females). The government suggests that adults take the test once a year, and awards certificates in the 'outstanding, good, or pass' categories. The test items include two sets for Group A and Group B. The first set is considered to reflect basic fitness, and the second set overall health. However, the two sets of adult tests are not discrete and also lack certain tests that might be expected, such as blood pressure and cholesterol level (see Table 13.2).

Table 13.1 Test items for young people in the National Fitness Standards

	Age 9–12	*Age 13–15*
Speed:	50 metre run 4 × 10 metre shuttle 10 second, 25 metre shuttle	50 metre run 100 metre run 4 × 10 metre shuttle 10 second, 25 metre shuttle
Endurance:	1 minute, skipping 8 × 50 metre shuttle 400 metre run 2 minutes, 25 metre shuttle 100 metre swim 500 metre ice skating	1,000 metre run (male) 1,500 metre run (male) 800 metre (female) 3 minutes, 25 metre shuttle 200 metre swim 1,000 metre ice skating
Jumping:	high jump long jump standing broad jump	high jump long jump standing broad jump
Throwing:	softball sandbag ($\frac{1}{4}$ kilogram) stuffed ball (1 kilogram)	shotput (3 kilograms) stuffed ball (2 kilograms)
Strength:	1 minute, sit ups 20 seconds, burpees inclined pull ups	1 minute sit ups (girls) pull ups (boys) inclined pull ups (girls) timed, bent arm hang
	Age 16–18	*Age 19 or over*
Speed:	50 metre run 100 metre run 4 × 10 metre shuttle 10 seconds, 25 metre shuttle	50 metre run 100 metre run 4 × 10 metre shuttle
Endurance:	1,000 metre run (male) 1,500 metre run (male) 800 metre run (female) 4 minutes, 25 metre shuttle 200 metre swim 1,500 metre, ice skating (male) 1,000 metre, ice skating (female)	1,000 metre run (male) 1,500 metre run (male) 800 metre run (female) 200 metre swim 1,500 metre, ice skating 1,000 metre (female)
Jumping:	high jump long jump standing broad jump	high jump long jump standing broad jump

Throwing:	shotput (5 kilograms, male,
	    4 kilograms, female)
	stuffed ball (2 kilograms)
		shotput (5 kilograms, male,
		    4 kilograms, female)
		stuffed ball (2 kilograms)

Strength:	1 minute, sit ups (female) pull ups (male) parallel bar dips (male) inclined pull ups (female) timed, bent arm hang	1 minute, sit ups (female) pull ups (male) parallel bar dips (male) inclined pull ups (female) timed, bent arm hang

Table 13.2 Test items for adults in the National Fitness Standards

Set 1, Fitness Test items

Type	*Group A*	*Group B*
Size	height and weight	height and weight
Function	maximum VO2	maximum VO2
Fitness grip	strength sit and reach vertical jump push ups (males) one minute, sit ups (females)	grip strength sit and reach one foot balance (eyes closed) reaction time

Set 2, Health Test items

Type	*Group A*	*Group B*
Size	height and weight	height and weight
Function	maximum VO2 step test	maximum VO2 step test
Fitness grip	strength sit and reach vertical jump 4 × 10 metre shuttle push ups (males) 1 minute, sit ups (females)	grip strength sit and reach one foot balance (eyes closed) reaction time

CHINA'S 'FITNESS FOR ALL' PROJECT

In 1995, the government introduced the national 'Fitness for All' project. Its purpose was:

1   to promote national fitness for the benefit of economic development;
2   to improve the overall fitness and health of the nation; and
3   to establish a national fitness network.

While a primary focus of the project is on children and young people, most groups, including people with disabilities, were targeted. To achieve the goals, the government established a four-stage plan. The introductory stage (1995–6) was to establish the plan at different experimental locations. In the second stage (1997–8), promotion of the fitness concept and participation in fitness activities was to be gradually expanded to other places. The third stage (1999–2000) would spread the basic structure of the Fitness for All project to the whole nation and the fourth stage would continue to raise the fitness levels and establish a broad network of fitness organizations.

To carry out the project, the SPESC proposed a 1–2–1 plan:

1 Every individual should participate in at least one daily fitness activity, learn at least two kinds of sports or activities, and have one annual fitness test.
2 Every family should have at least one piece of fitness equipment, participate in at least two outdoor fitness activities for every season, and take at least one fitness journal or newspaper.
3 Every community should provide at least one fitness or sport facility, organize two community-based fitness events, and develop one team of mass fitness supervisors.
4 Every school should provide students with at least one hour, daily, of fitness activity and organize two camping or long-distance hiking excursions.

The SPESC also developed several strategies:

1 To include fitness projects in the national economic development plan, balancing competitive sport and mass fitness.
2 To raise awareness of fitness through intensive national propaganda.
3 To carry out the existing law and develop new laws for mass fitness; improve the management of mass fitness; and plan regular, formal, sport and mass fitness events.
4 Gradually increase the involvement of sports associations and communities in mass fitness.
5 Increase resources from the government and encourage institutions and individuals to invest money in fitness activities.
6 Establish fitness testing and publicize the results. Train mass fitness supervisors to teach, supervise and manage mass fitness activities at beginner, intermediate, advanced and national levels.
7 Encourage personalized fitness activities and promote traditional fitness and health activities.
8 Conduct intensive research in mass fitness and provide feedback for further improvement.
9 Include the development of fitness facilities in the overall planning of any city or countryside area.
10 Request all sports and fitness facilities be open for mass fitness.
11 Request all institutions to regularly organize exercise to music.
12 Reward outstanding institutions and individuals in the mass fitness movement.
13 Draw up a national list of the various fitness activities.

The Fitness for All project has been in existence since 1995 and some descriptive reports and observations suggest the project is going well, although there are few research data currently available. The following statistics were published in articles appearing in the *People's Daily* (the official government newspaper) between November 1996 and December 1997. In Guangzhou (the capital of Guangdong province), a fitness network has been established, and more than 4 million people participate in fitness activities, accounting for 60 per cent of the total population. In the whole of Guangdong province, 40 per cent of the population participate in regular exercise, and the same was true in Dalian, northern China. In Chengdu (capital of Sichuan province), gymnasiums or fitness facilities (more than 100) were open to the public during the 1997 Chinese New Year, and all of them were full. The city also built a sports equipment shopping centre, which has become very popular. In Gansu province, 90 per cent of the institutions and industry have participated in the Fitness for All project. More than 50,000 fitness events were organized and more than 8 million people participated in the events. In Inner Mongolia, 35 per cent of the people participated in fitness or sport events, and more than 1 million people participated in 2,000 organized fitness and sport events. An estimated 150 million elderly people throughout China participate in regular exercise, and several hundred new organizations for different groups have been formed.

Although mass fitness in China has been developing rapidly and the national Fitness for All project has many achievements to its credit, there are still problems that need to be solved. For historical reasons, competitive sport has been the major focus of the Chinese government. China was weak and had been invaded by other countries before 1949, and the government and people wanted to regain their dignity by standing at the top of the world. However, the development of the economy is a long-term task, and the government turned to sport with high expectations, hoping that victories in sport would show to the world that China was a strong nation. Thus, winning gold medals has been the dominating force in Chinese sport. Under this pressure, the SPESC spent 90 per cent of its sport budget on competition-related activities. An investigation in Dalian city (a well-developed area with a high participation rate in sport) indicated that only 1 per cent of their budget in 1997 (two years after the Fitness for All project started) was used for mass fitness activities. The total amount of money was about US$12,000, and that was for almost 4 million people.

The 'gold medal syndrome' has also had a negative influence on people's fitness. Many people, from top leaders to ordinary citizens, have become sport spectators rather than participants. They are concerned about the achievements of national teams and they get very excited when Chinese athletes win gold medals in the Olympic Games. However, they do not participate in sport themselves. For example, soccer is the favourite spectator sport, but it does not have the highest number of participants. People forget their own need for exercise when they watch sport on TV.

Another source of confusion is that the SPESC classifies chess and card activities as sport. The result is that many people participate in these activities, which have no value for fitness – and these are counted in the various statistics.

Newspapers also focus their reports on professional sports, and the small number of professional athletes, instead of on fitness for more than a billion people. One statistic indicated that among the 3,722 reports and articles in the *People's Daily* (the most popular Chinese newspaper), in 1997, 62.5 per cent were on professional sport competitions, 17.5 per cent on chess or cards, 18.7 per cent on meetings and information on famous people in sport, but only 1.3 per cent on fitness, and this at the time of the second stage of the Fitness for All project.

Although there have been changes in the fitness levels of city people, those in the countryside still lag behind significantly. As many as 80 per cent of the population are farmers, whose living conditions and health care differs considerably from that in the cities. Exercise and sport could therefore play an important role in helping to keep farmers fit. However, except for a few regions, where fitness is part of the rural way of life, fitness is still a remote concept in the countryside. There are several reasons for this:

1   *Working patterns*. Farmers spend most of their time in the fields, following traditional work patterns. They have no time or energy for exercise or sport after working from early morning to evening. There is less government sport provision in the countryside compared to cities, and few farms organize their own sport or fitness activities.

2   *Concept and atmosphere*. Most farmers believe that exercise and sport are a waste of time and energy; they feel that fitness activities are not necessary, since they do daily physical labour. This concept sets a mental block for most farmers and has a negative influence on their motivation to participate. Furthermore, the fitness movement has not yet created significant interest in the countryside, even though it is becoming popular in the cities.

3   *Economy and living level*. The economic development of farms and the living standard of most farmers in China are far below city level. Most farmers have just achieved, or are still trying to achieve, a living-wage level which allows them to have ample food and improved living conditions. Fitness is not yet on their agenda. The economy of farms changes very slowly in comparison to cities, and farm areas cannot afford gymnasia or equipment for fitness. Rudimentary outdoor basketball courts are still the only fitness facilities on most farms.

LACK OF RESOURCES

China is still a developing country even though its economy has been growing relatively quickly in recent years. The limited resources have had to be used on other things deemed more important than fitness; the resources the government can provide for fitness are limited, even for the Fitness for All project, and this situation is unlikely to change. Because gold medals are still a high priority, competitive sport continues to attract major funding and the only way to raise additional money for fitness is to count on donations from society and industry.

The lack of facilities is a key factor hampering the development of fitness. According to national statistics, by the end of 1995, 615,693 standard sports facilities covered 1.07 billion square metres, averaging 0.65 square metres per person. The government only invests 80 million yuan (approximately US$10 million) annually on building sports facilities, and about 80 per cent of existing facilities are inadequate. Most communities do not have exercise and sport facilities, and one-third of elementary schools do not have standard sports fields. Many schools are losing existing facilities because businesses are looking for space for new construction and often the school sports fields are targeted. Because education in China does not have enough resources, many schools have to find ways to support themselves to some extent, and selling parts of the sports field is one possibility.

SUMMARY

Throughout China there is a huge range of popular sports, traditional activities, children's and adult games and pastimes that reflect climate, regional differences, ethnic minority groups and overseas influence. According to figures collected in 1997 by the SPESC, the activities include formal sports (e.g. basketball, volleyball, soccer, badminton, table tennis, track and field, swimming, gymnastics, ice skating, weightlifting and social dance), fitness and health-oriented activities (e.g. aerobic dancing, cycling, jogging, *tai ji quan, qi gong* and *wushu*), play-oriented activities (e.g. tug-of-war, hopscotch, skipping, jumping rubber bands, shuttlecock kicking), and ethnic minority-related activities (e.g. horse riding, dragon dancing and dragon boat racing). Mass fitness has a long history, but with the growth of the Chinese economy and opening doors to the world, mass fitness at the end of the 1990s has been accepted by many people and the government.

NOTE

1 The author would like to acknowledge material and advice contributed by Ji-Hong Cao, Wen-jian Zhang, Xiao-chun Wang and Xiao-ru Liu of Shenyang Physical Education Institute, and Gong Chen of San Jose State University.

REFERENCES

Olympics (1993) Beijing: People's Sport Publisher.

Mass Fitness (1990) Beijing: People's Sport Publisher.

Fitness for All (1996) Beijing: National Physical Education and Sports Commission.

Fitness for All Documents (1995) Beijing: National Physical Education and Sports Commission.

Mass Fitness Supervisor's Handbook (1994) Tianjin: Tianjin People's Publisher.

Fitness Assessment Manual for Adults in China (1996) Beijing: Standard Publisher of China.

Essays on Play and Sport (1996) Hainan: Hainan Publisher.

Lu, C. (1992) *Chinese Gongfu*, Canton: Canton Tour Publisher.

Ke, Y.L. (1993) *Chinese Oigong*, Shanghai: Writers Publisher.

Shu X.W. and Liu, P. (1993) *Chinese Defeated Chinese*, Shanghai: Hua Yi Publisher.

Knuttgen H.G., Ma, O. and Wu, Z. (1990) *Sport in China*, Champaign, Illinois: Human Kinetics Publisher.

People's Daily (1996, 1997), Beijing.

Appendix
Administration of sport

Shirley Reekie[1]

China has traditionally been a highly centralized nation, although the situation has begun to change in recent years. The administration of physical education and sport is undergoing similar change although it is still dominated by three government structures. The first is the National Physical Education/Sport Commission (a ministry or government department) which is in charge of general professional and amateur sport training and competition, mass fitness and research. The second is the National Education Commission which is in charge of physical education and sport in school, and the third is a collection of industry and business ministries responsible for fitness and sport for their employees and families. These three organizations have a vertical administration system at provincial, city and district division levels to carry out their duties, with lateral networking among them. For example, two of them may work together to organize sports events. These three systems are all responsible to the head of government.

Besides the above three government-controlled administrations, there are two other types of major organization which co-ordinate with these government structures and have their own specific professional duties. One is comprised of professional organizations, including the Chinese Olympic Committee, the All-China Sport Federation and the Chinese Physical Education Association. The second embraces a variety of other organizations, including the trade unions, the national youth association, the national women's association, the national student association, business/industry-sponsored sport clubs and spontaneously organized groups in the community.

NATIONAL PHYSICAL EDUCATION/SPORT COMMISSION

The National Physical Education/Sport Commission is the major sport/fitness administrative organization in China, and although groups share similar responsibilities, this commission does most of the work in nationwide sport/fitness. It has several sub-structures. The first is its vertical administration from national through district level offices, with each office working at its own administrative level. The second is the collection of special departments responsible for research and education which govern six teaching institutes and one research institute, one mass fitness department in charge of national mass fitness affairs, one sport training and competition department which governs nationwide professional sport training and competitions through nearly twenty newly-established sport training centres, and one training division responsible for the training of national teams.

In early 1998, the Chinese National Congress passed a bill to eliminate the National Physical Education/Sport Commission and delegate its duties to the All-China Sport Federation, which would itself be placed under the prime minister at a level of administration lower than a ministry. This decision ran into extremely strong resistance and resulted in the prime minister deciding to maintain the commission as part of the government, but to change its name to the National TiYu (Physical Culture) Bureau. Its functions will thus remain the same as before, but it is no longer listed as a ministry.

Structure of the commission

National commission

The national commission administers, co-ordinates and supervises nation-wide sport and physical education/fitness, and has several major functions:

- makes policies, regulations and guidelines for nationwide activities
- establishes and carries out nationwide annual and long-term plans
- supervises its vertical administration and special organizations
- organizes nationwide sport events
- approves national sport records, awards athletes' degrees (somewhat similar to the old Soviet Master of Sport titles, achieved by attaining certain high standards in a specific sport; they are not academic degrees in the western sense of the word 'degree') and approves referees
- supervises and co-ordinates community fitness and sport affairs
- organizes publications, conducts research and trains administrators
- plans and organizes nationwide professional and amateur sport training
- organizes international exchange programmes and competitions
- selects and trains national sport teams

Provincial commission

Each province in China has a provincial commission on physical education/sport. The provincial commissions are supervised by the national commission, but they are part of provincial governments. Their major functions include:

- carrying out the national plans and developing provincial plans on sport/fitness
- supervising and co-ordinating provincial sport/fitness events
- organizing provincial competitions and co-sponsoring some national competitions
- approving athletes' degrees and provincial referees
- planning sport training in the province and establishing proficient professional and amateur sport teams
- organizing publications, research and administrator training
- supervising the city commissions
- selecting and training provincial sport teams

City commission

Each city in a province has a sport/physical education commission supervised by the provincial commission, but belonging to the city government. Their major functions include:

- carrying out provincial plans and developing city plans on sport/fitness
- organizing citywide competitions and co-sponsoring provincial competitions
- planning sport training in the city, and establishing proficient amateur sport teams and networking with its districts
- supervising the district commissions
- selecting and training city sport teams

District commission

Just as at city level, each district in a city has a sport/physical education commission supervised by the city commission and belonging to the district government. Their major functions include:

- carrying out city plans and developing district plans on sport/fitness
- organizing district competitions and events
- planning and carrying out amateur sport training and networking with schools, institutions industries and farms
- supervising and co-ordinating sport/fitness schools and other organizations
- selecting and training district sport teams

Research and education department and its institutes

The research and education department of the National Physical Education and Sport Commission has several functions. The first is to train and assess the administrators of the commission system. The second is to supervise the National Sport Research Institute and the six physical education institutes with national importance – Beijing Physical Education University, Shanghai Physical Education Institute, Shenyang Physical Education Institute, Wuhan Physical Education Institute, Chengdu Physical Education Institute and Xi An Physical Education Institute.

A major function of the National Sport Research Institute is to conduct research related to the national sport teams and sometimes related to mass fitness. The six physical education institutes have several functions. The first is the training of university and high school teachers, fitness supervisors, sport coaches and physical education administrators. These institutes have their own youth sport schools and sport teams for national competitions. Conducting research is another function of these institutes. In 1980, Shenyang Physical Education Institute was the pioneer in conducting intensive fitness assessments of high school students.

Besides these commission-supervised institutes, there are provincial physical education institutes and research institutes. These provincial institutes have the same functions as the national institutes, except that they serve their own provincial needs.

Training/competition department and its centres

This department used to be comprised of three departments in charge of all national professional sport training and competitions. Following a major reform in November 1997, the three departments were replaced by the new training/competition department. All functions of the former three departments were distributed to the newly-established national sport training centres. Over eighty sports, which used to be administered by the National Physical Education and Sport Commission, are now managed by these centres. The purpose of this reform was to delegate work from the commission to the centres and sport associations. These training centres and the events they manage are as follows (they are responsible for all training and competitions of their sports at national level), by sport:

- archery and rifle shooting
- basketball
- cycling, motor-cycling
- chess
- fencing (also includes horseriding and pentathlon)
- gymnastics
- martial arts (non-Chinese martial arts: boxing, weightlifting, judo, wrestling, taekwondo)
- mass fitness and sport
- model racing (includes model airplane and model sailboat racing)

- mountaineering
- small ball sports (baseball, softball, team handball, field hockey, golf, bowling, racquetball, etc.)
- soccer
- swimming (includes swimming, synchronized swimming, water polo and diving)
- table tennis and badminton
- tennis
- track and field
- volleyball
- water sport (water polo, power boat racing, sailing, etc.)
- winter Sport (speed skating, figure skating, skiing, ice hockey)
- *wushu* (Chinese martial arts)

Sport training division

This department is in charge of the training of national teams. All professional athletes and their coaches, as well as the sport training bases across the nation, come under this department. They provide all resources for training at the highest level. They select professional athletes for each national team for either short-term training for upcoming sport competitions or long-term training, such as for the national table tennis team. The coaches for each national team are also chosen by this department.

Following the recent reform of sport administration in November 1997, the function of this department has also changed. It now shares responsibilities with the national sport training centres and the national sport associations, and co-ordinates training and competition with these centres and associations. The format of financial support for these sport teams has now changed from being solely government-supported to being government and business/industry co-sponsored. Professional sport competitions are also moving away from government sponsorship alone and are changing to the government and industry/business co-sponsorship operational pattern.

Mass fitness department

Five government organizations are involved in the administration of mass fitness. The most important is the Department of Mass Fitness attached to the National Physical Education/Sport Commission which is in charge of nationwide mass fitness. Similarly, sport commissions at provincial and city levels are in charge of the mass fitness at their respective levels. The second is the Department of Health, Physical Education and the Arts attached to the National Education Commission. This department is responsible for school physical education and fitness, and the subordinate commissions are responsible for the administration of fitness and physical education in schools. The third is the National Ministry of Health and its subordinate levels. The duties are to conduct sport rehabilitation and therapy, health examinations and fitness assessments. The fourth is the National Minority Population Commission whose duty is to organize traditional minority population sport events. An example is Mongolian 'nadamu' sport which includes Mongolian wrestling, horse racing and goat chasing. The fifth is the National Ministry for the Disabled which promotes and organizes sports and fitness for people with disabilities. All five ministries or commissions are responsible to the head of government. Most of them have several levels of operation – national, provincial, city, district and institution or 'dan wei' (work unit such as company, factory or school). These are all government departments funded by taxation.

The National Physical Education and Sport Commission is the major organization with overall responsibility for mass fitness. Its duties include the development of annual and long-term planning for mass fitness, development of the budget for mass fitness, management of mass fitness organizations, making mass fitness policies and rules, supervision and evaluation of the procedures and organization of comprehensive fitness events. There are two departments directly involved in national mass fitness related activities and events: the Mass Fitness Department and the Society Fitness Centre (the latter is less of an administrative group and more a body involved with health promotion and conducting research). In 1997, the Department of Mass Fitness had seven types of work, which included conducting research, establishing laws and regulations, organizing meetings, tournaments and national fitness events, welcoming international delegations and running workshops for them, and administrative work such as fundraising, writing publications, overseeing supervisor and instructor training, giving awards, and fitness equipment testing. The Society Fitness Centre has four types of basic work: organizing meetings and training courses, organizing fitness or recreational activity events, organizing international fitness and recreation events, and other activities such as organizing youth fitness camps and youth weight control camps.

NATIONAL EDUCATION COMMISSION

The National Education Commission is responsible for physical education and sport in schools and colleges, including elementary schools, middle and high schools, and universities, across the nation. The Department of Health and Physical Education is the major unit for sport and physical education. Its major responsibilities include making policies, establishing sport and fitness standards, organizing national sport and fitness events, supervising the assessment of fitness levels, establishing national curricula for physical education instruction, and publishing standard textbooks. The commission carries out its duties through the Department of Health and Physical Education in its provincial commissions which, besides carrying out policy, is also able to adjust policies to fit specific regional needs. The provincial commissions supervise the work of the Department of Health and Physical Education at city level, and the city departments of health and physical education supervise the same department at district level. The district level departments organize and co-ordinate sport events and fitness activities at schools within the regions for which they hold responsibility. University sport events or fitness activities are usually organized and supervised at provincial or city levels.

MINISTRIES

Each ministry in China has its own vertical administrative structure. The ministry usually controls personnel, budget and academic aspects of local offices. The local offices are partially controlled by local government for community-related activities or city-organized activities. The ministries usually control the sport activities through their internal sport associations, but also through women's associations, trade unions (which are actually a part of government), or youth associations whenever there is no sport association within that ministry. These ministry-wide organizations include, but are not limited to, the following:

Armed forces sport association (National Armed Forces Political Department)
Automobile industry sport association (National Automobile Industry Ministry)
Aviation sport association (National Aviation Industry Ministry)
Chemistry sport association (National Chemical Industry Ministry)
Coalmine sport association (National Coalmine Industry Ministry)
Collegiate sport association (National Education Commission)
Disabled population sport association (Benefit Affairs Ministry)
Electric power system sport association (National Electric Power Ministry)
Farmer sport association (National Farm Ministry)
Forestry sport association (National Forestry Ministry)
Geographic industry sport association (National Geographic and Mine Industry Ministry)
Engineering and electronic industry sport association (National Engineering/Electronic Industry Ministry)
Middle and high school sport association (National Education Commission)
Minority population sport association (National Minority Commission)

Premium-oil system sport association (National Premium-oil Industry Ministry)

Police sport association (National Public Safety Ministry)

Post office sport association (National Post Ministry)

Railway sport association (National Railway Ministry)

These ministry-supported levels of administration occasionally receive financial support from the National Commissions for important events. They used to be comparatively weak owing to dominant control by the National Physical Education/Sport Commission; however, they are developing rapidly and will take over major responsibility of national/local fitness events in the near future. The major duties of these organizations include providing facilities/equipment and consultation, organizing fitness activities or recreational events, and organizing sport competitions within their ministry system. They often co-ordinate events with the National Physical Education/ Sport Commission, such as at national or local sport competitions or tournaments. These organizations usually serve their own employees and families.

PROFESSIONAL ORGANIZATIONS

The Chinese Olympic Committee

The Chinese Olympic Committee is not a part of the government. It is a small organization with most of its officers working as administrators within the National Physical Education and Sport Commission. The Chinese Olympic Committee represents China in the activities of the International Olympic Committee. The major functions of the committee are to:

- establish the constitution of the Chinese Olympic Committee based on the constitution of the International Olympic Committee
- organize trials and select Chinese teams and athletes for Olympic competition
- supervise the training of each sport association which participates in Olympic competition
- participate in all activities organized by the International Olympic Committee.

The All-China Sport Federation

The All-China Sport Federation is not an official part of the government and its officers are not in paid positions within this Federation. Most officers are administrators of the National Physical Education/Sport Commission and are distinguished experts in their sports. The major duties of the All-China Sport Federation are:

- promotion of mass fitness and raising skill levels
- co-ordination with the government and other organizations of the development of sport and physical education in China.
- co-ordination with related groups of organizing national sport events
- development of international relations and co-organization of international competitions
- supervision of national sport associations, system-wide sport associations and provincial branches of the federation
- participation in training of sport teams at national and provincial levels

The All-China Sport Federation supervises three types of sport organizations. The first consists of the divisions of the All-China Sport Federation at provincial level. These branches have similar functions to those at headquarters, but at the provincial level. There are thirty divisions in the entire nation. The second type is made up of the national sport associations of which there are forty-one. The third type is comprised of the ministry sport associations as previously described.

The major national sport associations are all grouped by sport:

Chinese Archery Association
Chinese Badminton Association
Chinese Basketball Association
Chinese Baseball/Softball Association
Chinese Bicycling Association
Chinese Boxing Association
Chinese Chi Gong Association
Chinese Fencing Association
Chinese Field Hockey Association
Chinese Gymnastics Association
Chinese Horse Racing Association
Chinese Ice Hockey Association
Chinese Ice Skating Association
Chinese Judo Association
Chinese Power Boat Racing Association
Chinese Sailing Association
Chinese Shooting Association
Chinese Skiing Association
Chinese Soccer Association
Chinese Swimming Association
Chinese Table Tennis Association
Chinese Team Handball Association

Chinese Tennis Association
Chinese Track and Field Association
Chinese Volleyball Association
Chinese Weightlifting Association
Chinese Wrestling Association
Chinese *Wushu* (Chinese Martial Arts) Association

The major duties of these specific sport associations are:

- promotion of their sport nationwide
- conducting of research and organization of annual conferences
- training of coaches
- co-selection and training of amateur and professional athletes
- co-organization of tournaments and competitions
- provision of consultation to coaches

In addition to the sport-focused organizations, there are also those which cross horizontal boundaries, such as:

Collegiate Sport Association
Disabled Population Sport Association
Elderly Sport Association
Farmers' Sport Association
Middle and High School Sport Association
Minority Population Sport Association

The major duties of these specific associations are:

- promotion of fitness for their designated population
- co-organization of sport tournaments and competitions

Chinese Physical Education Association

The Chinese Physical Education Association is an academic organization for national physical education. It is a part of the China Science and Technology Association. Its major functions are:

- organizing and co-ordinating essential research
- publishing books and journals
- spreading knowledge on physical education, research and training
- advising and counselling the government on sport, mass fitness and physical education
- organizing seminars and workshops for improvement of professionals
- organizing national and international conferences

The members of this association are professors and researchers in physical education and sport, as well as some coaches and administers.

The Association also has its provincial and city divisions. These divisions have a similar function to the national association, but serve at provincial level and city level.

The Association has twelve divisions which cover:

- computer/technology physical education
- fitness
- kinesiology
- physical education information
- physical education statistics
- physical education history
- school physical education
- sport equipment
- sport medicine
- sport psychology
- sport sociology
- sport training

The major functions of these divisions include organizing and co-ordinating professional conferences, organizing research in their fields, and establishing networking with national and international experts in their specific fields.

OTHER ADMINISTRATION SYSTEMS

There are other types of informal administration of sport and physical education in China. These include the national trade union organization, the national youth association, national women's association and national student association. However, these organizations usually organize short-term or a limited range of events, and mostly they co-ordinate events organized by the formal administrations, such as the sport commission or ministry.

National Trade Union Organization

Despite its name, the organization is part of the government, rather than being an organization of workers. The trade union system has its vertical administration all the way from the national division through provincial, city and district divisions, and down to an office at each government-owned institution, school, factory and business. The major function of the union from national through city level on fitness and sport is to co-ordinate competitions and fitness events with the sport commissions or other administrations on sport. The union offices at the institution level are directly involved in organizing or co-organizing the actual fitness/sport activities or events. For example, the union office within a factory organizes basketball games, table tennis games or other events for the employees at that factory. The offices at this level usually organize their own sport teams to participate in competitions at city- or ministry-wide sport events.

National Youth Association

The National Youth Association is also part of the government. It functions as the Communist Party at youth level, so that it is a kind of political organization. But it does provide many opportunities for young people besides the political function. The youth association has its vertical administration all the way from the national office through provincial, city and district divisions to all government-owned institutions, schools, factories and businesses. The major function of the youth association from national through city levels on fitness and sport is to co-ordinate with the sport commissions or other administrations such as the ministries on youth sport competitions and fitness events. The youth associations at factory or school level are directly involved in the youth fitness or sport events within their factory or school. For example, the school youth associations organize activities such as basketball games between cohort-group classes (in China, high school students stay with the same classmates until they graduate) or co-ordinate with school physical education departments to conduct campus-wide fitness displays or annual track and field competitions which are popular in almost every school. The youth association in a department store often organizes fitness activities, such as soccer or chess, for young employees.

National Women's Association

The National Women's Association is also part of the Chinese government. The association has its divisions all the way from the national through provincial, city, district to all government-owned institution, school, factory and business. The major function of the women's association from national through city level on fitness and sport is to co-ordinate with the sport commissions or other administrations, such as the ministries, on advocating sport and fitness for women. The women's associations at factory or school level are directly involved in fitness or sport events within their factory or school, but their function is limited to assisting other organizations such as the trade union, youth association or physical education department to organize fitness or sport activities. For example, the school women's associations encourage women to participate in activities such as basketball or co-ordinate with school physical education departments to conduct campus-wide annual track and field competitions. The women's association in a factory often encourages employees to participate in fitness activities, but it rarely organizes a sport or fitness event for women only. Its major function in sport or fitness is mainly replaced by the youth association and trade union.

National Student Association

The National Student Association is not part of the government, but it has divisions such as the youth association from the national level though the institution level. The major function in sport and fitness is limited to advocating school students' participation in fitness/sport and to co-ordinating with sport/fitness government agencies at national or provincial level. At school level, the student association co-ordinates with the youth association or physical education department to organize sport tournaments, such as volleyball or annual track and field events.

Business/industry-sponsored sport groups

As the reform of China's economy progresses from planned to free market, sport is entering the free market economy as well. In recent years, sport groups owned by industry/business or institutions have boomed in China. These groups have corporate sponsors and attract national and even international sports stars to join. Examples include Beijing Duck Basketball Team (owned by Beijing Steel Company), Beijing Jing-shi Basketball Team (co-owned by the Beijing Teachers' College of Physical Education and a business company), Wang Kui Race-walking Club (co-owned by a company and the world-renowned coach Wang Kui). These teams and clubs directly participate in national high-level competitions. As the Chinese government is determined to change the sport system from government sponsorship to private sponsorship, professional sport in China is likely to become much more highly commercialized in the near future.

Spontaneous community organizations

These organizations are not part of the government, but serve the people who share an interest in the same sport or activity. These kinds of organizations are usually local groups. They often start with several people interested in one type of exercise or activity and gradually expand by the snowball effect. Some spontaneous groups have formal constitutions and regulations, but most do not and they are loosely organized. There are three types of spontaneous groups. The first is the sport group, usually formed by young people. They meet whenever they have time and just play for fun. These groups play a formal sport, such as basketball, soccer or martial arts. The second type is the fitness group. These groups usually serve the retired population and people who do not have access to an exercise facility, or do not have time to participate in other organized exercise during the day or evening, or do not have money for clubs. These groups usually meet in the early morning for a couple of hours and finish their activities before breakfast. The exercises or activities they participate in include social dance, Chinese folk dance, Tai Chi, Chi Gong, walking or jogging, and winter outdoor swimming. The third type is made up of recreational activity groups and often they are not sport or fitness oriented (however, in China these activities are all classified as fitness). These groups participate in activities such as bridge, chess, fishing and pigeon racing.

Even though these spontaneous organizations are not of major administrative importance in sport or fitness in China, they are nonetheless very popular and active. What they do represent is the direction of mass fitness in China in the future — that is, that this level of sport participation will be increasingly run by the people themselves with very little government support.

RELATIONSHIP OF THESE ADMINISTRATIONS

The previous sections introduced each sport/physical education administration. These systems all have several functions and they overlap and co-ordinate with each other to carry out fitness/sport activities. In this section, the inter-relationship of the various organizations will be discussed from the perspective of the overall organization of sport and fitness.

Professional competitive sport

Professional sport competitions, such as national games, national basketball championships or provincial games, are all organized by the National Physical Education and Sport Commission at national and provincial levels. All training of Chinese professional sport teams and their participation in international sport competitions are organized by this commission (the department of training and competition, the training division and the national training centres). Their work is co-ordinated by the All-China Sport Federation and the Chinese Olympic Committee. The costs are borne mainly by the government and co-sponsored by industry/business. The professional teams are either owned by the sport commissions at national and provincial level or by industry/business.

Youth competitive sport and amateur competitive sport

Youth competitive sport is under the administration of the National Physical Education and Sport Commission and yet forms part of the professional sport training pyramid. The national teams choose their athletes from the provincial professional teams, the provincial teams choose their professional athletes from the provincial and city amateur sport schools. The city and district amateur teams choose their athletes from the schools. Youth competitive sport is handled at provincial and city level by the Sport Commission. The youth sport schools are at amateur level, but their purpose is really to prepare athletes who will become the professionals of the future. All financial support comes from the National Physical Education and Sport Commission.

Examples of amateur competitive sport include the national coal-mine industry basketball games or provincial business track and field tournament. They are controlled by the ministries with support from the Sport Commission and sport associations. The provincial games and city games are also a part of amateur competitive sport, mainly organized by the National Physical Education and Sport Commission, and co-sponsored by other organizations.

Physical education in schools

Physical education in schools and universities is organized by the National Education Commission. All education system amateur sport competitions and training are also under the administration of the National Education Commission at different levels. Examples of these sport competitions include the national university games, national middle school basketball tournament or city level school track and field events. Their work is co-ordinated by the department of school physical education within the National Physical Education and Sport Commission, and other organizations such as the youth association or national or provincial level student association.

Mass fitness

Mass fitness in China is encouraged and led by the National Physical Education and Sport Commission, together with various ministries, the National Education Commission, and other organizations such as the trade unions and youth association. Actual fitness activities are carried out at the institution and local levels. Business-oriented clubs and spontaneous groups are part of the informal administration.

Research in sport and physical education

Research in sport, physical education and fitness in China is conducted at national and provincial research or teaching institutes, and at physical education departments within universities. The major administrators and leaders of research are the Chinese Physical Education Association and the National Physical Education/Sport Commission.

Training of administrators, teachers and coaches

The responsibility for training administrators, teachers and coaches is shared by several administrations. The top leaders at national and provincial levels are trained by the Communist Party, and very often these people do not have a background in sport or physical education. On the other hand, some national and provincial administrators are former world-class athletes or coaches who were assigned solely because of their excellent reputations in sport or coaching. The administrators of fitness and sport attached to education commissions, ministries and city sport commissions are trained by the physical education institutes, but some are former athletes or coaches who came directly from the sport teams.

Physical education teachers at university and high school are trained by physical education institutes and departments of physical education within universities. Physical education teachers at elementary schools are trained by the teacher schools (which are of high school level). The mass fitness/instructors/supervisors are trained by the Sport Commission and physical education institutes.

Coaches for professional and amateur sports come from two sources. One source is graduates from the physical education institutes and the other is former athletes. In practice, most coaches, especially at professional level (provincial and national level) are former athletes. Some of them attend short workshops but most are assigned to the coaching position without any training. A few coaches who lack formal training receive education from various correspondence courses offered at physical education institutes.

THE CURRENT SITUATION

The administration of physical education, sport and fitness in China is undergoing major change, and this reform may take many years to establish a new administrative system. The basic changes include six aspects: (1) the focus of physical education and sport in China may switch from a gold-medal-winning orientation to a more balanced view of both professional sport and mass fitness; (2) mass fitness will transfer from government to private sponsorship and, at the same time, participants will be required to bear more of their own costs, or so the government hopes; (3) the government will maintain general control of sport and physical education, but the major functions will be delegated to professional organizations, society and the community; (4) the administrative style will change from being experience-oriented to being more scientifically supported and trained; (5) sport and fitness will increasingly be seen as an industry and enter the free market; and (6) administration will be based more on formal regulations and law.

Results of these reforms have yet to be realized, and there may well be problems that develop during the reform process. What is clear, however, is that the direction being taken is towards internationally-recognized patterns, including having more experts participating in the decision-making process, and also moving towards a more commercial basis for sponsorship.

NOTE

1 The author would like to acknowledge material and advice contributed by Xiaoe-chun Wang, Xiao-ru Liu, Ji-hong Cao, Wen-jian Zhang and Gong Chen.

REFERENCES

Documents on reforming the sport administration (1997) Beijing: National Sport/ Physical Education Commission.

Essays of Play and Sport (1996) Hainan: Hainan Publisher.

Fitness For All Monograph (1996) Beijing: National Sport/Physical Education Commission.

Knuttgen, H., Ma, Q. and Wu, Z. (1990) *Sport in China*, Champaign, Illinois: Human Kinetics Publisher.

Ke, Y. L. (1993) *Chinese Chi Gong*, Shanghai: Writer's Publisher.

Mass Fitness (1990) Beijing: People's Sport Publisher.

People's Daily (November 1996–November 1997) Beijing: People's Daily Publisher.

People's Daily, 11 March 1998.

People's Daily, 19 March 1998.

Olympics (1993) Beijing: People's Sport Publisher.

Shu, X. W. and Liu, P. (1993) *Chinese Defeated Chinese*, Shanghai: Hua Yi Publisher.

Index

acrobatics 26, 31, 42, 43, 65
active man, Manchu emphasis on 57–65
All-China Achievement Programme
   225–6
All-China Sports Federation 229, 240,
   262–4
American College of Sports Medicine
   (ACSM) 241
Annals of Lu 26
archery 24, 27–8, 30, 32, 36, 39, 49, 53,
   59, 66, 67, 72, 124
aristocratic empires (581–960) 38, 43;
   civilian recreations 39–42; health and
   exercise 42–3; military activities 38, 39
Asian Games 125, 126
athlete development 126–7; in Beijing
   131; central sports school 128–31;
   national team 136–8; provincial team
   132–6; spare-time sports schools 127–8
athletics 78, 121, 152

Ba Duan Jin (Exercises in Eight Forms)
   48
Ba Shan 36, 43, 47, 48
badminton 124, 129, 152
Bai Juyi 48
Ban Duan Jin 232, **235**
Bao Sheng Yau (Lu Essentials of
   Maintaining Health) 48
Baoding Zhiyan 41
baseball 73
basketball 78, 121, 133, 135, 151, 152,
   153, 154, 157
Beijing Institute of Physical Culture 234,
   239
Beijing Medical College 239
Beijing Normal University (BNU) 156–8
Beijing Sports Competitive School 131

Beijing University of Physical Education
   (BUPE) 150–1
board games 25, 32, 57, 65, 66
board hitting 28
Bonavia, D. 77
boxing 31, 54–5, 62, 65, 135, 156
Boxing of the School of Shaolin 37
Brownell, S. 63, 72, 75, 77, 81, 82, 84, 85,
   169, 170–2, 173, 175, 176–7
buda qin (ball striking on foot) 41
Buddhism 36, 62
bull fighting 47–8
business/industry sponsored sport groups
   267

Chai, C. and Chai, W. 76
Chang, J. 175
Chao Yuanfang 43
charioteering 26–7, 30, 65
Ch'en Jerome 72, 74, 76, 78
chess 57, 66, 72
Ch'ien-Lung 60
children: coaching for 127–8, 133; fitness
   testing procedures for 247; sport for 47
China 86–7; end of old order 74–9;
   establishment of Republic 79–86; and
   introduction of western physical
   education 71–4; post-imperial 79–86;
   rebellions in 74–6; social, economic,
   political background 70–1, 74–6
China Sports Medicine Association 229
Chinese Association of Sports Medicine
   (CASM) 229, 240–1
Chinese Olympic Committee 262
Chinese Physical Education Association
   264–5
chiuwan (hitting the pellet) 49–50
Chou dynasty (1112–770 BC) 231

Clumpner, R.A. and Pendleton, B.B. 78, 83, 85, 86
coach education 142–3; course organization 144–5; funding 145; information service 147–8; national coaches 146–7; part/full-time courses 145; participants 145–6; refresher courses 143–4
community organizations, spontaneous 267–8
competitive sport: domestic 122–5; growth of 78–9; international 84–6, 125–6; national 84–6; professional 268; youth/amateur 268–9
Confucianism 24, 172–5
Crew, C. 72–3
cuju 32–3, 41, 56, 57
cycling 135, 253

dance 25, 26, 28–9, 31, 32, 33, 41–2, 47, 65, 253
daoyin 23, 34, 37, 43, 232, **233**
Deng Xuezheng 174
Dong Jinxia 166, 168, 172, 174
dragon boat racing 33, 48, 65, 253
drugs 7–8, 160–1, 178–81
Du Jin 56

elite sport 120–2; athlete development 126–38; domestic 122–5; international 125–6; major competitions 122–6; trends/observations on 138–41
equestrianism 8–9, 26–7, 30–1, 53–4, 59, 253
exercise: and health 34, 36–7, 42–3, 48, 56, 66; with padlocks 59–60; status of 14; and women 42

falconry 63–4
fencing 31, 59, 135, 151
festivals 25, 33–4, 41, 43, 72
feudal society (476 BC–AD 220) 29–30; festival recreations 33–4; health and exercise 34–5; military activities 30–3
field/track events 155, 156, 157, 159
fitness: in 1980s and 1990s 244–5; between 1949 and 1979 243–4; business-oriented clubs 246; government level 245–6; and lack of resources 252–3; mass 269; pre–1949 243; specific organizations 246;

spontaneous groups 246–7; testing procedures 247–9
Fitness for All project 14, 249–52
football 32–3, 41, 56, 65, 66, 67–8

Georges, P. 174
Gernet, J. 20, 36, 46–7, 51, 57, 58, 65, 70, 74, 79
golf 49–50, 66, 68, 73
Gu Shiquan 78, 82
Gu tinglin 55
Guangdong Research Institute of Sports Science (GRISS) 224–6, 240
Guangdong Sports Technical Institute 134–5
Guangzhou Institute of Physical Education 151–2
gymnastics 129–30, 133, 136, 156, 157

Hackensmith, C.W. 76
Han dynasties 29
Han Fei Zi 24, 34
Han period 34–5
hand fighting 31, 68
hockey 66
Hong Kong Sports Institute (HKSI) 130, 134, 224, 225, 229
Honig, E. and Hershatter, G. 177
horse racing 8–9
Howell, M. 4
Hsu Yi-hsiung 78, 83, 86
Huan Di Nai Jing 232
Huang Haiwen 178
Huang Li-chow 55, 62
Hughes, E.R. 75, 77, 78, 79, 83
Hung-wu 52
Hunter, W.C. 71, 72
hunting 64

I Zhuan (Book of Changes) 22
ice sports 60–1, 65, 157
International Federation of Sports Medicine (FMS) 241

Jiang Yun 165, 166, 167
Jiangsu Research Institute of Sports Science (JRISS) 222–4
Jiao Di games 31, 66
Jin dynasty 45–51
Jones, R. 166, 168
Ju Cheng Ming 33
Junior Games 123–4

kangding (tripod lifting) 31
Kanin, D.B. 82, 86
kite-flying 42, 43, 65, 72
Knuttgen, H.G. 78–9, 82, 84, 86
Kolatch, J. 77
Krotee, M.L. and Wang Jin 83
Ku Ting-Lin 62
Kung-fu 62

Latham, R. 53, 54, 55, 56
Lewis, T. 168
Li Hongbing 167
Li Ning 13
Li Sao 34
Li Shih-chen 53
Li Shu-Ku 62
Li Yen 33
Li You 33, 67
Liao dynasty 45–51
Liaoning Research Institute of Sports
    Science 226–8
Liaoning Sports Training Centre 135–6
Liu Lingling 40
Liu Pingchung 51
Liu Qian 172
Loh, M. 180
Lui, S. 83

Macleod, I. 168
Manchus 57–65, 72
martial arts 36, 65, 151; emergence of
    53–5; and influence of shaolin 62–3
middle ages (220–589) 35–6; exercise and
    health 36–7; military life 36; religious/
    social influences 36
military sport 22, 32, 47, 65–6;
    aristocratic empires 38, 39;
    examinations in 61–2; feudal 30–3;
    middle ages 36; Mongol 53–5;
    primitive 26–7; Qing dynasty 59–62
Ming Dynasty (1368–1644) 21, 51–7, 68

Nanjing Institute of Physical Education
    (NIPE) 129–30, 152–3, 222, 223, 224
National Education Commission 260–1
National Games 11, 84–5, 106, 122–3,
    159, 171, 229
National Games of Minority
    Nationalities 124–5
National Physical Education/Sport
    Commission 255–6; city 257; district
    257; functions 257–8; mass fitness

department 259–60; national 256;
    provincial 256–7; sport training
    division 259; structure 256–7; training/
    competition department/centres 258–9
National Research Institute of Sports
    Medicine (NRISM) 221–2, 226, 229,
    240
National Research Institute of Sports
    Science (NRISS) 214–19, 226, 229, 240;
    coach–scientist link 220; degree
    programmes 219–20; working within
    the system 220–1
National Student Association 267
National Trade Union Organization
    265–6
National Training Bureau of the State
    Physical Culture and Sports
    Commission 136–8
National Women's Association 266–7
National Youth Association 266
Needham, J. 10
Northern Chou dynasty (557–581) 38

Olympic Achievement Programme 225–6
Olympic Games 4, 10–11, 86, 87, 121–2,
    125–6, 136, 202; and bid for 2000 208;
    and conflict with sport
    commercialization 211–12; controversy
    over 205–6; further development in
    206, 208; future trends 209–13;
    historical background 202–4; initial
    involvement in 204–5; and integration
    of Chinese culture with 210; new era
    in 206; potential contribution to 210,
    212–13; social dimension 202–3; sport
    dimension 203–4; western
    ethnocentrism of 210–11; women in
    161–5, 167–8

Pai Yu-fung 55
Pan Gu 32, 68
Pendleton, B. 84
People's Liberation Army (PLA) team
    136
Percival, W.S. 73
physical education: curriculum 101–4,
    149; funding 149; general sports
    classes 104–5; inspections 102;
    institutes 148–58; introduction of
    western 71–4; in middle schools
    95–104; modernization of 76–7;
    outline health plan for 115–19; in

overall structure 94; in primary schools 94–5; problems facing introduction of 77–8; research in 269; in schools 90–3, 269; science/science research institutes 113; in the service of the Republic 81–3; special schools for 110–13; in specialist institutes 108–10; standards 103–4; tertiary level 104–13; in universities 93–4, 105–7
Physical Education Law (1929) 82–3
P'ng, C.K. and Donn, F.D. 63
polo 39–41, 43, 49, 65, 66
Polo, Marco 52, 55–6
Powell, D. 173, 176
primitive society (3000–476 BC) 26–9

Qi 22, 23, 24, 232
qi gong 14, 244, 247
Qi Jiguang 55
Qin dynasty (221–206 BC) 31
Qing dynasty (1644–1840) 57–65, 171
Qu, M. and Yu, C. 232
quan 31

Radice, B. 28
Rai, S. 172, 176
recreational sport 20; in aristocratic empires 38–43; development of, in Ancient China 20–43; in feudal society 29–35; in middle ages 35–7; military, medical, philosophical, social factors 22–5; political/economic influences 20–2; in primitive society 26–9
religion, influence of 61–2, 65
Ren Hai 24, 34, 68
Riordan, J. 81, 86, 168, 170
Rizak, G. 77
running 48, 56, 168

Sasajima Kohsuke 41
Schirokauer, C. 70
self-sufficiency movement 74–9
Semotiuk, D. 82, 85
Sewell, W.G. 84
Shan Hai Jing 23
Shang civilization 26
Shang Shu (Book of History) 23, 29
Shanghai Baseball Club 73
Shanghai Boat Club 73
Shanghai Institute of Physical Education 153
Shanghai Sports School 128–9

Shanghai Yacht Club 73
Shaolin, influence of 61–2, 65, 68
Shenyang Institute of Physical Education 154
Shi Ji (Historical Records) 32
Shi Jing (Book of Songs) 28
Shu Shi 49
shuttlecock 47, 67, 72
Sima Qian 32
soccer 9–10, 136, 157, 168; buying/selling of players 193–4; club system 187, 190–2; in international arena 194–5; international comparisons 197–9; observations/trends 199–200; opportunities in 195–6; professional emergence of 186, 196–7; promotion of 192; women in 197; world trappings 192–3
social recreation 72–4; Mongol 55–6; Qing dynasty 63–4; Song to Yuan dynasty 47–8
Song dynasty (960–1279) 21, 45–51, 67, 68, 170
Song He 167
sport: background 1–2; decline in non-Olympic events 11–12; effect of political/economic change on 3–5, 10, 13–14; funding for 4–5, 12, 13–14, 136; future direction of 10–12; and gender 175–6; groupings of 12; growing sophistication of 45–51; high performance/mass sport linkage 210; infrastructure 168; and lack of pure competition 67; as lower-class activity 171–2; modern 71–4; outline health plan for 115–19; professionalism in 9–10, 185–200; as Recreation for All 5–6; regional/other differences in 8–9; regulations for 6–7; research in 269; role of in society 165–9; rural–urban difference 12; in the service of the Republic 81–3; status of 14; structure/strategy of 15–17, 209; texts on 68; traditional 14; traditional/modernist combination in 2–3; and transport/communications 13
sport administration 84–6, 255; current situation 270–1; ministries 261–2; National Education Commission 260–1; National Physical Education/Sport Commission 255–60; other systems 265–8; professional

organizations 262–5; relationship between organizations 268–70
Sport for All Programme 225, 228
sport medicine: future development 241; post-1949 period 232, 234–5; pre-1949 period 231–2; professional institutions 239–40; professional organizations/ activities 240–1; professional preparation 237–9
sport science: NRISM 221–2; NRISS 214–21; observations/trends 229–30; PE institutes 228–9; provincial research institutes 222–8
State Physical Culture and Sports Commission 228
State Physical Education and Sports Commission of China (SPESC) 15, 244, 245–6, 249–51, 253
stilts walking 72
Sui dynasty (581–617) 38
Sun Simiao 43
sunbathing 48
swimming 28, 56, 66, 121, 129, 135, 151, 152–3, 157, 159–60, 168, 174
swing 32, 42, 43, 65, 66
swordplay 31

table tennis 152, 156, 168
tai ji quan 14, 232, **236–8**, 244, 247
Tait, P. 180
Tan Hua 28, 42, 67
Tang dynasty (618–907) 34, 38
Tao Hou-jung 37, 68
Taoism 23–4, 30
tennis 73
ti cao 244
Tian Ma 64
Tian, M.J. et al. 241
touhu 28, 32, 47, 68
Traditions of Tso 26
training 168; administrators and teachers 270; coach education 142–8, 270; physical education 148–58
tug-of-war 27, 42, 65, 253
tuoguan (lifting a city gate bolt) 31

Urban Games 124, 126

Van Dalen, D.B. and Bennett, B.L. 81, 84
volleyball 124, 133, 135, 152, 153, 154, 155, 156, 168

Wang Chuan-shan 62
Wanjing 49
Warring States period (476–221 BC) 29–30, 31, 32
weight training 151
weightlifting 31, 124, 134, 168
Wen Jiang project 8–9
Wenli Yehuopian 57
Werner, E.T.C. 71–2, 73–4
Western Han dynasty (200 BC–AD 25) 31, 231
Western Wei dynasty (535–557) 38
women: 'Chinese first, women second' 169–70; contribution to Olympics/ world championships 161–5; countryside/Confucian philosophy 172–5; and drugs 160–1; and exercise 42; physique, medicine, science 178–81; reasons for progress 181–2; recreational activities of 56; and social change 175–6; and socialism 176–8; and sport 66–7; strength of 54; success of 159–60; as swimmers 28; traditional attitudes towards 170–1; as wrestlers 47, 67
wrestling 27, 41, 43, 47, 49, 54, 60, 65, 67, 124, 135, 151, 168
Wu Quan Xi 232, **234**
Wu Shao Zu 7, 166
Wu Weng-chung 37, 41, 47, 60–1, 62
Wuhan Competitive Sports School 130–1
Wuhan Institute of Physical Education (WIPE) 154–6, 228
wushu 14, 22, 31, 150, 152, 153, 155, 156, 237–8

Xie Kainan 178
Xie Yanmin 169, 173, 178
Xie Yunxin 36, 59, 63
Xu Qi 166, 167
Xun Zi 24

Yan xixhai 55
Yang Wanhua 174
Yen Shi-chai 62
Yen Yuan 58
Yin and Yang 22–3, 24
YMCA/YWCA 78–9, 84–5, 87
Yu Daiyou 55
Yuan dynasty (1271–1368) 51–7, 68
Yue Fu institute 32

Zhan Guo Ce (History of the Warring States) 32
Zhang Li 5
Zheng Chuhai 42
Zhong Bian 53–4, 56

Zhou Bangyan 48
Zhou civilization 26–8
Zhou Mi 48
Zhou Xikuan 24, 67, 76, 82, 84
Zhu Ming-yi 85